X 7
F 156

W9-CED-398

Praise for *A Smile as Big as the Moon*

"Kersjes's refreshing, heartwarming account proves that faith and vision can yield great things."

—*Publishers Weekly*

"A moving, true-life account. . . . Genuinely inspirational."

—*Booklist*

"Like the U.S. Space Program, this is a compelling story that shows what can be accomplished when you are only limited by imagination and ingenuity. The reader can readily sense the personal dedication and love that Coach has for his students."

—Bob Springer, astronaut

"Those of us who have witnessed Mike's wonderful work are very happy that it is evident and celebrated in this great book."

—Tom Rooney, president of Team Lemieux, LLC

"*A Smile as Big as the Moon* is a terrific book. At once uplifting and thought provoking, it pulls no punches in depicting the hardships encountered by a group of special education students and the teacher who believed in them. A remarkable and unforgettable story."

—Jerry Bruckheimer

MICHAEL KERSJES *with Joe Layden*

A SMILE
AS BIG
AS THE
MOON

A SPECIAL EDUCATION

TEACHER,

HIS CLASS, AND THEIR

INSPIRING JOURNEY

THROUGH

U.S. SPACE CAMP

 St. Martin's Griffin 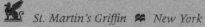 New York

A SMILE AS BIG AS THE MOON: A SPECIAL EDUCATION TEACHER, HIS CLASS, AND THEIR INSPIRING JOURNEY THROUGH U.S. SPACE CAMP. Copyright © 2002 by Michael Kersjes and Joe Laydon. All rights reserved. Printed in the United States of America. No part of this book may be used or reproduced in any manner whatsoever without written permission except in the case of brief quotations embodied in critical articles or reviews. For information, address St. Martin's Press, 175 Fifth Avenue, New York, N.Y. 10010.

www.stmartins.com

Library of Congress Cataloging-in-Publication Data

Kersjes, Michael E.
    A smile as big as the moon : a special education teacher, his class, and their inspiring journey through U.S. space camp / Mike Kersjes with Joe Layden.—1st ed.
      p. cm.
   ISBN 0-312-27314-2 (hc)
   ISBN 0-312-30314-9 (pbk)
   1. Special education—United States—Case Studies.
2. Handicapped children—Education (Secondary)—United States—Case studies. 3. U.S. Space Camp (Huntsville, Ala.)
4. Kersjes, Micheal E. I. Layden, Joseph, 1959– II. Title.

LC3969.4 .K47 2002
371.9'0473'092—dc21   2001048779

10 9 8 7 6 5 4 3 2

This book is dedicated to all special-needs children

and their families, who work so hard

every day to hold their vision steady . . .

until their dreams become reality.

AUTHOR'S NOTE

This true story took place more than ten years ago, so the dialogue has been reconstructed. The names and certain identifying characteristics of the following participants have been changed: Denise Boitano, Andrea Burke, Ross Fullerton, Shannon Hathaway, Tom Keller, Grant Plunkett, Marge Sheffield, Rebecca Shriver, Karen Treffiletti, Mark Tyler, and David Ward.

ACKNOWLEDGMENTS

I would like to take this opportunity to acknowledge the following people for their positive spirit and support in helping me and our special-needs children reach for the stars.

I would like to start by thanking Daniel Trierweiler and Burger King for believing that the underdogs could win. To my teaching partner, Robynn McKinney, who kept a level head and positive outlook through the good and bad times.

To my wife, Darcy, and my sons, Shawn and Ryan, who tried to understand my dreams and the obsession I have with Space Camp.

My mentor, Dr. Lynn Bondurant, and his wife, Kay, who opened so many doors for us. To all the Space Is Special board members, especially our chairman, Robert Springer, and his wife, Debbie, and our vice president, JoAnne Kochneff, and her husband, Doug.

I also want to thank Dr. Michael Washburn for giving Robynn and me the opportunity to pursue our dreams, as crazy as it might have seemed to so many other people. To Linda Vanderjagt, my current supervisor, for helping me make the right decisions toward the growth of our program.

To Mr. Larry Capps, CEO of the Space & Rocket Center, and the entire Space Camp administration and staff, for their hard work and dedication in helping to give these children an experience of a lifetime.

I would also like to thank the following for their funding and support: Mr. Edson (Ted) Arneault, CEO for the Mountaineer Race Track & Resort, and Mr. Ted Dragisich, who have brought our program into the state of West Virginia; the entire Pittsburgh Penguins organization, especially Mario Lemieux and Chief Operating Officer Tom Rooney; Martin Wegener and Peter Riley, from the New England Financial Group, and their entire staff for their ongoing fund-raising efforts.

To Sandy Colegrove, for caring that all children have a chance in life.

To Bobbi Peterson, Peggy Brumley, Shelley DiCesare, and Melissa Slendak, for keeping my travel plans straight.

To Frank and Jodi Stanley, for their continued support.

To all of the people who helped make this book a reality: Mickey Freiberg, my agent, who never gave up and is always there for me; Frank Weimann of the Literary Group, who brought Joe Layden to our team; Neil Russell, for being with us through the good and bad times; Homer Hickham, who connected me with the right people so that our story could be told.

To Joe Layden, who was so dedicated in writing this story.

To St. Martin's Press, and especially its publisher, Sally Richardson, who understood my vision. To my editors, Michael Denneny and Christina Prestia, who worked so closely with Joe and me in shaping this book.

Thanks to all the Forest Hills Northern special-needs students portrayed in this book, and to the rest of their classmates, for making my first trip to Space Camp such a memorable experience.

Finally, I would like to thank my mother for instilling within me the drive and passion to never give up . . . regardless of the odds.

*Great spirits have always encountered
violent opposition from
mediocre minds.*

—ALBERT EINSTEIN

PART

ONE

PROLOGUE

MAY 7, 1989

After two layovers and nearly ten hours of travel, the cabin is quiet. The serving carts are gone, the flight attendants seated for our descent. We're cruising along at ten thousand feet, about to begin the final leg of an extraordinary quest that has spanned a year and a half. I look around at them now, twenty kids between the ages of fourteen and seventeen, some slumped down in their seats, sleeping, exhausted even before the game begins, others with their faces pressed into the windows, the glass fogging with each anxious breath. This morning, when we boarded the first plane in Grand Rapids, Michigan, they were a wild and frenetic bunch, so excited they could barely stand still. A decision was made then that the adults in our group—me, my wife, my teaching partner, a couple of aides from our classroom—would be distributed evenly throughout the cabin, to comfort and reassure those who hadn't flown before and, more important, to make sure that all hell didn't break loose at the top of the world.

Seems silly now, for the trip has been blissfully uneventful. Not one air sickness bag needed, not one kid injured on a moving walkway, not one smoke alarm accidentally or otherwise activated . . . not a single flight attendant or pilot traumatized. Twenty kids from five different schools, each with some type of learning disability, and so far, at least, they have been model citizens. There is Steve, the boy whose flatulence and mischievousness can sometimes, but not always, be attributed to his battle with Tourette's syndrome; Lewis, the wiry and angry kid who has lived in twenty-seven foster homes; Marion, whose inability to focus and concentrate is due at least in part to her ongoing struggle with leukemia; Ben, a sweet-natured boy with Down's syndrome; Stephanie, a tall and awkward girl with a ferocious temper; Scott, a dyslexic kid who is trying to live up to his father's grand expectations; and Mark, a dead ringer for Alfalfa on the old television show *The Little Rascals*. These kids, and thirteen others, have all been collectively lumped under the umbrella of special education, a euphemistic brand if ever there was one, with its implications of uniqueness and undertones of helplessness, stupidity, and trouble. And yet throughout this long day they have caused barely a ripple of unintended or unwanted interest. How surprised the folks back home would be: the principal who thinks this whole adventure is nothing more than a mad quixotic joke; the regional coordinator of special education who, though she'll never admit it, wants nothing more than to see us fail, to see these kids disheartened and disappointed once again; the teachers who regularly gather in the faculty lounge and trade cruel and sophomoric insults about these children over lunch, despicable behavior that makes the taunts of the mainstream students seem benign by comparison, and that has prompted both me and my partner to routinely brown-bag it in the classroom. What would they say now? What will they say when we return?

There is a nervousness in the pit of my stomach, a rolling reminiscent of Friday nights in the fall. I'm a football coach as well as a teacher (actually, I've always believed that a football coach—a good one, anyway—*is* a teacher), and the atmosphere on this plane right now reminds me of a locker room fifteen minutes before kickoff. The stillness is deceiving; cut through it and you'll find a swirling mass of conflicting emotions: fear, excitement, anticipation, dread. And it isn't just the participants, the players, who are susceptible—I feel it, too.

We've spent so much time—so many hours, days, weeks, and months—preparing for this opportunity. But it isn't the possibility of losing that scares me; it's the possibility of something more palpable, more devastating: failure. They aren't the same thing, loss and failure. Losing I can handle, provided the effort and intentions are honest, the teamwork consistent with the values we have stressed and taught. Failing is something else, especially in this case. These are special ed kids, and as such they are accustomed to being criticized, laughed at, scorned . . . and worst of all, ignored. I've seen them transformed over the course of the past eighteen months. Once a motley collection of misfits and troublemakers, most of whom expected nothing from themselves because nothing was expected of them, they have metamorphosed into a group bonded by a common goal, a group that has a chance to achieve something akin to a miracle, something no group of learning disabled students has ever accomplished.

Not that I romanticize their accomplishments. I've worked with special-needs students for far too long to take a simplistically optimistic point of view. These are basically good kids who have been dealt a bad hand—by God, by their parents, by their teachers, by their peers, by the system. They've lived most of their lives on the margins, and sometimes the damage that has been done is so great as to be irreparable. These kids can try your patience and they can break your heart. There are no simple solutions for any of them. There are, however, times and circumstances, remarkable moments, when they can and do remind you of the overwhelming power of the human spirit.

I'm confident this week will bring out the best in them, in all of us, though there is no way to know for sure. I hope all goes well. I hope there are no fights, no emotional meltdowns, no screwups of such magnitude that they cause embarrassment for our school district. That, inevitably, would result in failure, which in turn would lead to the closing of a door that has been opened just a crack, after so many years of being locked tight. And that would be a tragedy.

The kids know all of this. We haven't tread lightly on their fragile egos, haven't spared them lectures on the consequences of their actions. They are nothing less than trailblazers: the first group of special education students to attend Space Camp at the United States Space & Rocket Center in Huntsville, Alabama. For the next six days they will live and train like astronauts, and how they perform—how they acquit themselves academically, intellectually, emotionally, competitively—will go a long way toward determining whether this bold experiment continues or ends. These twenty young men and women represent not only Forest Hills Northern High School, where I am a teacher and they attend classes, and not just the city of Grand Rapids, Michigan. They are the first, and so they represent learning disabled children from all over the world. It's quite a burden to shoulder.

I don't know whether these thoughts are racing through their minds right now, as they're racing through mine. I'm not sure what they're thinking. As the plane drops slowly from the sky, and a disembodied voice reminds everyone to make sure his or her seat is in a locked and upright position, I glance out the window and see the bright orange and crimson clay of northern Alabama glistening in the late-afternoon sun. The silence in the cabin is broken by the voice of Mark Tyler, who, like many of these kids, has never been on a plane, never strayed far from the state of Michigan.

"Hey, Coach," he says.

"Yeah, Mark?"

"It's all red down there. Is Huntsville like Mars or something?"

I smile to myself. *Not a bad analogy, Mark: red planet, red clay.* To these kids, Alabama might as well be a different world. And ready or not, our ship is about to land.

1

The first time I heard about Space Camp was in the late summer of 1987, on one of those long, sweaty August days when you're in the classroom, trying to clean up and get ready for another year of school. At the time I was a special education teacher whose primary responsibility was to run a self-contained classroom for students from five different schools in and around Grand Rapids, Michigan. Our program was housed at Forest Hills Northern High School, where I was also the defensive coordinator for the varsity football team.

I'll admit that my mind in those days often wandered. I'd been teaching special ed for more than a decade, and the strain of taking the work home with me night after night, year after year, was beginning to take its toll. It's no great secret that teaching is demanding and often rewarding work, but teaching special education is uniquely challenging. If you care about what you're doing, the kids have a way of getting inside you, becoming a part of your life in ways you never imagined. You end up being much more than their teacher—you become a psychologist, social worker, doctor, foster parent, and friend. With twenty to twenty-five kids in your caseload, representing a broad spectrum of learning disabilities and social and emotional deficiencies, you learn very quickly that it's not possible to save them all. You try, of course, but some things are out of your control, and, to be honest, some kids want no part of you or your rescue attempts. Some kids turn out well, some go bad, and that's just the way it is. You accept it, but you don't stop caring. When you stop caring, well . . . then it's time to move on.

After so many years in the classroom, I recognized the telltale signs of burnout—the listlessness, the lack of enthusiasm on the eve of a new semester, the inability to focus. I was thirty-five years old and getting stale, but I wasn't ready to change careers or ask for a new assignment—not yet, anyway. Instead, I searched sort of aimlessly for something, some way, to regain the vigor that had brought me to this line of work in the first place.

Inspiration came in the form of an article that appeared in an issue of *Scope* magazine, which was published by Scholastic, Inc., and distributed in classrooms throughout the United States. The story was about a program in which students were given an opportunity to attend an intensive, week-long session at the U.S. Space & Rocket Center, a 450-acre theme park, museum, and educational center located next door to the U.S. Army's Redstone Arsenal in Huntsville, Alabama. The students, almost all of whom were labeled "gifted" or "talented," participated in a variety of activities similar to those experienced by astronauts in training for missions on the space shuttle. The week included simulated missions and competition with other similarly bright and ambitious kids. I can't explain what came over me, what possessed me to read this article, the clean-cut subjects of which were uniformly brilliant and well-heeled—the kinds of students destined for Harvard, Yale, or MIT—and think: *Our kids would love this!* Maybe it had something to do with my own childhood infatuation with space and science. Or maybe it was born out of desperation, out of a need to do something so unlikely and improbable that it would require nothing less than a complete and blind commitment. A leap of faith, so to speak.

I was reading the article a second or third time when my teaching partner, Robynn McKinney, approached my desk. Robynn and I shared a classroom in a remote part of the school, not far from the gym, but well out of the way of most traffic, and a good distance from the nerve center of the school: the main entrance and the front office. Literally and metaphorically, we worked on the fringes of the school, making the most of our own decisions and trying to do the best we could for our students, getting little feedback from our principal or other teachers, except when one of our students got into some sort of trouble. Our kids generally were not mainstreamed—other than home economics and automotive repair, the great majority of their classes were taught by Robynn and me. She usually had the emotionally impaired students, while I had the learning disabled students, although it really didn't matter since we split teaching duties down the middle. The room was divided by a retractable partition, and we were free to switch kids from one class to another, exchange subject matter . . . whatever we wanted. We were a self-contained classroom, all right, so much so that most of the school barely recognized our existence. Our room was like a big cell block: no windows, bad light, bad air. My first special ed job was in an inner-city school, and my room there had been little more than a closet next to the steam room. A cubicle that barely fit five people comfortably, it was a pitiful excuse for a classroom and sent a clear message to the kids who were taught there: *You are worthless.* The setting at Forest Hills Northern was vastly superior, but nonetheless inadequate for the function it was given. The implication, again, was that these were kids who didn't deserve the same opportunities or consideration as the rest of the school population, and that made it less than a healthy environment in which to learn.

This sort of second-class treatment bothered me more than it bothered Robynn. She was no less committed, no less inspired in her devotion to teaching special-needs students, but she was better at shrugging things off, at refusing to take these inequities personally. She simply did her job, and she did it extremely well, regardless of the obstacles placed in her way. Me? I would do a slow boil.

Now, though, I was merely excited. The more I read about Space Camp, the more I liked the sound of it.

"What are you looking at?" Robynn asked as she glanced over my shoulder.

I pushed my chair away from the desk, leaned back, and gave her some room. "Here. Check this out."

She picked up the magazine and began to read. I didn't watch her, didn't wait for a reaction, because I was reasonably sure that it would not exactly mesh with mine. After a couple minutes Robynn slapped me on the back of the head with the magazine and fairly shrieked, "Are you out of your mind?"

"What?" I replied innocently. "It's a good story."

"Yeah, right, Kersjes. I know what you're thinking."

"You do?" Of course she did. One of the reasons we worked so well together was a tacit understanding of the other person's personality, including all strengths and weaknesses. Robynn knew me as well as anyone on the planet, with the possible exception of my wife.

"Yeah, this is another of your nutty ideas," she said, admonishing me with a wag of her finger. "And you should put it out of your mind right now. You know what kind of kids we have in this classroom. How in the world do you see them doing something like this?"

I shrugged. "It's just a thought."

"Uh-huh . . . a bad one. Forget about it."

Robynn knew how I felt about taking chances, about how strongly I believed in teaching kids to challenge themselves, to question the labels that had been thrust upon them. On occasion I had done some odd things to get this point across, and more often than not Robynn had enthusiastically supported me, even though it sometimes meant incurring the wrath of our superiors. This time, though, she was certain I had lost whatever tenuous grip on reality I had previously held. I couldn't blame her. Special ed kids at Space Camp? *Good God!* The mind boggled at the potential for mayhem.

She tossed the magazine on the desk and began to walk away.

"There's an eight hundred number," I said, somewhat sheepishly.

"Excuse me?"

"Here, in this little box." Robynn had turned around and come back. "See? Can't hurt to make a phone call, right? Won't cost a dime."

She rolled her eyes. I could see she was exasperated. Sometimes Robynn would lose patience with me and she'd end up dancing around my desk, waving her arms, her voice rising steadily as she tried to talk some sense into me. We were headed in that direction now.

"I don't believe you," she said. "Think about this, Mike. It's nuts."

I stood and began walking toward the door, *Scope* magazine in hand. Robynn was a step behind me—this, too, was typical. If she couldn't talk me out of something, Robynn usually became an accomplice. "I'll just make one call, see if they have any programs for kids with disabilities."

"And that's it?"

"That's it."

"If they say no, you'll drop the whole thing?"

I nodded. "Absolutely."

AS ROBYNN AND I squeezed into the little phone booth outside the main office, I could see Marge Sheffield peering over the top of her computer monitor. As an administrative secretary, Marge was Forest Hills' chief traffic cop and gossipmonger. She always wanted to know what was going on and usually she had a way of finding out. Robynn and I were offering no information, though. Not yet, anyway.

With Robynn pounding me on the shoulder, simultaneously laughing and admonishing me—"I can't believe you're doing this!"—I dialed the 800 number for Space Camp. A woman picked up on the first ring.

"Good morning, Space & Rocket Center, may I help you?"

I took a deep breath. "Hi, my name is Mike Kersjes and I'm calling from Forest Hills Northern High School in Grand Rapids, Michigan. I'd like to speak to someone about the Space Camp program."

"One moment . . ."

I was quickly transferred to an administrator named Heiko Enfield, the assistant director of camp programs. He was pleasant and well spoken, and listened patiently as I explained who I was. I told him I was a football coach who worked with special education students, and I was wondering whether Space Camp offered any types of programs for kids such as ours.

My question was met with dead air.

"Mr. Enfield?"

"Yes, I'm here," he said, the tone in his voice reflecting a mixture of apprehension and irritation. "I'm afraid we don't have anything like that right now. Space Camp really is a program for gifted and talented children, as you probably know."

"I understand. But I was hoping there might be opportunities for kids who are a little less fortunate but no less enthusiastic."

Another long pause.

"Not that I know of. However, if you'd like, I'll be happy to transfer you to my boss, Dr. Deborah Barnhart—she's the director of our camp programs."

"That would be great. Thanks."

"Okay . . . hold on a minute."

As Muzak poured out of the phone, Robynn gave me a nudge. "What's going on?"

"I'm moving up the chain of command."

She slapped me again on the back of the head. "You're insane, you know that?"

I looked at Marge, who was now whispering to another secretary and occasionally glancing in our direction. I could just guess what they were talking about.

Suddenly the Muzak stopped.

"Deborah Barnhart speaking."

"Hi, Dr. Barnhart," I began. "This is Mike Kersjes calling."

"Yes, Mike . . . Heiko briefed me. What can I do for you?"

For the next five minutes I proceeded to give Dr. Barnhart a pitch. I told her what types of kids we had and why I thought they would benefit from Space Camp. As I listed the various disabilities exhibited by our students, I could sense her interest waning. Bad karma was flowing out of the receiver.

"I'll tell you what," she finally said. "Why don't you and your partner put together a formal proposal, something that outlines your students' disabilities, their strengths and weaknesses, and why you think this would be a beneficial experience."

Hmmmm . . . Isn't that what I just did?

"Give me something very detailed . . . very precise," she went on, "and I'll take a look at it."

Now, I'd been involved with enough bureaucrats and administrators to know a kiss-off when I heard it. This proposal was going straight into the circular file. Deborah Barnhart would never see it; in fact, I doubt she thought we'd actually write a proposal. This was merely her way of sidestepping a potentially distasteful and uncomfortable issue. I knew all of this, but I didn't let on. I simply exited the conversation politely.

"Okay, Dr. Barnhart. Let me talk it over with my partner and we'll see what we can do. Thanks for your time."

"Thank you, Mike."

As we left the phone booth and began to walk back to our classroom, Robynn continued to berate me for being such a dreamer. She vowed not to help with the proposal, though I knew she would. Standing just a few yards away, eavesdropping on our conversation, was our principal, Tom Keller. Like me, Tom loved sports, especially football—and since I'd been a coach on a state championship team, there was a degree of respect between us. But it was a small degree. Tom was new to Forest Hills Northern, had in fact just completed his first year as principal. He struck me as a climber, someone who had no intention of staying in one job for very long; he made few attempts to connect with anyone—students or faculty—on a personal basis. Tom stressed nothing so much as curriculum (in fact, in just a few years he would leave to become superintendent of curriculum in another district), and so he had little use for vocational education of any sort. His mission was to improve the test scores of the top students in the school, thereby making the town a more attractive place in which to live and raise children, and greatly improving the chances that he'd soon be promoted into a new position. It was a sound, ego-driven strategy that had worked for administrators at any number of schools. Unfortunately, there was no place in this master plan for special education. Special ed just didn't fit in.

Tom asked, slickly and casually, what all the commotion was about. I held up *Scope* magazine and said, "Space Camp, Tom. We're looking into it."

He held his hands out, palms up. "Why? What would you do there?"

Already I was annoyed. I could feel the hairs on the back of my neck standing on end. "The same thing other kids do there: learn about space," I replied. "They've asked us to write a proposal, and I think we're going to do it."

Robynn didn't say anything. She wasn't on board yet. As for Tom, well, he smiled thinly, arrogantly, and said, "Come on, Mike. Think about what you're doing here. Some of these kids have IQs below eighty-five. They come from broken homes, foster homes. This is ridiculous." He smoothed his neat silk tie with his hand, straightened his jacket, and added, "Besides, I want you guys concentrating on curriculum, not this kind of . . . nonsense."

Tom's response was entirely predictable. In general he disapproved of the way Robynn and I did things, the way we ran our classroom with complete disregard for the principal's wishes. We broke a fair number of rules and regulations, although not because we wanted to be difficult, and not because we were stupid or pigheaded (okay . . . maybe a little pigheaded). Rather, we just wanted to do what was best for our students, and sometimes that meant getting involved in an intensely personal way—finding jobs for them, creating alternative types of curriculum, treating them as family. Sometimes our approach backfired, but we were always willing to accept the consequences. Our attitude was this: *We're with these kids for seven hours a day, so don't tell us what's best for them. You don't even know them.* Did we miss department meetings? Yes. Did we do what we were told? Not always. Did we regret any of it? Not in the least.

"Well, I think it's worth a shot," I said to Tom as we walked away. "I'll keep you posted."

"Yeah, Mike. You do that," he said.

I was pretty sure Tom's attitude mirrored that of Dr. Barnhart: *They won't even write this proposal, so I'm not going to get all worked up about it.* To be perfectly honest, I wasn't so sure myself.

THAT DAY, AT football practice, the idea rattled around in my head. I was having trouble concentrating, which was unusual for me. I loved football and was typically fixated on it throughout the fall. We were going to have a very good team that season, so I shouldn't have been prone to distraction. For some reason, though, I couldn't shake the idea of Space Camp. I'll admit that part of it was being told no. Here I had this idea—admittedly, an idea that was a little odd, a little adventurous—and everyone was responding to it negatively. The people at Space Camp wanted no part of our kids. Our principal thought the notion was laughable. Even Robynn was expressing doubt. Of course, in her case, I understood where it was coming from. She didn't want to see me get hurt, didn't want to see the kids embarrassed. I sensed that she just wanted to gauge my level of commitment before allowing herself to be dragged into something she might regret. I trusted Robynn implicitly. Although we'd only worked together for a few years, we'd known each other since high school. I'd been a football player at Catholic Central High in Grand Rapids and Robynn had been a cheerleader at nearby Ottaway Hills. She had later attended dental hygiene school with my wife, Darcy. It became a career for Darcy, but Robynn lasted only a short time as a hygienist before returning to school, at Texas Christian University, where she earned a degree in teaching. Some fifteen years after graduating from high school, we found ourselves working together in our hometown. Our relationship was comfortable, respectful, professional, and undoubtedly strengthened by something of a "foxhole" mentality. Still, in this case, Robynn was wary. Maybe there was a reason they didn't have a program for special education students at Space Camp. Maybe it was simply too demanding, too risky.

After practice I picked up my two sons, five-year-old Ryan and nine-year-old Shawn, and went home. Darcy was still at work, so I started dinner and tried to keep those two wild little boys from tearing the house apart. It was no small task, since I was tired and having trouble concentrating. Eventually I took a seat at the kitchen table and began fiddling with a napkin. Without even really thinking about it, I folded the napkin into a paper airplane and zipped it at Ryan. He reached up, snatched it out of the air, and giggled uncontrollably.

"Show me how to make one, Daddy!" he squealed. *"Please!"*

So I did. For the next half hour we sat there, me and my two kids, and constructed airplanes out of paper napkins. The first few didn't turn out so well, and some of them didn't fly quite right, but the boys were undeterred. Eventually they each built an airplane that flew straight and true. As I watched them, two little boys completely enthralled by something so simple and elegant, I thought, *Look how quickly they picked this up. Our students can do this, too.*

And that was it. I made a decision that night. I didn't say it out loud, to my wife or my children, but I said it nonetheless, just moments before giving myself over to sleep: *We're going to Space Camp!*

2

Most of the students who found their way into our classroom did so only after numerous missteps. Robynn and I represented one last, desperate chance—we were the final stop before they were placed in some type of alternative school or, worse, institutionalized. A few of the kids came from middle- and upper-middle-class families, but most were from the lower end of the socioeconomic spectrum. Nearly all of them were convinced of their own worthlessness. They were special ed kids, and everyone knew it. They might as well have had the word *stupid* tattooed on their foreheads.

That sort of self-loathing is tough to break down, which is one reason I always kept in my classroom a poster bearing a quote from Albert Einstein, one of my personal heroes, and a man who overcame a childhood learning disability to become one of the most revered and influential mathematicians in history:

"Imagination is more important than knowledge, for knowledge is limited and imagination can encircle the world."

At the start of each year I'd point out this poster, talk about Einstein, and then ask the students, "How many of you have an imagination?" And, of course, virtually every hand would rise.

"Good," I'd say. "Because I don't care about your IQ. I don't care about your standardized test scores. We're all equal here, and we're all going to work together, and imagination is going to play an important role in how well you do."

Getting the kids to embrace this notion was a challenge, especially when it seemed as though the whole school was united against them, from the administration right down to their own peers. I avoided the faculty lounge because I got tired of listening to teachers complaining about the kids they were supposed to be helping. The most bilious remarks often were reserved for the least fortunate kids, the ones with learning disabilities. After hearing, "Hey, Kersjes, you know what your idiots did today?" for the hundredth time, I decided I'd had enough of the faculty lounge. I began eating in my classroom with my students. And we'd talk. There, in the privacy and safety of that room, they would open up. This was new to me when I first came to Forest Hills Northern. When I'd taught in the inner city, my special education kids didn't seem to mind eating in the cafeteria; they were more readily accepted by the mainstream students. Out in suburbia, though, the meanness was palpable. Many of my students hated going to the cafeteria, where they would be subjected to all kinds of nasty and confrontational behavior, so they begged me to let them eat in my room. Even though it was a violation of school policy, I agreed. Interestingly enough, when people would walk by the room, the students would slide their chairs away from the doorway, try to blend into a wall. They didn't want to be seen, didn't want to be identified as "special ed." And yet they willingly spent their free time in that room because it was the one place where they felt secure. It was their sanctuary.

THE FIRST WEEK of that new year was like any other: wild, exhausting, chaotic. Robynn and I spent most of our time arranging schedules for the students, carefully selecting the teachers we thought would work well with our kids in the handful of classes in which they were going to be mainstreamed. From an organizational standpoint, scheduling was always a nightmare. We tried our best to make everyone else happy— the students, the parents, the other teachers—but, typically, each day brought a barrage of new complaints.

And, of course, a barrage of behavior problems. Some were benign, some fairly serious, but all had to be addressed in a timely fashion. Predictably, Steve Bennett was the subject of a good percentage of the calls that came to my room that week. Steve was essentially a good kid, one of the most spirited, funny, and interesting students I've ever taught, in fact, and one of my all-time favorites. That said, I can't deny that he was capable of great and premeditated mischief. Steve was born with Tourette's syndrome, a neurological disorder characterized by "tics"—involuntary, rapid, sudden movements that occur repeatedly in the same way. Tourette's syndrome usually presents itself in the teenage years and is frequently accompanied by attention deficit hyperactivity disorder. In Steve's case, Tourette's manifested itself most often in the form of facial grimaces and arm movements. He would also fart and belch at the most inopportune moments, and seemed to delight in making all kinds of outrageous comments, often peppered with vulgarities.

One of the interesting things about Tourette's is that while it surely is a maddening disorder that has a powerful grip on its victim, it also allows someone who has been diagnosed to . . . shall we say . . . take advantage of the situation. Some things were beyond Steve's control, but he also knew how to get under a person's skin. There were many times when he'd cut loose with a stream of expletives or interrupt a classroom discussion with a powerful display of flatulence, and you could tell by the look on his face that he was doing it strictly for his own amusement. Steve also had a fascination with toys and gizmos of all kinds. He was like Captain Kangaroo, forever pulling yo-yos, kazoos, harmonicas, model cars, and tiny plastic mice out of his pockets. I'd be standing in front of the class and hear a loud crackling from the back of the room, and then the sound of voices rattling across the airwaves, sometimes accompanied by a siren. And there would be Steve, his ear pressed against a police scanner, holding up a finger, saying, "Big fire downtown, Coach. Sounds pretty bad." It was Steve's goal in life to be a paramedic, and listening to a scanner was his way of preparing, studying. "Just doing my homework," he'd say, and I couldn't help but laugh.

The school bus brought out the best in Steve, or the worst, depending on your point of view. He loved an audience, and here were fifty or sixty kids all jammed into one small space, just waiting for Steve to amuse them. He rarely disappointed. Unfortunately, the bus driver on Steve's route failed to see the humor in Steve's performance, and as a result Steve very nearly lost his riding privileges in the first week of school. Each day I was handed a new disciplinary report, and each day I had to sit Steve down and try to explain to him that he could not indulge his every compulsion. With an impish grin on his face, and his foot tapping the floor in a staccato rhythm, he'd just nod. "Okay, Coach. It won't happen again."

While some teachers had little tolerance for Steve, I found him to be an immensely likable kid. The same odd wiring that resulted in his Tourette's syndrome also seemed to fuel an industriousness that you couldn't help but admire. Granted, Steve had trouble concentrating at times, but he was far from a slacker. In fact, he held numerous jobs and even started the first recycling program at Forest Hills Northern. Steve was one of the wealthier kids in our program—his father was a financial adviser and his mother was extremely active in the school arts programs—but I never sensed that he was spoiled. In fact, while he was quick-witted and capable of some remarkably acerbic comments, often directed at his classmates, he was also one of our most caring and thoughtful students, as evidenced by his relationship with Ben Schmidt.

Ben was the first student with Down's syndrome to attend Forest Hills Northern. Heavy-lidded, a bit overweight, and nearly always with a smile on his face, Ben had the typical look of someone with Down's. How far he had come in his fifteen years was especially clear to his parents, who had been advised, shortly after Ben's birth, to place their son in an institution. "He will never be able to take care of himself," they were told. "He will never have a normal life." "Normal," I've discovered, is a hard thing to define. Ben had a speech impediment and wore thick glasses to correct his vision. He was prone to catching colds and thus always seemed to have a runny nose. He'd frequently have to be reminded to zip up his pants after returning from the bathroom. Because Ben was gullible and generally trusting, he was an easy mark for other students, including some of those in our own program, but he was also an irrepressibly affectionate young man who was quick to wrap his arms around anyone he considered to be a friend. Steve Bennett was at the top of that list, for it was Steve who looked after Ben, who made sure that Ben ate his lunch every day and who quickly interceded when others tried to humiliate or embarrass Ben. Steve was Ben's surrogate brother, and anyone with the temerity to attack Ben was sure to experience Steve's response in short order. Sometimes Steve retaliated by leaping directly to Ben's defense and getting in the face of his tormenter. Usually, though, the retort was more clever than that. There was the time, for example, when Steve used his position as clerk at the school store to exact his revenge on some kids who had been teasing Ben. While serving hot cocoa one chilly winter morning, Steve decided he would prick their Styrofoam cups with a tiny pin, releasing a slow trickle of liquid over the customers' gloves and sleeves. By the time they realized what had happened, they were halfway to their homerooms and covered with thick, sweet chocolate.

Bad behavior, to be sure, but nonetheless admirable on a purely visceral level.

A harder case was Lewis Dayhuff, who was bused in every day from East Grand Rapids. Although he was a fourteen-year-old freshman that year, Lewis read at a second-grade level; even a cursory glance at his profile revealed that he had thus far been denied any semblance of a typical childhood. Abused as a young boy, and a veteran of more than two dozen foster homes, Lewis was an angry kid prone to violent outbursts. Lewis was mad at the world, and you really couldn't blame him for feeling that way. He and his younger brother were currently living with a miserable set of foster parents who viewed the two boys as nothing more than cheap labor for their dairy farm. The foster father was a heavy drinker, too. They were the types of people you see all too often in foster care: cynical, callous men and women who take in children not because they have love to give, but because they're looking for a handout from the government. There is no caring, no nurturing. They are professional foster parents, interested only in the almighty dollar.

An angular boy with unruly hair, Lewis was deceptively strong, at least in a physical sense. Never one to turn the other cheek, he was involved in three fistfights in the hallways during his first week at Forest Hills Northern. Not that he was merely a victim—Lewis was antagonistic and hotheaded, with a foul mouth and a fondness for rude comments. He fancied himself quite the ladies' man and could not understand why the girls in suburbia failed to swoon when he winked and said, "Nice set of jugs, baby." At the slightest provocation Lewis would fly into a rage, turning even the smallest disagreement into a physical confrontation. Hostile to the point of being dangerous, Lewis rarely gave even the slightest consideration to the consequences of his actions; he merely reacted in whatever way felt appropriate at the time.

It was obvious from the first day that hanging on to Lewis, preventing him from becoming a casualty of the child welfare system, would be a full-time job. Reaching him, on any level, would be one of the most challenging experiences of my teaching career.

Robynn and I used the proverbial back door to accomplish a lot of our goals in that first week, especially when it came to getting the kids in the classes they needed. Thankfully, we had an ally in Judy Brey, one of the guidance counselors. Judy had tremendous empathy for our kids, and she worked all kinds of magic to help them fit in. Regrettably, the students could not always be counted on to hold up their end of the bargain.

"Please, whatever you do, just don't screw up," we'd say after handing them their schedules. They'd nod, say "Thanks," and within a few hours, maybe a few days, the disciplinary problems would begin. Some of our more talented kids would start the year mainstreamed in three or four classes, but invariably, after confrontations with teachers, habitual tardiness, and absenteeism, they'd end up back in our classroom for six out of seven periods a day. They were simply too disruptive, too much work, for even the most energetic teachers to handle. The only thing that made those first few weeks bearable was that I was generally allowed to handle the disciplining of my own students. Most of the other teachers were good about that—when they had a problem with one of our students, they'd bring the student directly to me or Robynn and let us determine the consequences, rather than marching the kid right to the principal. If disciplinary matters were handled in the customary manner, I never would have gotten any work done. I'd have spent nearly all of my time running back and forth to the front office.

IT WAS IN that first week of school that I decided to introduce our students to Space Camp. Some caution was required when floating the idea, for I didn't want to present it as something that was a legitimate possibility, at least not yet. Moreover, I had no way of knowing how they might react. So, in an effort to test the waters, I passed out a bunch of the *Scope* magazines.

"Open to page sixteen," I said. We were supposed to be looking at an article that highlighted a number of books students might be interested in reading during the upcoming year. I chose that article first, however, because on the facing page was the story about Space Camp.

This was a not-so-subtle way of eliciting a reaction from the kids. It worked, too, although not quite the way I had planned.

"Hey! Look at this," Steve Bennett said. "Coach—you see this Space Camp thing? It looks kind of cool."

"Huh?" I responded, feigning ignorance and indifference. "Oh . . . yeah . . ." I paused and looked at the article, as if reading it for the first time. "That is interesting. What do the rest of you think?"

A lot of the kids just shrugged and grumbled. Our classroom was hardly a place of solidarity. The kids did not see themselves as a group of special students united in some great cause. In many ways they resented one another, for the simple reason that they did not want to be identified as being part of this group. It was sort of like Groucho Marx's old joke about not wanting to be part of any club that would have him as a member. As a result, our kids sometimes behaved terribly toward one another. While they would occasionally fight with mainstream students, they saved their most callous and insensitive remarks for the people who were most like themselves.

So when Stephanie Reinks leaned forward in her seat and shouted, "I think it would be fun, Coach!" I could almost smell blood in the water. Stephanie was emotionally impaired and learning disabled. She wanted nothing more than to be liked by everyone, but her physical appearance made her a target for all types of cruel behavior. Stephanie was nearly six feet two inches tall and overweight; she wore thick glasses. She also had a speech impediment. Other students often referred to her as "Alice the Goon," the unfortunate moniker of an old cartoon character so homely and frightening that she routinely sent the great Popeye the Sailor Man running for a can of spinach so that he could rebuff her advances. Imagine how hard it would be to go through each school day knowing other kids were going to address you as Alice the Goon, and you can understand why Stephanie spent so much time crying, and why she periodically slammed the door in our room so hard that the glass would shatter.

The words of approval were barely out of Stephanie's mouth when her nemesis, Scott Goudy, jumped in. Scott was obviously learning disabled (among other problems, he was dyslexic), but he resented, perhaps more than any of our kids, the label of special education. He didn't want to be in our class, and in fact many of his friends, including his girlfriend, were regular education students. Scott also suffered from alopecia, so he had smooth, hairless arms and the receding hairline of a middle-aged man, which didn't exactly help his self-confidence. Stephanie, for some reason, brought out the worst in Scott; so when she voiced some enthusiasm about Space Camp, Scott leaped all over her.

"Shut up, Alice! You big gump!"

"You shut up!"

I put up my hands. "Settle down." Too late. I'd lost control already. As Stephanie and Scott shouted at each other, the other students began to toss out comments, some in favor of Space Camp—and remember, we were talking simply about the concept of Space Camp; I hadn't yet suggested that it might be a place they'd like to visit.

Suddenly, Ben stood up at his desk, and with a big smile on his face, said, "Space? Cool!" Meanwhile, in the back of the room, there was Steve, taking full advantage of the chaos around him. "Three . . . two . . . one . . . blast off!" he shouted. And then, as only Steve could, he perfectly mimicked the sound of a rocket ship pulling away from the launch pad. "WHOOOOOSH!" As the bickering continued, Steve made a loud whistling sound, "Eeeeeeewwwwwwww," punctuated by a cry of "Incoming!" and the sound of an explosion, in this case signifying our room being blown to bits.

I looked over at Robynn, who was rolling her eyes and giving me an "I told you so" look.

"All right, everyone quiet down," I said. "Space Camp isn't quite like that. There are no bombs, and you don't really go into outer space. You learn how to be an astronaut. You learn how to prepare for a mission, you learn about space history. There's structure to it, and there's a lot of hard work."

Several of the kids began moaning. "Oh, you mean we gotta study? Forget it!"

Now I was losing my patience. "Dammit, guys! Listen for a minute, will you? That's not what I'm talking about. The students who attend Space Camp have a lot of fun. It's a great opportunity, and you know what? I think it would be great for us."

Ben thrust his hand into the air. "Coach?"

"Yes, Ben."

"I have a question."

"I know, Ben . . . go ahead."

"Isn't Space Camp for smart kids?"

The whole room, with the exception of Scott Goudy, cracked up. Steve resumed his rocket sounds, and the others pounded their desks in approval. The reaction was profoundly disappointing, for it mirrored the response of our principal. So ingrained was the notion of being stupid, pathetic losers that they couldn't imagine a place for themselves at Space Camp. It would have been easy to let it go then, to collect the magazines, toss them away, and never mention Space Camp again. But I didn't. Sometimes our kids needed more than a gentle nudge to explore their own limits, and this was obviously one of those times. Truth be told, I needed it, too. So, when the commotion subsided, I read the article aloud. I let it sink in for a few moments and then said, as directly and calmly as possible, "Guys . . . I think you can do this."

3

Within a week I had cobbled together a proposal. Having never written anything like it before, I really had no idea what I was doing, so I decided to simply give Dr. Barnhart precisely what she had requested. Robynn and I compiled short profiles of each student in the program, and I supplemented those with an impassioned essay about Space Camp and how it might boost the self-esteem of our students. All of this was done in relative secrecy. I didn't seek approval from our principal or the regional coordinator of special education. I didn't even tell my wife. With two small boys running around the house, and both of us working full time, our lives were wild and stressful enough at that point. I was pretty sure Darcy wouldn't have been thrilled with the idea of me taking on more responsibility at school, especially something as strange and problematic as preparing a group of special ed kids for Space Camp. Anyway, I figured there was a reasonable chance the proposal would be either ignored or shot down, so why bother getting her all worked up about it? No . . . better to ship it off quietly, with no great expectations.

A week passed without a response from Huntsville. Then two weeks . . . three weeks.

"This is killing me," I said to Robynn at the end of the third week. "I'd better call and see if they've at least read the proposal."

"Why?" she asked. "Don't you think it's pretty obvious that they don't care? If they liked the idea, they'd call."

She was right, of course. Robynn was usually right. She was much more logical than I was, much less likely to act on impulse. Still, I needed some sort of closure.

"We put quite a bit of effort into that proposal," I said. "The least they can do is give us an answer. They owe us that much."

By now some of the students had gotten excited about the idea of attending Space Camp. We had been talking about it a little bit, and they had become increasingly curious, although they were still plagued by self-doubt, saying things like, "Coach, they won't even let us into the regular ed science classes here. How can we go to Space Camp?" A valid point, and one that I couldn't answer.

So I called the Space & Rocket Center, and once again I was transferred to Heiko Enfield. He apologized for the delay, informed me that Dr. Barnhart was in a meeting, but assured me that she would return my call that day. To my surprise, she did exactly that. A short time after lunch one of the secretaries from the office poked her head into our room and said, with an arched eyebrow, "Mike, you have a phone call. It's from Space Camp." She smiled and walked out of the room, leaving me standing there with a golf ball–sized lump in my throat. I hurried to Robynn's side of the room and told her what had happened.

"I'm going with you," she said.

I was fortunate to have a wonderful aide in my classroom, a woman named Ginny Sieracki. Ginny was at once a mother hen and a drill instructor. Her husband had been my football coach in high school, and now she was working for me, which was kind of strange, but I loved having Ginny in the room. She was smart and forceful, and I could always count on her to maintain order if I had to attend to other business, as I did right now.

Robynn and I rushed right past the main office and took the call in the phone booth, but not before Tom Keller flagged us down. "I want to talk to you after this," he said, the tone in his voice making it clear that he'd been briefed by one of the secretaries, and he wasn't particularly happy. Not that I cared.

I took a deep breath and picked up the receiver.

"Mike Kersjes speaking."

"Hi, Mike, this is Deborah Barnhart." I gave Robynn the thumbs-up sign and mouthed the words *Dr. Barnhart*. She smiled approvingly. "I'm sorry it's taken so long to get back to you, but it's been very busy here lately. I'm sure you understand."

"Of course."

"I haven't had a chance to look at your proposal yet, but I want you to know that I have every intention of reading it, and as soon as I do, I'll give you a call."

Something in her voice told me this was another kiss-off, so I decided to press the issue.

"Any chance you can read it tonight?" I asked.

Dead silence. She hadn't expected that. But Dr. Barnhart was not easily swayed. "Actually, I'm kind of busy tonight," she finally said. "But I'll get in touch with you soon. You have my word."

After hanging up the phone I turned to Robynn.

"Well?" she asked.

"They're never going to read it . . . unless we call their bluff."

"What do you mean?"

"I mean they're just waiting for us to give up and go away. If we're serious about this thing, we're going to have to apply some pressure."

Robynn laughed. "Yeah, right. We're going to put pressure on Space Camp. How do you figure that?"

I smiled. "With a little help from Paul Henry."

Paul Henry was our congressman, as well as the cochairman of the Space and Technology Committee in Washington, D.C., which meant he was deeply involved in determining the allocation of federal funds to NASA, and, by extension, to places such as the United States Space & Rocket Center. A call from Congressman Henry would surely make Dr. Barnhart take notice. The challenge, obviously, was convincing him of the merit of our plan. He was an extraordinarily busy man, after all. My only hope was that he would recognize my name, since my sister had been deeply involved in his most recent campaign.

So, with the principal eyeing us from his office, and with Robynn once again pounding me on the back in disbelief, I called Paul Henry's office in Grand Rapids. His secretary answered and I quickly told her who I was, dropping my sister's name in the first few sentences. She explained that Congressman Henry was in Washington and probably would not be back in town for at least another month. I was just be-

ginning to deflate when she added, "But I can connect you to his autobahn line in Washington."

"Autobahn?"

"Yeah . . . it's like a hot line."

Cool!

"You'll be speaking to Mary Dunn, Congressman Henry's assistant.
Tell her what you need, and I'm sure she'll do whatever she can to
help."

The next thing I knew I was telling Ms. Dunn the entire story—how
we wanted to take a group of special education kids to Space Camp, but
had thus far been unable to get a response from the camp's administration. To my surprise, she seemed legitimately moved.

"Special ed kids at Space Camp," she said. "How exciting."

"Thank you, ma'am. The kids are excited, too."

"Paul is in session right now," she went on. "But as soon as he gets
out, I'll have him give you a call."

Oh no . . . here we go again. Another runaround.

"Do you have any idea when that might be?" I asked, trying to be
forceful but polite.

"He'll be through at the end of the day. Would you like him to call
then?"

"Uhhhh . . ." I stammered. She had caught me off-guard with that
one. "Well, I have football practice this afternoon. How about tomorrow
morning?"

"That would be fine. Why don't you call here before nine o'clock?"

"You want me to call him?"

"Uh-huh. I'll set up a conference call and you can give him your
pitch then."

As we left the phone booth, Robynn looked at me. "Good news?"

"Yeah. We have a conference call with Congressman Henry first thing
in the morning."

"All right!" Robynn shouted, but her jubilance was interrupted by
Tom Keller.

"In here," he said, wagging a finger at us. "Now."

The secretaries stared as we disappeared into the principal's office,
the looks on their faces saying, "Dead man walking!" Tom was pacing

back and forth, agitated but not really angry. "I thought we had an understanding that this was not the smartest thing to do," he began.

Robynn and I looked at each other. It was time to play dumb.

"What?" I said.

Tom shook his head. "Come on, Mike. You know what I'm talking about—sending special ed kids to Space Camp. We agreed that it was a bad idea."

"No, Tom . . . *you* said it was a bad idea. *We* didn't agree on anything."

Robynn shot me a look of admonishment. The last thing we needed now was a fight with the principal. Better to play it cool. But, then, Robynn was much more of a diplomat than I was.

"It doesn't look like it's going very far, anyway," she said.

"Oh?" Tom replied.

I picked up on Robynn's cue. "Yeah. Turns out they haven't even read our proposal yet. We may hear something tomorrow, though."

That last statement, which wasn't a lie, but wasn't quite the truth either (I didn't say anything about calling Congressman Henry's office), seemed to placate Tom. He dismissed us with a wary glance and went back to doing whatever it was that he did all day, while Robynn and I returned to our classroom and went about the business of teaching.

WHEN I ARRIVED at school the next morning, with hollow eyes rimmed by dark circles, the result of having tossed and turned all night, the kids immediately sensed something was up.

"Hey, Coach, you seem nervous," Stephanie said. "Everything all right?"

"Yeah, I'm fine. I just have an important phone call to make this morning."

I'd never been one to believe that nervousness was a sign of weakness. Over the years I'd seen enough kids throw up in the locker room before a football game and then perform brilliantly on the field to know that anxiety was merely one way in which the body prepared for stress. So the fact that I'd spent most of the previous night conducting an imaginary dialogue with Paul Henry really didn't concern me. I'd never spoken to a congressman before, and I wanted to be prepared. Was I nervous? Absolutely. I was also fairly confident.

I made the call at precisely nine A.M. and was immediately patched through to Congressman Henry. When he began the conversation with, "Hi, Mike . . . how's your sister?" I felt a surge of adrenaline: *Great! He remembers!*

"She's fine, sir."

"Good, good. Now . . . what can I do for you?"

"Well, Congressman Henry, I have this idea for sending my special ed kids to Space Camp. I think—"

He cut me off. "Great idea!"

"Thank you, sir. I think so, too. Unfortunately, I'm not making much progress. I wrote a proposal three weeks ago, and the people at Space Camp haven't even read it yet."

He sighed. "Why not? What's the problem?"

"I don't know. The person who has the proposal is Deborah Barnhart, and I know she's a very busy lady, but I'm starting to feel like she just doesn't want to deal with me or my kids."

That was all Paul needed to hear. He was a man of enormous energy, a man of action. "Okay," he said. "Here's what we're going to do. I have to go into session right now, but I'll be out around lunchtime, and I'll make a call down there on your behalf. We need to move this thing forward . . . *now.*"

The entire conversation lasted perhaps five minutes, and yet in that brief period of time I felt as though I had made more progress than in the previous month. I had never really been much of a political person, never had all that much faith in the political process. I'd never even considered writing a senator or calling a congressman, even though, in theory, it is their responsibility to serve their constituency and to listen to people such as myself. At the same time, I realized this was an unusual situation. I had a personal connection with Congressman Henry, and I had a hunch that he might be interested, that he might consider the notion of backing a program for learning disabled students at Space Camp to be a politically prudent thing to do.

One thing I hadn't really taken into consideration was the impact this would have on Dr. Barnhart and the other administrators at the Space & Rocket Center. So concerned was I with getting them to give our proposal a good and thoughtful read that I neglected to consider the possibility that my obstinance might make them angry. At the time, though, it seemed the right thing to do; in fact, it seemed like the only option.

At two o'clock that afternoon I was paged by the front office: "Mike, Congressman Henry's office is on the phone. Can you come down here, please?"

Robynn covered for me while I sprinted to the office and picked up the phone.

"You'll be hearing from them in about an hour," Paul said.

"From whom?"

"Space Camp." He paused. I could almost hear him smiling. "It's up to you now, Mike. Let me know how it goes."

"Thank you, sir."

"My pleasure."

Practically numb with excitement, I hung up the phone and froze. How could I do this without attracting the attention of the principal and his nosy secretaries?

"Marge?" I said. "I'm going to be getting a call around three o'clock. I'll be down in the coaches' office getting dressed for football practice. Can you transfer the call down there, please?"

She nodded politely and jotted something down on a piece of paper. I could tell this was eating away at her. She desperately wanted to know what was going on.

"Thanks," I said, and I started to walk out of the office. I was almost in the clear when Marge said, inquisitively, "So . . . what did Mr. Henry want?"

I stopped and turned. With a poker face I responded, "He'd like me to run for Congress."

Marge's eyes began to bulge. "Really?"

"Nah . . . I'm just kidding. It's nothing important."

"Ohhhh."

Gotcha!

AN HOUR LATER I was back on the telephone, this time with Dr. Barnhart. She was courteous but cool, her tone suggesting displeasure at having received a grumpy call from the cochairman of the Space and Technology Committee.

"I've read your proposal," she began. "It's very interesting."

Uhhhhh . . . is that good or bad?

"Congressman Henry thinks it would be a good idea for us to talk about this in greater depth," she went on. "Can you make a trip to Huntsville?"

"Yes," I answered, without giving it much thought.

"How soon?" she asked.

Uh-oh. Suddenly, this was moving more quickly than I had anticipated. I had sought nothing more than a fair chance, an honest appraisal of our proposal. Clearly, though, Congressman Henry had recommended a bit more. What he had suggested, I later found out, was this: *Have these people fly down and meet with them face-to-face. They have a good idea, and you should hear them out.*

"It'll have to be in the middle of the week," I said, "because I have football on the weekends."

"All right."

"Also . . . I have to get permission from our principal and special education coordinator."

Silence on the other end.

"Oh . . . I assumed you had that already," Dr. Barnhart said.

"No, not really." *Time to do a little tap dancing.* "I've kept this mostly to myself, so as not to disappoint too many people. You understand."

"Of course."

"I'm confident they'll support this," I lied. Then, slinging even bigger handfuls of crap, I added, "They're big fans of our program and our kids. I'm sure it won't be a problem."

Dr. Barnhart seemed to accept that explanation. She asked me to get together with Robynn and come up with a few possible dates that would work for us. Before ending the conversation, though, she let me know that we still faced an uphill battle.

"I have to be honest, Mike. Edward Buckbee, the chief executive officer of the Space & Rocket Center, is not really high on the idea of having special-needs students here, because this camp was founded as a place for gifted and talented kids. I told him about your proposal and, to be quite frank, he didn't like it at all. But he's willing to take a meeting."

That made sense. If I had been in charge of Space Camp, I'd probably have reacted the same way. Special ed kids were problematic. Doubtless it was a hassle Mr. Buckbee didn't need. At the same time, he, too, was a political creature, and thus smart enough to know that he had nothing to lose by giving us an hour of his time. That, he probably figured, would get us off his back, and satisfy Congressman Henry at the same time.

I knew this was the case; nevertheless, I was thrilled at having gotten this far. Each phone call peeled away anther layer of bureaucracy and brought us one step closer to achieving the impossible. I hung up the phone, finished getting dressed for football practice, and then sprinted back up to my room. Robynn was still there, along with several of the students.

"Well?" they said.

I was training for a marathon at this time, so I was in pretty good shape, but for some reason I couldn't catch my breath. So excited that I was practically hyperventilating, I choked out a few words.

"They . . . want . . . to . . . meet . . . us."

The kids looked at each other. Robynn cocked her head in disbelief. "Who?"

I paused, bent over, and let the blood rush back to my head. After a few seconds I stood back up and said, slowly and calmly, "We're meeting with Mr. Buckbee, the CEO of the Space & Rocket Center."

A moment or two passed as they measured the gravity of this statement. Finally, Grant Plunkett spoke up. "You know, I'll never fit into one of those damn flight suits."

This was typical of Grant's outlook on life. He was generally a quiet young man with a terrible outlook on life, mainly because his own life was so miserable. Overweight, badly dressed, and thoroughly disinterested in personal hygiene, Grant was achingly lonely. His father was gravely ill with kidney disease, and his mother did not work. The family was desperately poor. To say Grant was a pessimist would be to say that Johnny Unitas was a pretty good quarterback. The description, while accurate, just didn't do him justice. He reminded me of Eeyore, the sad-eyed donkey from *Winnie the Pooh*. To Grant everything was gloom and doom: "Oh, no, not this. Here we go again. This will be terrible." You could finish a hike with Grant and be sitting at the top of a mountain, looking out at some beautiful, breathtaking vista, and his response would be, "Oh, God, it's a long way down, I think I'm gonna be sick." There was never any light at the end of the tunnel with Grant, never a silver lining. Life simply sucked.

So it was no great surprise that Grant extracted only bad news from my announcement. The other kids, however, reacted in their typically quirky way.

"Does this mean we're going to Space Camp, Coach?" Ben asked.

"Sure it does, Ben," Steve Bennett piped in. "Let's get ready for liftoff. *Three . . . Two . . . One!*"

As Steve's rocket sounds filled the room, Scott Goudy pointed at Stephanie Reinks and shouted, "We're not taking Alice, are we?"

Stephanie jumped up, raced over to Scott, and smacked him on the back of the head. "Don't call me that!"

Robynn jumped in to break up their fight as the room fell apart again. As erasers flew and chairs toppled over, I thought, *It's a good thing Dr. Barnhart isn't here to see this.*

4

Even the most noble of plans can dissolve without the assistance of a few influential friends. In addition to Paul Henry, we were fortunate to have on our side a man named Mike Schmidt. Mike was an executive at Amway Corporation and a member of the Forest Hills Northern School Board. He also happened to be the father of Ben Schmidt, which meant he was a tireless advocate of our program. Robynn and I needed the support, or at least the tolerance, of the administration in order to pursue this thing any further, and there was no guarantee we'd get it. Mike knew of our plans and, of course, approved wholeheartedly. He and his wife had always pushed their son, but in a loving, gentle way. They had challenged the opinions of physicians and other specialists, the ones who thought Ben would spend his entire life in diapers, and together they'd raised a son any parent would be proud to call his or her own. If Ben wanted to go to Space Camp, and we were willing to take him, then they were going to do everything in their power to make it happen.

"If you get rejected by the principal, you call me," Mike had said. "Then we'll take it to the superintendent."

In early October Robynn and I had a meeting with Tom Keller. It was supposed to be the first of two meetings—the second would involve Denise Boitano, the regional coordinator of special education. That was the plan, anyway. We had barely sat down, though, when Tom said, "By the way, I've already talked to Denise, and she said she doesn't like the idea of you taking these kids to Space Camp. I'm just trying to give you a heads-up—she's dead set against it, so there's probably no reason for you to meet with her."

Robynn and I were stunned. We hadn't even made our pitch yet, and already we were being rebuffed.

"How about you, Tom? What do you think?" Robynn asked.

He shifted in his seat and then leaned forward, folding his arms on the desk in front of him. "To be perfectly honest, I don't think it's a very good idea, either. I know you've done a lot of work on this, and I know you believe in it, but I have a hard time rationalizing the expense. You're going to have to raise a lot of money for these kids, right?"

I nodded. There was no arguing that point. Robynn and I had done the math and estimated we'd need at least fifteen hundred dollars per student. We'd also need money to cover our own expenses, which included the upcoming trip to Huntsville, as well as the expenses of our aides. To be on the safe side, we settled on a figure of fifty thousand dollars. In every sense of the word, this was an ambitious project.

It wasn't just the money that concerned Tom. He made it very clear that he wanted us in the classroom, that he did not think it was our place to be delving into experiential education, especially with these kids.

"You should be *teaching*," he said. "You should be preparing these students as best you can for life beyond this school, not chasing some crazy dream that won't help them in any tangible way."

"This *will* help them," I said. "They'll be learning about science, history . . . they'll have a chance to accomplish things they never thought possible. Isn't that valuable?"

Tom shrugged. "You'll be out of the classroom too much, you won't be covering the prescribed curriculum, and you will all fall hopelessly behind. This is not the way I want to run my high school."

Your high school? Excuse me . . . I thought it belonged to the students.

There was no swaying Tom. He rattled off a laundry list of reasons why our idea had no merit whatsoever. I kept my cool, as did Robynn, but inside I was seething, thinking, *The hell with you! We're going to do this anyway.*

The conversation eventually withered and we were left sitting in Tom's office, staring at each other, trying to figure out where to go next. If looks could kill, Tom and I both would have been dead. I'm sure he was thinking, *You'd better not try to go around me on this one, Kersjes,* and I was definitely thinking, *Tom . . . I'm going right over your head.* I didn't like Tom in the first place, didn't respect him as an educator or as a man. Part of this, I'll admit, stemmed from the fact that Tom beat out a close friend of mine for the job of principal at Forest Hills Northern. I had supported Larry Curtis, an assistant principal and football coach who treated students and teachers with the respect they deserved. Larry was wonderful about letting me run the special education program the way I saw fit. He knew me and trusted me—more to the point, he knew I had the best interests of the students at heart, regardless of my methods.

Larry wanted to be principal of Forest Hills Northern in the worst way. It was his dream job, and he had spent years preparing for it. But, as often happens in these situations, a search committee decided to choose someone from outside the district. Along with a lot of other teachers, I was disturbed by the choice of Tom Keller, whose administrative experience had been limited to a principalship of a small, rural school. Nevertheless, I was willing to give him the benefit of the doubt. Regrettably, Tom made a terrible first impression, using the word "I" two or three times in every sentence, and almost never using the word "we." With his expensive suits, neatly trimmed hair, and athletic physique, Tom looked great, but he didn't look or sound like a team player. The job, to him, was all about personal opportunity and advancement: *"Look at me and what I can do!"*

Someone confronted me once and suggested that I was merely bitter that my buddy hadn't gotten the job, and because of that I was incapable of seeing Tom's strengths. "Come on," I was told. "This guy must be good at something, right?"

"Yeah . . . he's good at bullshitting."

In retrospect, though, I have to admit that Tom did have his strengths. He knew curriculum, and he was good at getting teachers—some of them, anyway—to work harder than they had in the past. He was good at running meetings and creating new . . . *things.* He had a real corporate mentality. I have no doubt he would have fit in well with any number of Fortune 500 companies.

Me? I was a teacher, and that's all I wanted to be. I wanted to be left alone to do my job in the way I knew it should be done, and that did not include excessive fretting about curriculum or wasting a lot of time in senseless meetings. To me, teaching was, and is, all about rolling up your sleeves and connecting with your students on a human level, as well as an intellectual level. With special-needs students, the obvious path is not always the best path. Sometimes you have to take chances. As someone once said, "If you want to make an omelet, you have to break a few eggs."

The mess that invariably comes with such endeavors didn't seem to appeal to Tom. The way I saw it, he wanted a neat, orderly school, one whose hallmark would be rigidity as well as academic excellence. Some people surely saw this as a good thing, but it sickened me. A high school principal is in the unique position of being able to have a profound effect on the lives of hundreds of young people. He can make a difference—I've known many principals who *have* made a difference. Tom Keller did not. I never really saw him deal with kids on any substantive level. He was just . . . *there*. He was the principal of Forest Hills Northern; the name tag said so.

Tom's rejection meant zero to me. If anything, it served as a galvanizing gesture. "Since you're saying no, and Denise is saying no, I guess we'll have to think about our next move," I said.

Tom stiffened. He didn't plan on there being a next move. Robynn, sensing a confrontation, jumped in.

"Tom," she said sweetly. "I think you might be making a mistake on this one. Mike has a pretty good idea here. We've thought it out together and we really believe this can work. It can be a boon for the entire school district."

Tom was unmoved. He shook his head, stood up, and walked to the door.

"This meeting is over," he said. As we left, he delivered a parting salvo: "Robynn, do us both a favor. Try to talk some sense into your partner."

That evening I vented to my wife, told her how unreceptive Tom had been, and how angry I had felt. I think, in a way, she was relieved. The principal had turned us down, the regional coordinator of special education had turned us down, and surely that would be the end of it. I would concentrate on teaching and coaching, and put aside all this nonsense about Space Camp. A sense of normalcy would return to our lives.

What I really had in mind was something else entirely. I'd already told Mike Schmidt about our disastrous meeting with Tom Keller, and he had reiterated his willingness to intercede on our behalf. Mike Washburn, superintendent of the Forest Hills School District, would be attending a regional meeting of superintendents from the Kent Intermediate School District (of which our school was a part) the next morning at East Grand Rapids Elementary School. It was Mike Schmidt's plan for us to accompany him to this meeting and ask for an audience with Mike Washburn. In other words, we were about to sail high over the heads of our supervisors.

Darcy was not exactly pleased with this idea. Rather than applaud my determination, she reacted, as most spouses would, I guess, with a mixture of trepidation and anger.

"Mike, what are you trying to do?" she said. "Do you know how much this will disrupt our lives? Defying the principal . . . your special ed boss? Do you realize what this could do to your reputation in this community? And to our family's reputation?" She shook her head disapprovingly. "You're possessed!"

She was right. I was possessed, because it was the right thing to do. But Darcy didn't see it that way. She felt that I was placing my students ahead of my family.

"What if you get fired?" she wondered. "What if you lose your health insurance?"

"Give me a break. They can't fire me for fighting for my own kids. Besides . . . I have tenure."

To be perfectly candid, part of the reason I was so adamant about pursuing this dream was that I didn't like being told no. I've been accused of having a problem with authority, but that really isn't quite true. I have a problem accepting orders from people I don't respect, people who seem to be making decisions based purely on promoting their own agendas. That is not what teaching is all about. I did a lot of soul searching in those days because I wanted to make sure that my motives were pure, that I wasn't simply being as stubborn and self-absorbed as the administrators surrounding me. Eventually I came to the conclusion that

I wasn't. I didn't like being rejected—that's true. The reason, however, had nothing to do with me . . . or with Robynn. These kids deserved a shot at going to Space Camp. A wonderful opportunity had been presented to them, and petty jealousy and bureaucracy were standing in the way. Robynn and I were the voice of these kids—no one would let them speak for themselves—and they wanted to go. They wanted to try. What was the harm in that? Why was everyone so opposed to their ambition?

The next morning Mike Schmidt picked us up at the high school and we drove together to East Grand Rapids Elementary. Through a glass door I could see more than a dozen superintendents conducting business. There weren't a lot of smiles in that room; it seemed to be a serious meeting. Nevertheless, Mike Schmidt walked right up to the door and knocked. This was a completely cold call, which I guess was appropriate for a guy who worked for Amway. Mike Washburn peered out, recognized one of his board members, and came to the door.

"Dr. Washburn, I'm sorry to disturb you," Mike Schmidt said.

"That's all right. What's going on?" He was polite, but obviously a bit distracted.

Mike Schmidt then threw the ball into my court. "Tell him," he said.

Mike Washburn and I knew each other pretty well. I was a football coach, and he loved football. In fact, I'd coached both of his sons at Forest Hills Northern. I knew him as a fair and decent man. Still, this was more than a little awkward and intimidating, to be making a pitch under these conditions, with a roomful of superintendents awaiting his return.

I swallowed hard and jumped right in.

"Mike, we've been given an opportunity and I can't see us passing it up." He was sort of half listening—as I talked, he periodically glanced over his shoulder at the stalled meeting. "With the help of Congressman Henry"—I thought it was a good idea to throw that in—"we've been asked to make a presentation at the U.S. Space & Rocket Center about bringing our special ed kids to Space Camp."

Mike blinked. "Say that again."

I repeated it, and added, "The problem is, Tom Keller and Denise Boitano are vehemently opposed to this whole idea. And I think they're wrong. I think this can work."

Before Dr. Washburn could answer, Mike Schmidt said, "I've talked to a couple of these kids, including Ben. They want to go down there, Mike, and they should have the opportunity. Will you give them a chance?"

Without answering, Mike Washburn motioned for us to follow him back into the room. We did. Everyone in the room stared at us. "Tell them what you just told me," he said. There wasn't even time to be nervous. I simply blurted out another sales pitch, this time cutting right to the chase. "Robynn and I have students from each one of your districts in our special education class," I said. "I know you probably won't believe this, but we think they can compete against gifted and talented kids at Space Camp."

All around the table, jaws hung slack. The reaction was stunned silence.

"We have an opportunity to do something unique," I went on. "But first we have to make a formal presentation in Huntsville, Alabama, at the U.S. Space & Rocket Center, and in order to do that we need your support."

Still there was no response. Finally Mike Washburn turned to face his peers and said, "I'm in favor of it. What do you think?"

Slowly they began to nod their approval. Then they began to ask questions. The more they asked, the more enthusiastic they became. Before leaving I said to Mike Washburn, "We've still got a little problem."

He waved a hand dismissively. "Yeah, yeah. Don't worry. I'll tell Denise and Tom it's okay."

"Thanks. But that's not what I meant."

"Oh?"

"Uh-uh. We don't have the money to get down there."

He smiled. "I'll tell you what. If you promise to pay back the school district, I'll get you the money for the initial trip."

I extended my hand. "Deal!"

IT DIDN'T TAKE long for word of our meeting to reach the principal and special ed coordinator. Tom was predictably enraged. He marched right down to my room after getting the call from Mike Washburn, pulled me aside, and vigorously expressed his displeasure.

"What are you doing?" he said. "I gave you my answer."

"Tom, I don't know if you were ever in the military, but I was. And there is such a thing as chain of command. If your chief says no, you go to your captain. If your captain says no, you go to the commander. If the commander says no . . . well, you keep right on climbing."

The veins in Tom's forehead were pulsating. He was having trouble keeping his composure. "What are you talking about?"

"Sometimes people are close-minded," I said, "and other people are more open-minded. We made our presentation to people we thought would be open-minded. And we had parent involvement."

That really set him off. "Who?" he snarled.

"Mike Schmidt."

With that, the air seemed to rush out of him. Tom was naturally threatened by Mike Schmidt because Mike had a lot of power and disagreed with Tom on a number of issues. Mike's involvement meant Tom was effectively defeated. The superintendent and a prominent member of the board of education had publicly supported our plan. There was nothing Tom could do but walk away and hope that we fell flat on our faces.

If the principal was angry, the special education coordinator was positively livid. Like Tom, Denise seemed more concerned with her own image and accomplishments than with the problems faced by her students. Denise and I had conflicting personalities, as well as conflicting ideas abut how to run a classroom for children with special needs. That my coaching schedule often caused me to miss department meetings during football season didn't help matters any. She saw me as a malcontent . . . a rebel . . . a pain in the butt. So it was no shock that Denise summoned me to her office within seconds after being informed by Mike Washburn that full support and consideration were to be given Mike Kersjes and Robynn McKinney in their effort to win approval from the Space & Rocket Center.

"You know, I don't appreciate being embarrassed in front of the superintendent," she said as she stormed around her office.

"Embarrassed in what way?" I responded. "You mean because we work harder than you do?"

Denise slammed a fist into her desk and shouted, "Do you know how much time I spend in meetings every day?"

I shrugged. "Meetings? Who cares? What do you do for kids?"

Her face was flushed, her teeth clenched. "I do a lot of things that you never see."

I laughed out loud at that one, which only made her more hostile. To Denise, I was like Henry Fonda in the movie *Mister Roberts*, always stirring up trouble, always making life miserable for poor James Cagney, the ship's captain. She was obsessed with beating me in some way, with catching me in some act of insubordination so severe that it would cost me my job.

"This isn't over," she said. "We'll see what happens."

I turned to leave.

"One other thing," she added. "When are you going to come to one of our special ed meetings?"

I didn't even look back. "Mike Washburn wants me coaching football," I said. "Take it up with him."

5

As much as Robynn and I believed in our students and wanted them to have an opportunity to attend Space Camp, and to push themselves in ways they'd never imagined possible, we were realistic about the obstacles that stood in our path. Most special education teachers, especially the good ones, manage to shed their naïveté without acquiring an armor of cynicism. They learn to work with their students, challenge them, support them . . . but they understand the reality of the situation. The kids in my class were there for a reason. They had serious problems, serious emotional, psychological, behavioral, and educational issues. Some had spent time in juvenile court. Most had known trouble in some form. To expect that every one of these kids would be instantly and miraculously transformed into something out of *Goodbye, Mr. Chips* was to expect the impossible.

Space Camp represented a dream for all of us, but to make that dream come true, Robynn and I had to remain rooted in reality. There is nothing wrong with hugging a student, either when he's performed well or when he's had a rough day. Equally important, though, is the ability to be tough, to recognize when a student is trying to con you, or when he's simply losing control. It's not all that much different from being a football coach. We wanted to get our kids into shape—we wanted to somehow persuade them to think and act like a team, and to believe in themselves perhaps for the first time in their lives. In pursuit of this goal, a warm and fuzzy attitude would take us only so far; in fact, it would likely result in failure.

By late autumn of 1987 Robynn and I had laid down the law with our students. We hadn't made any promises yet—our trip to Huntsville was still a few weeks off, and we'd have a better idea then whether Space Camp might truly be in our future—but we were talking about it almost every day in fairly concrete and sometimes threatening terms.

"If this happens," I would say, "things are going to change drastically around here. You guys are going to have to toe the line, because everyone will be watching us."

I looked around the room and began addressing the students, one by one.

"Lewis . . . you can't be running around pinching girls in the butt."

Everyone laughed, except me and Robynn.

"I'm not kidding. It can't happen anymore."

I addressed Scott Goudy: "You have to stop mocking other kids in our halls, and especially in our classroom." Scott rolled his eyes. I jumped all over him. "That's the kind of thing I'm talking about—your attitude. You need to grow up, Scott. Fast!" That was true, and not just because he was capable of causing considerable trouble. Scott was one of the smartest kids in our class. He was also a pretty good athlete (he was on the swimming and football teams), and it wasn't hard to envision him playing a vital role at Space Camp. We needed him, physically and intellectually. Without an attitude adjustment, though, Scott would be dead weight.

Steve Bennett reacted to my scolding of Scott in predictably scatological fashion, unleashing a torrent of belches. As the guys laughed and the girls cried, "Gross!" I moved slowly, assuredly down the aisle toward Steve. I'd never had a kid I liked quite as much as I liked Steve Bennett—he was funny, clever, and, as I've said, extremely protective of some of the other special ed students. But he was quite capable of driving you over the edge.

I stopped at Steve's desk and bent down, until our noses were only a few inches apart. "That's enough," I said. Steve closed his mouth. The noise subsided. "You have to control yourself a little better. No more toys, no more farting in the hallways."

Steve nodded. Like most of our students, he knew when I was kidding, and he knew when I was serious. This was no time to be a wise guy. Looking around the room, I couldn't help but wonder whether we had set our sights too high. We had students with significant health problems, like Marion Mills, whose treatment for leukemia had left her overweight and chronically fatigued. A few others had severe emotional problems that might be exacerbated by stress, and if there was one thing we were sure to encounter at Space Camp, as well as in the months of training beforehand, it was stress. I was concerned specifically about Andrea Burke, an intensely sensitive girl whose emotions always bubbled just below the surface. The slightest negative or critical comment, from peers or teachers, would reduce Andrea to tears. Insecure and starved for attention, Andrea was an inveterate tattletale and whiner, which naturally did not endear her to her classmates. It didn't help matters any that Andrea had an older sister at Forest Hills Northern who was everything that Andrea wanted to be: pretty, smart, athletic, popular. For some reason Andrea was virtually ignored by her sister whenever the two were in school. If Andrea was walking to class and spotted her sister (usually hanging out with the most popular crowd), she'd smile and wave and yell "Hi!" Big sister would simply turn her head and pretend that Andrea didn't exist. Not surprisingly, this just devastated Andrea. How she would respond to the demands of Space Camp was difficult to predict, but I wasn't optimistic.

In general, whatever concerns I might have had were alleviated by my belief that most of these kids, if given a tangible goal, would actually experience a diminishing of symptoms. Few of them had ever strived for anything in their lives, had never allowed their reach to exceed their grasp. In preparing for Space Camp they would have to focus on a specific task, one that would require greater commitment and energy than anything they'd ever known. Maybe, just maybe, this would take their minds off their other problems and disabilities, or at least make those disabilities more manageable. In my heart I believed that to be the case, but I had to remind myself of it every day. Each time a student got into a fight or was summoned to the principal's office, I told myself, "Don't worry. Once we're in training, they'll settle down."

There were, however, incidents that tested my faith, the most memorable of which occurred just a few weeks before Christmas, as Robynn and I were preparing for our trip to Huntsville. One afternoon I was in the auto shop, helping some of our students with a class on small-engine repair, when Robynn stumbled into the room, her hair and face a ghostly white. At first I thought she was ill, but as she spat and sputtered, and white dust swirled around her head, I realized that she was covered with . . . *flour!*

"Help! Come quick!" she shouted.

The students stared in disbelief as Robynn turned and ran out of the room, with me giving chase.

What had happened was this: Robynn had been assisting in a home economics class at the same time that I was in the auto shop. A lot of our kids were in that class, along with several regular ed students. The project for the day was pumpkin pie. Well, everything was going just fine until one of the students (not one of ours) began picking on Stephanie. According to Robynn, the student made fun of Stephanie's pie, said Stephanie didn't know how to cook, and, of course, made some crack about "Alice the Goon." Stephanie took this rather personally and, as was her wont, began fighting back. She lost her temper, yelled at the kid, and he responded by dumping a handful of flour on top of Stephanie's pie.

Well, that was the beginning of the end. Steve Bennett, who was working nearby, came to Stephanie's rescue, retaliating in precisely the way you might expect. He took a bag of flour and chucked it at the kid, dousing him completely and triggering an all-out war. Pretty soon flour and pumpkin and piecrusts were flying in all directions, as this little bit of bickering escalated into a full-scale food fight. By the time I entered the room, the home economics teacher had regained control, but it looked as though every oven and refrigerator in the place had exploded simultaneously. And in the middle of it all was Ben Schmidt, his face and glasses covered with flour and pie guts, smiling, looking like he was having the time of his life.

"Don't worry," I said to the home economics teacher. "Our kids will clean up the whole mess." With that, Stephanie began stomping her feet and cursing.

"But, Coach!" she screamed. "They started it!"

"I don't care who started it. We will clean up."

"*But, Coach!*"

"Stephanie, come to my room. *Now!*"

I faced the home economics teacher. "If my kids take care of this—"

She finished the sentence for me: "Then it stays in this room."

She was doing us a big favor by choosing not to report the incident, especially when we were about to make a presentation on behalf of our special education students at Space Camp. I could only imagine that if Mike Washburn had been in the room at that moment, he might have questioned his own judgment.

"Thank you," I said, and led Stephanie into the hall.

No one is really equipped to cope with being provoked and attacked on a daily basis, but Stephanie was more vulnerable than most kids. Unfortunately, as in any school, there were heartless kids at Forest Hills Northern who were drawn to her fragility like a buzzard to a carcass. They'd pick at Stephanie until they hit bone, or until they provoked the desired response, either her running away with tears streaming down her cheeks, or cutting loose with a profanity-laced tirade, punctuated by the slamming of a door. Stephanie would get on the bus each morning and immediately be placed on the defensive. By the time she arrived at school, she'd already be crying, and by lunchtime she'd be fighting back, challenging the jerk who called her "Alice" or tripped her up as she walked from the lunch line to a table, spilling food all over the floor in the process. Most of our kids hated gym class because they were clumsy or underdeveloped, and Stephanie certainly fell into this category. Unlike most of our kids, Stephanie would not walk away from a fight, would not turn her back on her tormenters. She was more like Lewis—she'd been hurt so often that the pain of a physical confrontation didn't even frighten her. She was big enough that she could do some damage, too, regardless of whether her opponent was a boy or a girl.

It broke my heart to see Stephanie that day, sobbing uncontrollably, asking why people were so mean, and why she was in trouble for simply defending herself. I tried to explain that things were changing, that she'd have to somehow find a way to rise above the ugliness of other students, to be stronger than they were, to be more mature than they were . . . to be better than they were. She just shook her head. It wasn't fair, and she knew it. When she slammed the door on her way out, putting yet another crack in the glass, I just let it go.

6

"Where's Alabama, Dad?"

My older son, Shawn, was seated at the kitchen table, pawing at a map of the United States. Robynn and I were scheduled to leave first thing in the morning, and I was more than a little apprehensive, not only because we were going to be making a crucial presentation at Space Camp but also because I had never really been away from my family before. Oh, I'd spent a couple days at football camp, but never had I traveled out of state, on an airplane, to a place that seemed so distant, so remote, so . . . unfamiliar.

"Right there," I said, pointing to the southeastern United States.

My other son, Ryan, spread his fingers across the map. "That's not so far," he said.

I laughed. It's hard to teach a five-year-old about space and distance, and my wife wasn't helping matters any. "Your father is going far, far away, boys," she said, instantly reducing Ryan to tears. Darcy remained convinced that I was wasting my time, and she wasn't about to absolve me of the guilt I was feeling. Rather, she was laying it on thick.

"What if the plane crashes?" she said later, before we went to bed. "What happens then?"

"Huh? God almighty, Darcy, the plane is not going to crash. Everything will be fine."

The next morning, at the airport, Darcy barely spoke to me. And while I didn't know Robynn's husband very well, standing there with his little boy, sleep still in his eyes, he seemed to be reacting to this entire venture with about as much enthusiasm as Darcy. There was, to put it mildly, a lot of tension in the room.

When it came time to board the plane, Shawn and Ryan clutched at my legs. "Come on," Darcy said. "Give your father a kiss." *Oh, good,* I thought. *She's softening.* "You may never see him again."

What?!

Shawn and Ryan both began to wail. I held them close, told them everything would be okay. Darcy was crying, too, and Robynn's husband was giving me a look that could charitably be described as "disapproving," as if he was thinking, *You're getting Robynn into this mess, buddy—you'd better know what you're doing.*

To be perfectly honest, I was thinking the same thing.

WE ARRIVED IN Huntsville in the early afternoon, rented a car, and drove to the Marriott Hotel, located on the grounds of the U.S. Space & Rocket Center. Having never visited the South before, I was fascinated by the red clay, the oppressive heat (nearly ninety degrees in December), and especially the pace. Everyone seemed to be moving in slow motion. It was instantly apparent that I'd have to make a conscious effort to throttle back a bit if I didn't want the locals to think I suffered from attention deficit disorder.

After checking in, we met Heiko Enfield at the security desk of the Space & Rocket Center. He offered to give us a tour of the facility in advance of our late-afternoon meeting with Deborah Barnhart (our other big meeting, with CEO Edward Buckbee, was scheduled for the next day). Well, I was like a kid in a candy shop, my head on swivel for the better part of two hours. The first thing we saw was a real Mercury rocket, standing seven stories high, towering above the entire complex, an omnipresent reminder of the vastness of space, and the tools required for even minimal exploration. We visited the space habitat, a futuristic dorm where students lived while they were attending camp, and a museum that offered an overview of the history of space exploration. Wherever we went, we were surrounded by kids in crisp blue jumpsuits, impressive replicas of the uniforms worn by astronauts on space shuttle missions. The students were all so busy, so completely engrossed in their work, although much of that work seemed like play: bouncing across the floor of an open room in a contraption that simulated the reduced gravity of the moon, or spinning madly in a gyroscope-like device known as a "multi-axis trainer." They piloted a space shuttle replica, issued commands in Mission Control, and conducted experiments in a space lab.

"Is this fantastic or what?" I said to Robynn.

She smiled and tugged gently at my elbow. "Slow down," she whispered. "Try not to seem so anxious. You're acting like a tourist."

I didn't care. I was so excited that I could barely control myself.

"Can we see the cockpit?" I asked.

Heiko nodded. "Sure. Right this way."

We walked through the shuttle and into the cockpit, and here, for the first time, I felt a surge of anxiety. Lights flashed on and off, voices crackled through an intercom. There were literally hundreds of dials, switches, and knobs. It looked like . . . well, like the cockpit of a space shuttle, so complicated that you'd need a Ph.D. to pilot the thing.

"The campers don't use all of these instruments, do they?" Robynn asked sheepishly.

"Oh, yeah," Heiko said proudly. "But that's only part of it."

He led us into the space lab, where a group of students were immersed in some type of work.

"What are they doing?" I asked.

"Conducting crystallization growths, microgravity experiments . . . things of that nature."

"How long do the experiments last?" Robynn inquired.

"About two hours."

Robynn's eyes widened. "Uh-huh."

As we left the space lab, Robynn said, quietly, so that Heiko wouldn't hear, "Our kids are going to do this?"

"Absolutely. We can teach them." In my head, though, a tiny voice whispered, *"Maybe we've bitten off a little more than we can chew."*

PRIOR TO TAKING over the directorship of Space Camp, Deborah Barnhart had been an officer in the U.S. Navy. She was a smart, determined woman with short, blond hair and an athletic build. Her handshake told me right away that this was a woman who was quite capable of supporting us (if she believed in our passion and commitment) or kicking us right in the butt (if she didn't believe in us). She had the handshake of a football player at a pregame coin toss . . . a handshake that said, "Don't mess with me." I kind of liked that.

"So . . . what do you think of the place?" she asked.

"It's great," I said. "I think our kids can really shine here."

"How so?"

I launched into an impassioned speech about the benefits of Space Camp, most of which I had gleaned from a promotional videotape provided by the Space & Rocket Center's public relations staff. It was all fairly obvious, the stuff about teamwork, building confidence, learning about science in a hands-on manner, but I believed in it, so I had no trouble parroting the information right back. Moreover, I said, "I think our kids can grasp the material. It's not so much about content here, it's more about concept. This program will test our kids, there's no question about that, but with Robynn and me training them, working with them, it's doable."

"Our kids have disabilities," Robynn chimed in, "but they can learn how to do everything you ask of your students here. Given the proper amount of time, and the right materials, we can prepare them. We just want a chance."

Dr. Barnhart seemed sympathetic to our cause, far more so than she had during our telephone conversations, anyway. Still, she was hard to read.

"What you're suggesting is all very new to us," she said. "We have one program here for students with disabilities. Those students are hearing impaired." She paused. "They also happen to be intellectually gifted."

The point was clear. Space Camp was not in the business of tutoring kids with special needs. It was a rigorous program for the academic elite. The subtext was that it was also a program for the social elite, since a high percentage of wealthy kids tend to be smart kids attending the very best public and private schools. In every way imaginable, our students would be out of place at Space Camp.

"I'm just letting you know what you're up against," Dr. Barnhart said. "Frankly, I'm surprised you've gotten this far."

"Thank you."

"Don't thank me yet. You still have a long way to go. Without Mr. Buckbee's approval, this is a dead issue."

"When do we see him?" I asked.

"Tomorrow at one. I'll warn you right now—Mr. Buckbee likes the give and take of negotiation. It's a game to him. So think about what concessions you might be willing to make. And be ready to deal."

Neither Robynn nor I had much experience in these matters, so once again we turned to Mike Schmidt for help, figuring that in his years of climbing the ladder at Amway, he no doubt had learned a thing or two about the art of the deal. Mike was typically gracious and accommodating. He quickly lined up a conference call with five members of his contracts department, and together they walked us through a standard business meeting.

"It doesn't matter what you're negotiating for," Mike said. "The important thing is to know the rules of the game. Robynn, I understand you graduated from Texas Christian University. Is that correct?"

"Yes, it is."

"Good. You'll be running the show."

"What?!" I said. I was somewhat offended . . . and confused.

"You guys are in the South," Mike said. "You're not in Michigan. If Robynn can play the role of the Southern belle, everything will go much more smoothly."

"And me?" I asked.

Mike laughed. "Mike, you're like a bull in a china shop. You won't negotiate, you'll argue. Believe me, that won't work in Alabama. I want you to sit there quietly and support everything Robynn says. Don't speak unless you're spoken to."

Although my ego was bruised, I had to admit that Mike's strategy made sense.

The next morning I ran for more than an hour, endless laps around the complex, trying to work off some of my excess energy. The more I ran, the more I saw of Space Camp, the more I wanted to make this happen. I wanted our kids to see this remarkable place, to live here for a week, and to prove that they were more than everyone thought they were. If that meant sitting back and biting my tongue in the most important meeting of my life, then that's what I would do.

Robynn and I met in the lobby of the Marriott. When she stepped off the elevator, wearing a frilly blue dress adorned with a little white ribbon, I nearly fell on the floor laughing.

"Is there a problem, sir?" she asked. Then she paused and curtsied, and added, with a genteel Southern twang, "I mean . . . I do have to play the part, now don't I?"

I laughed. "Ready when you are, ma'am."

EDWARD BUCKBEE'S OFFICE was designed with maximum intimidation in mind. He sat at one end of a long table, while Robynn and I sat at the other end. Also in the meeting were Deborah Barnhart and Heiko Enfield. Maybe it was my imagination, but it sure seemed as though the room sloped away from Buckbee, lending him an air of superiority; more likely, he simply had a bigger chair. Behind him, framing him almost, was a huge picture of the Space & Rocket Center. The entire setup fairly screamed: *I'm in charge here!*

Buckbee was an impressive man: tall, well-muscled, with thick black hair and very expensive taste in clothing. He was in his late forties, maybe early fifties, and appeared to be a man who lived for meetings such as this, where he'd have an opportunity to flaunt his power and authority. As with our encounter with Dr. Barnhart, this meeting began with some pleasantries, Buckbee asking us how we liked Space Camp, whether we'd had a chance to tour the facilities, that sort of thing. Very quickly, though, he got down to business.

"How do you see this program helping your kids?" he asked, looking directly at me. Mike Schmidt had told me to speak only when spoken to, so . . . I started to respond.

"Well, Mr. Buck—"

He cut me off. "I mean, aren't there other camps specifically designed for special education students?"

This time I hesitated, just to be sure he'd finished. "Yes, sir, there are, but not where they can learn math, science, and technology the way it's taught here. Not where they can use their imaginations and their hands." He leaned forward, apparently intrigued. "Mr. Buckbee, our kids can do amazing things with their hands . . . when they're given the opportunity. And if you give them the opportunity, I promise you we'll work with them over the next year to make sure they're thoroughly prepared."

"Next year, huh? When do you want to bring these kids down here?"

Easy question. If all went according to plan, Robynn and I would attend one of the teacher education programs at Space Camp in the spring or summer, use the information we gathered there to establish a curriculum, and then devote most of the 1988–89 school year to intense training. As I described the plan to Buckbee I could tell he was impressed. Most of the kids who came to Space Camp were exceptionally bright and affluent. They'd competed in science olympiads and math olympiads. Many of them were repeat visitors, and so they knew exactly what to expect from the camp. Their preparation amounted to little more than filling out a registration form and asking their parents to write a check. We were promising something far more ambitious, something I was certain Buckbee had never heard.

"What do you and Robynn hope to learn during your visit here?" he asked.

"Exactly what we want our kids to learn." I had him at this point. He was hooked . . . and then I nearly lost him. "By going through the teacher program, we'll have a chance to see what modifications will be necessary for our kids."

Oops!

Buckbee stiffened, cleared his throat. "Modifications? What kind of modifications? What are you talking about?"

Robynn kicked me under the table. I had dug the hole. Now she would try to hoist us out. "We're not talking about adapting Space Camp to fit the needs of our students," she said reassuringly. "Some of our kids have fairly serious learning disabilities, and it's important that we're thoroughly familiar with the program, so that we can tailor a training regimen that will address their various circumstances. Don't worry, it won't mean any additional work for you or your staff."

Buckbee nodded approvingly. For the next several minutes he focused exclusively on Robynn, drilling her with one question after another, questions about curriculum and preparation and the specific challenges facing our students. She fielded each inquiry gracefully. When he ran out of questions, Buckbee turned to Dr. Barnhart. "Deborah," he said. "You and I need to discuss this a little more."

What the heck does that mean?

Buckbee swiveled back toward Robynn and me. "You two are staying overnight, aren't you?"

I figured I could handle that one safely enough. "Yes, sir."

"Good." He tapped a pencil, gave me a hard look. "You do anything besides teach?"

"Yeah, I'm a football coach." *What kind of mind game is he playing?*

"You are, huh?"

"Yes, sir."

"Figures. You look like a football coach."

Thanks . . . I think.

"How did your team do this season?"

"Pretty good—we won the conference championship."

"Is that so?"

"Uh-huh."

He shuffled some papers, looked around the room. This was one of the strangest men I'd ever encountered. What was he doing? What was he thinking? Why the feigned interest in the Forest Hills Northern football team? It was almost as if he was getting some kind of perverse pleasure out of toying with us, watching us squirm.

Finally, he stood up and extended a hand. "It was nice to meet both of you," he said. Then he turned to Dr. Barnhart. "Deborah, I'd like you and Heiko to have breakfast with Mike and Robynn in the morning. You can give them my decision at that time."

And that was that. We'd made it to the Emerald City and gotten an audience with the Wizard of Oz. Whether he would grant our request remained to be seen.

THE WEIRDNESS CONTINUED that evening. Deborah Barnhart invited us to dinner at a wonderful Japanese restaurant, where we had a nice meal, shared some sake, and talked for a few hours about our work and families (Deborah also had two boys). It was really a very pleasant experience, so pleasant, in fact, that I didn't know what to make of it. Was the dinner her way of hinting that the answer was "yes," or was it merely a gesture of compassion, a way to ease the pain before delivering bad news? I had no way of knowing. Buckbee had been so cold and impersonal . . . so odd.

"We gave it our best effort," Robynn said when we got back to the hotel. "Nothing to do now but wait and see."

That night I barely slept at all. I couldn't stop thinking about the kids and how disappointed they would be if we came home defeated. What would we say to them? What would we say to their parents? The inevitable "I told you so" that would come from the administration didn't concern me in the least, but when I imagined the expressions on the kids' faces as we brought them together and delivered the bad news . . . when we told them that the people in charge of Space Camp had listened to our thoughtful presentation and had nonetheless determined that special ed kids were just too problematic . . . well, I knew how they'd react. They'd shrug it off, because rejection was nothing new to them. That was the most painful truth of all.

THE NEXT MORNING, when we arrived at the Marriott's dining room, Deborah and Heiko were waiting. They bellied up to the buffet table, filled their plates with grits and gravy and eggs. I took two slices of toast and a cup of coffee.

"Come on, Mike," Deborah said as she looked at my plate. "This is a big Southern breakfast. Dig in!"

Normally I would have obliged. I didn't get to be two hundred thirty pounds by turning down a free meal. But there was no chance of that happening now. Too much sake and not enough sleep, combined with a serious case of anxiety, had my stomach doing somersaults. I wanted an answer, and I wanted it right away. Then, maybe, I'd be able to eat. However, as with the rest of the trip, there was a protocol to follow. For the next forty-five minutes we sat at the table and politely chatted about the weather, the holidays, the Crimson Tide football team . . . anything and everything except the one subject that had brought us together in the first place: Space Camp.

Eventually Deborah got up, pulled out a credit card, paid the bill, and led us out of the restaurant. As we walked past the cashier and into the lobby, I whispered to Robynn, "Maybe Buckbee hasn't made a decision yet."

No sooner had the words left my mouth than Dr. Barnhart turned and said, almost as an afterthought, "Oh, by the way . . . we're going to give your kids a shot at Space Camp."

My knees went weak. I thought I was going to faint. *Oh, my God! Why couldn't you have told us earlier?*

"W-w-w-when?" I stammered.

"When did we know?"

I nodded.

"Before dinner last night. But I had to make sure of one thing."

"What's that?" Robynn asked.

"That you aren't just professors looking to pad your résumés or get advanced degrees or whatever; that this whole adventure is about the kids, and not about you." Deborah stopped, gave us a hard look. "I'll be honest. I told Mr. Buckbee that I'd put my job on the line for you guys. So you'd better pull this thing off. If you screw up, or if your kids screw up, we'll all be in big trouble."

7

This was a moment of clarity.

In a vast ballroom of the Hilton Hotel in Houston, on the first day of a NASA-sponsored Teacher in Space Conference, Robynn and I were searching for a table. We had registered for the evening's program, which included an address by Dr. Robert Brown, NASA's director of education, but had thus far been unable to locate our assigned seats. So we circled the room, looking . . . looking. Finally, we found it—our table! It was in the back of the room, nearly against the wall, in a dimly lit corner not far from the clatter and clutter of the kitchen. Seated alongside us were a low-level NASA administrator and two people from the Soviet Union, whose affiliation was never quite made clear. This much I knew: We were the only teachers at that table.

But then, no one really thought of us as teachers. My name tag read: MICHAEL KERSJES—SPECIAL EDUCATION, and that was all anyone needed to know. Nearly everyone I had met since arriving had treated me as though I had fleas or something, staring at that badge, giving me a quizzical look, and then asking, in a tone of bewilderment, "Why are you here?"

"Well, let's see . . . I'm a teacher, and this is a conference for teachers."

"Oh . . ."

The implied message was that we were not educators. People with good hearts, perhaps; people doing work that was on some level valuable, or at least necessary, but not teachers. Oh no. That designation was reserved for those who worked with real students, and those very same people were seated much closer to the front of the ballroom, where they could see the featured speaker, hear his every word, because obviously it was much more important, more vital . . . more relevant . . . to them than it was to us.

All of this hit me pretty hard. Never before had I felt the stigma of being associated with special-needs students. Back home in Grand Rapids, people had always thought of me as a football coach first, special education teacher second. In fact, if you had asked just about anyone: "Who's Mike Kersjes?" the response would have been, "He's a football coach."

"Anything else?"

"Yeah, he's a teacher."

"What does he teach?"

"Uhhhh . . . I don't know."

You see, it didn't matter. Now it mattered, and perhaps for the first time in my life I understood what my kids had been feeling. You wear a tag and that tag defines you. It becomes who you are. As I sat down at that table, so far from the center of activity, so utterly disassociated and ignored, it hit me: *Special ed kids . . . back of the room; special ed teachers . . . back of the room.* This is what it was like to be a second-class citizen. It was a lousy, dehumanizing experience, and it strengthened my resolve about meeting with Dr. Brown.

That, after all, was our reason for being in Houston in the first place. No sooner had we gotten the good news in Huntsville than we were informed that we'd need the cooperation and approval of Dr. Brown in order to obtain curriculum material that we could use to train our students for Space Camp. Without that material, our plan would disintegrate. So, less than two weeks after clearing what we thought would be the final hurdle, here we were, trying to clear another one. Having left our families behind and our students in the care of aides and substitute teachers once again, we had registered for this conference at the advice of Deborah Barnhart. She had described Dr. Brown as something akin to NASA royalty, with a degree from Harvard and a list of accomplishments and accolades as long as his arm.

"He's a serious man," Deborah had said. "I have only one piece of advice."

"What's that?"

"Never call him Bob."

I would keep that in mind, in the event that we were actually granted an audience. Things hadn't gone particularly well in the twelve hours since we had arrived in Houston. Wearing our Midwestern naïveté on our sleeves, we had strolled up to the conference registration desk and explained that the real reason for our visit was that we hoped to meet with Dr. Robert Brown. The registrar politely explained that such a meeting would not be possible without the approval of Ross Fullerton, a NASA public relations executive who was coordinating Dr. Brown's schedule during his trip to Houston (Dr. Brown was based in Washington, D.C.). So I called Fullerton's office from my hotel room. To say it didn't go smoothly would be a colossal understatement. Fullerton was a typically overburdened, hostile flack who took every request for an interview or meeting as a personal affront. After listening to an abbreviated sales pitch, during which I outlined our program at Forest Hills Northern and our reasons for wanting to attend Space Camp, Fullerton exhibited all the warmth of the Grinch on Christmas Eve.

"That," he said, "is the stupidest thing I've ever heard. I am not going to waste this man's time by helping you get an appointment to see him. He's a busy guy."

I was stunned. Practically speechless. Suddenly I felt a surge of paranoia. I wondered if Fullerton had been in contact with Ed Buckbee, and if perhaps this was an effort to sabotage our mission. I took a deep breath and said, as calmly as I could (what I really wanted to do was reach through the phone and rip out the guy's vocal cords), "Fine, sir. I'll be calling you back."

"I don't know why," Fullerton huffed, and then hung up.

This time I didn't even hesitate before calling in the cavalry. I reached into my wallet, pulled out a card with Congressman Henry's name on it, and began to dial. Fortunately he was in his office and happy to take the call.

"You want to see Dr. Robert Brown? You mean Bob Brown?" Paul said with a laugh, when I explained the purpose of our trip to Houston. "Gee, I think I can make that happen."

"Not according to Mr. Fullerton."

"Yeah?" Paul said, clearly annoyed. "Hang up and wait by the phone."

I did as I was told, and sure enough, not fifteen minutes later the phone rang. On the other end, screaming as if he'd been shot in the chest, was Ross Fullerton.

"You son of a bitch! You've got a red clearance."

Trying to remain calm, and trying not to laugh, I said, "What does that mean?"

"It means some congressman just called and ordered me to let you in!" I gave Robynn a wink. "Now get over here! I'll give you ten minutes."

Not bothering to change clothes, we jumped into a car and drove straight to Fullerton's office. We didn't expect a warm greeting, and we weren't disappointed. After being cleared to enter the building, we started walking down a long hallway, at the end of which was Fullerton's office. He had wheeled his chair into the doorway and was waiting for us to arrive. From twenty feet away I could almost see the beads of sweat forming on his brow. He wore a wrinkled white shirt that looked as though it had been pulled straight out of the dryer, and a rumpled blue suit. He appeared haggard, like a guy who probably got beat up by his bosses on a daily basis.

"You're Kersjes?"

"Yes."

He nodded, looked at Robynn. "McKinney?"

"Uh-huh."

"All right. Come in, take a seat, and tell me what this is all about. But make it quick."

For the second time in less than an hour I explained the entire project to Ross Fullerton, and for the second time he responded with sarcasm and negativity.

"Special ed kids at Space Camp," he said, shaking his head in disbelief. "You guys are crazy." He paused. "You know, there are more practical ways to introduce kids with special needs to space and science. Let me give you some examples." Fullerton picked up the phone and summoned one of his assistants. In walked a tall, thin man with a receding hairline and a slight smile. He wore khakis, a casual button-down shirt, and a big fish tie—staring out from the guy's chest was a walleye pike! He looked absolutely hilarious.

"Yes, Ross?" he said casually.

Fullerton did not introduce us. He simply said to the man with the fish tie, "I want you to take these folks around and show them what we do here at NASA for handicapped children."

Robynn rolled her eyes. I could tell what she was thinking: *"Handicapped?"*

Fish Man rubbed his chin. He seemed confused. "Uhhhh, what do we do for handicapped children, Ross?"

Fullerton leaped out of his chair and began to scream. "You know what I'm talking about! Take them over to that building . . . the one where the handicapped kids were building missiles, stuff like that."

Fish Man nodded. "Okay, Ross. Calm down. I'll show them around."

As we left Fullerton's office, Fish Man said, "Boy, you have ruffled his feathers. What did you do to make him so mad?"

"We got a red clearance," I said.

Fish Man laughed. "That'll do it." He looked over his shoulder, as if worried that someone might hear him. "Let me tell you something. What they do for special ed kids here is nothing. Take a look." He led us into a poorly lit room filled with desks and tables and boxes of miniature rockets.

"Why is it so dark?"

Fish Man picked up a booklet and flipped it open, revealing pages of instructions written in Braille. "This room is for blind people," he said. "They can't see anyway, so I guess no one cares if it's dark. Saves money, right?"

I was appalled. "This is it? What about getting out, visiting classrooms, explaining the space program to special education students. Do you have anything like that?"

Fish Man shook his head. "Heck, no. They wouldn't understand it anyway."

"They might . . . if you gave it a try."

Fish Man shrugged and led us back to Fullerton's office.

"So, what did you think?" Fullerton asked, seemingly proud of this meager effort.

"I think it's a joke," I said. "Anyway, we're not here to see what you do, or think you do, for special-needs kids. Frankly, I couldn't care less. We're here to see Dr. Brown, and I'd like to know when that's going to happen."

Fullerton's face flushed red. He tugged at his collar. "You'll get your meeting," he spat. "But I don't know when. You just be ready when I call, because you won't get a second chance."

WE WERE STILL waiting for the first chance when we took our seats in the back of the Hilton ballroom that night. When Dr. Brown walked to the podium to begin his speech, I withdrew a microcasette recorder and placed it in the center of our table. Then, to Robynn's dismay, I turned it on.

"What are you doing?"

"Hey, I'm a football coach. I like to have a game plan. Whenever you go into battle you have to know what type of offense you should use and how to defend yourself . . ." She looked at me as if I were talking nonsense. "Same thing here. Maybe we can learn something by studying his speech."

Dr. Brown's lecture lasted about twenty minutes and covered a number of topics, but the overriding theme was this: how he hoped to improve NASA's education program for all mankind. He used that exact word: "mankind." And so I sat there, wondering . . . *Does that include children with special needs?* Must be. After all, he had said "mankind." He hadn't said, "for all brilliant people." He hadn't said, "for all geniuses." Nope. He had said, "for all mankind." If he was a man of his word, a man of principle, there was reason to be optimistic. In all candor, though, I had my doubts. We'd spent the previous four months scaling a giant bureaucratic dung heap, and by now I had come to recognize a pile of crap when I saw it . . . or smelled it . . . or stepped in it.

THE NEXT MORNING brought more lectures, classes on satellite technology, chest thumping by representatives of the U.S. and Soviet space programs, each of which was still trying to establish supremacy. A lot of it was interesting in an Orwellian sort of way—when you realize that satellites have the ability to take clear, precise photos of a suburban mailbox from ten miles above the Earth's surface, well, that sends a chill down your spine. It was pretty cool . . . and pretty spooky at the same time.

Robynn and I were eating lunch when Ross Fullerton marched up to us and said, with no emotion whatsoever, "You'll be meeting with Dr. Brown in twenty minutes. Meet me in the lobby."

Fullerton walked away briskly without saying another word. This, of course, was his way of getting back at us. He had hoped to catch us off-guard, and it had worked, but only for a moment. We were prepared. Nervous . . . but prepared.

When we got to the lobby, two elevators were waiting. Dr. Brown's entourage consisted of seven or eight people, including Fullerton and Fish Man, who this time wore a tie emblazoned with a rainbow trout. Oddly enough, there were no introductions. Upon seeing us, Dr. Brown led his entourage into the first elevator. Robynn and I took the second elevator. As the doors closed, Fullerton said, "Top floor."

We gathered in a conference room, at the center of which was a large oval table. Dr. Brown sat at the head of the table; Robynn and I were invited to sit in the two seats closest to him. Everyone else sat back and watched. Before making formal introductions, Fullerton shot me a glance, and I thought for a moment he might actually smile, so much was he enjoying watching me sweat. I was in the roasting pan and he was getting ready to do a little basting.

Dr. Brown cleared his throat, pushed back his chair, and stood up. He pointed a finger at us and said, testily, "Who do you think you are, getting a red clearance and going over the heads of my people? What kind of tricks are you trying to pull?"

"Uhhhh . . ."

He didn't give me time to respond. He just kept hammering us. "What is so special about you and your program that you think you can waltz in here and make demands? Don't you understand protocol?"

It went on like that for several minutes, with Dr. Brown ranting and belittling and chastising us for our insolence. After a while it became clear that his primary goal was to scare the heck out of us, and he was doing a pretty good job of it. With the doors closed and the air conditioning apparently malfunctioning, and this guy reading us the riot act, I soon developed a case of the flop sweats. Perspiration rolled down my abundant forehead and into my eyes. Buckets pooled in my armpits.

Seeing I was in distress, Robynn passed me a handkerchief, but it was really inadequate. A beach towel might not have sufficed under the circumstances. Like Frosty the Snowman, I was having a meltdown right in front of this guy, and with each word, each question, he sliced off another chunk of ice.

Finally he stopped, sat down, and folded his arms on the table.

"Is someone going to answer any of these questions? Or should we just call it a day?"

Robynn kicked me under the table, as if to say, "It's your turn this time." So I raised my hand, like a nervous schoolboy.

"Go on," he said.

I took a deep breath, exhaled slowly. "Dr. Brown, I really enjoyed your speech last night."

That seemed to throw him a bit. He furrowed his brow. "Thank you."

"You're welcome. But what I really want to know is . . . do you stand behind what you said about your program being accessible for all mankind?"

He didn't hesitate. "Of course I do."

"Good. Then that means it should be accessible for special education kids, right?"

Dr. Brown stood up again, moved closer to me, as if to remind that he was in charge. "I just want to know how these kids will fit in at Space Camp, and I want to know why you need the curriculum material you've requested."

I wanted to remain polite, respectful, but I couldn't help thinking that he was being petty, so I decided to speak from the gut. I told him about a vocational program that Robynn and I had started with the cooperation of a local entrepreneur named Dan Trierweiler, who owned more than two dozen Burger King restaurants in the Grand Rapids area. "Our kids are working at these restaurants," I said. "They're collecting paychecks. They want to be taxpayers, not simply tax receivers. They want to be an intricate part of society, but that's pretty hard when everybody—their friends, their families, the school, even the federal government—keeps telling them, 'Don't take the risk. It's not worth the effort.' " I paused, surveyed the scene. Everyone was listening, even Fullerton. "Frankly, I've had it with that kind of attitude. That's why

I'm here today. That's why Robynn is here. To speak for these kids. They want to take the risk. They want to do something that really does make them 'special,' in a way that will make them proud. And we want to give them that opportunity."

Another pause.

"Let me ask you, sir . . . do you know our kids?"

He shook his head.

"Our kids have disabilities. They have problems. But you know what? They are contributing to the federal government. Part of the money they earn, and part of the money their parents earn, goes to your budget. There are seven million children in this country who are working and paying taxes despite suffering from some type of disability, and they're not getting any breaks. You take their money, you dole it out, you do all these elaborate, exciting things at NASA . . . but it's all designed for gifted and talented kids." I paused, gestured toward Fish Man, whose jaw suddenly went slack. "This guy tells me he's never even been in a special education classroom. Ever! I mean, that's just—"

"*Stop!*" Dr. Brown apparently had heard enough. He turned to Fullerton and said, "Ross, is this true? Have we never sent a representative to a special education classroom?"

Fullerton was so nervous, so angry, that he was literally shaking. "Well, yes, it's true, but in fairness I should point out that we've never had any requests."

That was the beginning of the end. Pretty soon Dr. Brown was shouting at Fullerton, and Fullerton was shouting at Fish Man, and then other members of the entourage jumped into the fray. Robynn and I watched in amazement. This was what happened when people were caught with their pants down: complete and utter panic.

After a while Dr. Brown grew tired of the bickering and put a hand in the air. "That's enough! We're losing focus here." The room fell silent. Dr. Brown pointed at Robynn and me. "I think you two should leave now."

"Leave?"

"Yes. We have some things to hash out in this room, and it's not appropriate for you to be here. You've made some valid points. I'll give you my answer tomorrow."

As I pried my sweat-soaked suit off the chair and excused myself from the room, it was all I could do to keep from screaming, *"Tomorrow? Not again!"*

SOMETIMES YOU JUST have to believe in fate, if only because there is no logical explanation for the way things unfold. After leaving the meeting Robynn and I agreed to get together in a few hours. She wanted to attend a couple lectures, while I merely wanted to go back to my hotel room, change into some dry clothes, and relax for a little while before getting ready for the evening's big event: a Hawaiian luau. God, however, must have had something else in mind.

Around four o'clock that afternoon I went down to the lobby to pick up a newspaper and some snacks. As I hopped back onto the elevator I heard someone say, "Hold that, please." So I put a hand on the door and waited as the other passenger stepped onto the elevator. Our eyes locked. I couldn't believe it!

"Hello, Dr. Brown . . . what floor would you like?"

My room was on the seventh floor, so that button was already illuminated. Dr. Brown nodded, looked at the panel, and said, flatly, "Looks like we're going in the same direction."

Oh, my God! He's on my floor! You've got to be kidding!

We rode up in silence, me in the front of the elevator, trying to blend into the wall, and Dr. Brown in the back, rocking on his heels.

Please hurry. Please hurry.

I could only hope that when we reached the seventh floor, and the doors opened, he would go left, and I would go right. It was obvious he didn't want to talk, hadn't made any sort of decision, so I just wanted to get out of his presence as quickly as possible.

"Ding!"

The elevator stopped, the doors slid open, I stepped out and immediately turned right . . . and so did Dr. Brown. *Oh no!* He trailed me down the hall, just a step or two behind. As I stopped at my room, number 712, and began nervously fidgeting for my key, Dr. Brown walked around me, but very slowly, almost as if he had something to say. No such luck. He was getting ready to stop, too. When I looked up, he was swiping a key into the door of room 710. We were next-door neighbors!

When I finally got into my room I collapsed onto the couch. This was incredible! It couldn't have been scripted any better. "I need a beer," I said out loud. So I snatched a Michelob out of the cheap Styrofoam cooler Robynn and I had picked up before checking in the previous day. Unfortunately, all of the ice had melted and now the beer was swimming in a pool of warm water. "Figures. It's been that kind of a day." With a heavy sigh, I emptied the water into the bathtub, grabbed the hotel ice bucket off the sink, and headed for the door. As I stepped out into the hallway I was shocked to see Dr. Brown exiting his room. Not only that, but he also held an ice bucket in his hand! There we were, the two of us standing outside our rooms, ice buckets at the ready, staring each other down, like the gunfight at the O.K. Corral.

The ice machine was at the end of the hallway, closest to my room, but still a good hundred feet away. I began to walk, with Dr. Brown, again, just a stride behind me. I could feel the perspiration forming on my brow all over again. Even in shorts and a T-shirt, I was beginning to overheat.

This is un-freaking-believable!

When we got to the ice machine I quickly filled my bucket and set it down. Then, for reasons I still can't quite explain, I held up the scoop and said, "Let me get that for you."

"Thank you," Dr. Brown said as I took his bucket and filled it with ice. As I handed it back to him, I added, "Do you mind if I call you Bob?" Don't ask what came over me. It just seemed like the thing to do at the time.

"What did you say?" Obviously, I had surprised him. I hadn't said, "Well, have you made a decision?" or "Man, you make me really nervous," both of which I was thinking.

"I said, 'Do you mind if I call you Bob?' "

He shrugged, and for a moment it looked as though he might smile. "No, I guess not."

As I saw it, the door was now ajar so I leaned into it. "Hey, are you going to the luau tonight?"

"Unfortunately, no. I didn't know anything about it because I got in late last night, so I really don't have appropriate clothing."

I looked him over. He was about my height and stature. A crazy idea entered my head.

"What size shoe do you wear, Bob?"

"Eleven and a half . . . why?"

"Because I'm a twelve, and I have an extra pair of sandals. How about your waist size?"

"Thirty-four."

"Great! Me, too. You can borrow a pair of my shorts." There was a lull in the conversation as Dr. Brown nodded approvingly. I decided to go for broke. "Would you like to come back to my room and have a beer?"

Without hesitation he said, "Sure. That would be great."

And so, for the next hour or so, Dr. Brown and I hung out in my room, drinking Michelob, eating pretzels, and chatting like a couple of guys at a neighborhood sports bar. Eventually the conversation turned to Space Camp, and the meeting we had endured that afternoon.

"You know," Dr. Brown said, "you're kind of direct."

"I'm sorry . . . I didn't mean to be rude."

He held up a hand. "No, no. That's all right. You really made me think about some things."

"Bob," I said, "I know some of the people at Space Camp aren't thrilled about this, but they did give us their blessing. All I need from you is some material from NASA's Research Center—stuff on astronomy, science, the history of space exploration—because our kids have never been exposed to any of it before. We want to work with them. We want them to be prepared. We want them to be pumped up. We want to do this the right way."

Dr. Brown took a swig of Michelob, then set the bottle down. "I've heard enough," he said. "We'll help you in any way we can."

The relief was instantaneous, and yet still it all seemed surreal. Here was the head of education for NASA, a man with a reputation for being completely unapproachable, and he was sitting in my hotel room, drinking my beer, about to wear my clothes, and agreeing to support our program. This was almost too good to be true. There was just one more thing to do.

"Bob, can you do me a favor?"

"Sure."

"In a few minutes Robynn is going to knock on that door. When she does, I'd like you to answer it."

"Why?"

"I just want to see the look on her face."

An impish grin crossed his face. "Okay."

We talked for a little while longer, until, right on time, there was a knock outside my room. I stood off to the side as Dr. Brown opened the door and said, "Yes?" At first there was silence. Complete silence. Then I could hear Robynn saying, "Oh, I'm sorry . . . I must have the wrong room."

Unable to control myself any longer, I stepped into the doorway, laughing so hard my stomach hurt. Dr. Brown also began laughing.

"You've got the right place, Robynn," I said. "Say hello to Bob Brown."

Robynn stood wide-eyed as Dr. Brown shook her hand. I then gave him a pair of sandals, shorts, and a Hawaiian print shirt. Dr. Brown excused himself. "I'll just be a minute," he said, and disappeared into the bathroom.

Robynn watched the door close, then turned to me, an expression of complete and utter befuddlement on her face.

"He needed some clothes for the luau," I said.

"Oh, well . . . that explains everything."

8

When Robynn and I returned to Grand Rapids we discovered that the rumor mill was in high gear. I should have anticipated this. A man and a woman can only spend so much time together before people begin to make assumptions, especially when the man and woman are coworkers. Some of the talk was merely that: relatively benign gossip, exchanged with a wink and a nudge. Some of it, however, was bilious. It was designed to hurt, to ruin careers and families and reputations.

One teacher, who was actually a good friend of mine, stopped me in the hallway one day after school, as I was on my way to the weight room.

"Hey, Mike," he said, smiling salaciously. "I hear you and Robynn are getting to be pretty close." He looked around, to make sure no one was listening, and then made a clicking sound with his mouth. "Didn't think you had it in you."

As a veteran teacher this type of reaction shouldn't have shocked me, but it did, at least coming from this guy. I expected more.

"What are you talking about?" I said.

"You know . . ." He pumped a fist in front of him, at chest level.

Something in me snapped at that, and I grabbed him by the collar, put him up against a locker. "Where did you hear this?"

"Easy, Mike! I didn't mean anything."

"Where did you hear it?!"

"In the faculty lounge. One of the front-office secretaries was talking about you guys, saying you were using Space Camp as an excuse to go on the road . . . to spend some quality time together." He paused, held up his hands, as if to surrender. "It's all over school. I thought you knew."

I loosened my grip, suddenly ashamed of having lost my temper. "Sorry."

He smoothed his shirt. "That's all right. I guess I'd be upset, too."

Upset didn't begin to cover the way I felt. Robynn and I had grown accustomed to the looks and comments from our peers, to the snickering that came from the faculty lounge. It wasn't just the fact that we had been working so closely—we'd been doing that for a few years. No, the hostility stemmed largely from jealousy. Robynn and I were traveling, attending conferences and meeting with powerful government representatives. We were working long and hard for something we believed in, and our passion for this project, for our kids, set a standard that made some other teachers, the ones who strolled out of school each day at three o'clock with not so much as a planning book in their hands, look incredibly bad. For the most part it was easy to ignore their behavior, to accept it as the pathetic by-product of being bitter and lazy. But this . . . this was reprehensible; it was the height, or depth, of unprofessional behavior, worse than anything our students had ever exhibited. In fact, their response to the swirl of gossip was nothing short of admirable.

I noticed one day in class that the kids were quieter than usual. They weren't speaking out of turn, stepping on each other's responses, poking fun at each other. There had often been days when they were lethargic, but this was different. This time they seemed to have something on their minds.

"What's wrong?" I finally asked.

Steve Bennett was the first to respond. Although typically quick with a joke or a sarcastic comment, he said, calmly and seriously, "Coach, we're hearing some things about you and Mrs. McKinney."

I stopped writing on the blackboard, put the chalk on my desk, and walked directly to where Steve was sitting. "Get up," I said.

Steve pushed his chair away from his desk and slowly stood up. His eyes were fixed on the floor. The fact that Steve, one of my favorite students, had initiated this conversation only made it more painful, and more critical.

"Look me in the eye," I said. Steve lifted his chin. Our eyes locked. "Exactly what do you hear, Steve?"

He looked around the room. The rest of the class sat quietly, awaiting his answer. "We hear you're having an affair."

Those words hit me with crushing force. I took several steps backward, until I was near my desk. I looked out at the class. "What do you guys think about that?"

There was no response . . . at first. Then Stephanie Reinks's hand went into the air.

"Yes, Stephanie."

"I think it's a lot of bull, Coach. You guys are good friends."

With that, a buzz filled the air, the humming of twenty kids agreeing on something, a sound rarely heard in our classroom.

"Let me tell you something," I said. "There is no affair. There's nothing going on." I hesitated, tried to think clearly. They deserved more than just a flat denial. They deserved an explanation. "Mrs. McKinney and I are very close," I continued. "We're like brother and sister. Do I love her? You bet I do . . . but as a friend. Some of you have boyfriends, girlfriends . . . and you have regular friends. You know the difference, right?"

They nodded, said "Sure, Coach," and we all went back to work. For these kids, who supposedly were socially inept, intellectually deficient, and morally bankrupt, that was explanation enough. They accepted it, embraced it, and never mentioned it again. The same could not be said of my coworkers, which begged the question: *Who has the disability here?*

9

N ot long after our trip to Houston, the euphoria dissipated and reality settled in. We needed money. A lot of it. We had constructed a carefully worded letter and sent it home with the students, so that their parents would know how much work still lay ahead, but we were optimistic, probably because we were so naïve.

My wife had been one of the first to throw cold water on our celebration. "I can't believe you really pulled this off," she had said upon hearing the outcome of our meeting with Dr. Brown. "Now what?"

"Now we need fifty thousand dollars."

Her face went ashen. "Mike . . . that's not a little thing. That's a *ton* of money."

"I know, but I think we can raise it. I mean, how hard can it be?"

As we soon discovered, in slow, painful fashion, it was nearly impossible.

Our students, bless their hearts, were unfazed by the Sisyphean nature of this task. To them, it was no different than trying to raise money for a dance. "Hey, why don't we have a car wash?" Steve Bennett suggested.

"Yeah, right, Steve," I said. "You'll be sitting in the front seat, playing with the horn, flicking all the switches, pushing the cigarette lighter, and God knows what else."

Another student, Pat Zerfas, suggested we take it one step farther and offer oil changes, lube jobs . . . even tune-ups. Pat was moderately autistic—he drifted in and out of his own private world, never really bothering anyone, but never paying full attention, either. Like so many of our kids, though, Pat was good with his hands. He could take an automobile apart and put it back together again.

"How about it, Coach?" he said. "I can bring my own tools."

As talented a mechanic as Pat might have been, I couldn't imagine him leading a pit crew comprised entirely of our students. I envisioned angry motorists lurching away in their BMWs, engines hiccuping and coughing, oil dripping from the doors and windows.

Lewis, a talented artist as well as a budding sexist, liked the idea of a car wash, but only if we could convince the prettiest girls in the school to help out. "I'll do a sign," he said. " 'Have Hot Chicks Wash Your Car!' That'll be cool."

Grant Plunkett, as usual, was playing the role of Eeyore, saying things like, "Oh, man, I don't want to stand out in the hot sun all day, washing cars, getting all wet. That sounds awful."

Robynn and I knew from the start that any money raised by the students would have to be purely supplemental, but even that didn't shake my confidence. I just figured we had a good idea and someone would give us the cash to bring that idea to life. After all, wasn't that the way things were supposed to work?

Among the many people who supported our adventure, none was more vital or enthusiastic than Dr. Lynn Bondurant, who worked out of Lewis Research Center in Cleveland and was in charge of NASA education for the Midwest. We had been referred to him by Dr. Brown, who had assured us that Dr. Bondurant would not only provide us with the curriculum material we needed but that we would also find him to be an enormously likeable and generous man.

Right on both counts.

This was a gentleman who, upon meeting Robynn and me for the very first time, greeted us in the hallway outside his office with a hug and a smile and these exact words: "I've been waiting thirteen years for you! Please . . . come in!"

As if that weren't enough, when we entered his office, the first thing I saw, hanging on the wall above his desk, was a framed picture of Albert Einstein. In big, sweeping letters across the bottom of the picture were the words "Imagination is more important than knowledge." I froze in my tracks. *Somebody pinch me!* Granted, it was an abridged version of the quote I loved best, but the implication was clear. In this room we had found a kindred spirit. And just as I was thinking, *This is too good to be true*, it got even better.

"Hey," Lynn said. "Did you guys know I used to be a high school principal in Michigan? Small world, huh?"

I nearly fell on the floor. After all we'd been through, after so many meetings with critics and skeptics and cynics, here, finally, was a true believer. An ally. A mentor. A *friend*.

We spent the next day and a half gathering information and material that could be used in our curriculum. The plan had to be palatable to the Board of Education, and that meant infusing the training with liberal doses of astronomy, geology, aerospace engineering, physiology, history. By the time we left Dr. Bondurant had assembled a neat outline for us explaining how everything would work perfectly in preparing our stu- dents for Space Camp. It was obvious that he was a visionary. In the ensuing months and years I would hear him lecture many times, and he never failed to hold the attention of his audience, mainly because he had the rare gift of being able to transport you to another time and place. That's what he did to Robynn and me that first day in Cleveland— he took us, and our students, to Space Camp. Dr. Bondurant was pre- cisely what I thought a leader should be: open-minded, fair. He believed in exciting people rather than intimidating them.

In addition to holding our hands as we attempted to formulate a training plan, Dr. Bondurant assisted us in the formidable task of raising funds for our venture. For starters, he suggested, "Try the local library. Gather as much information as possible on how to construct a decent grant proposal, and then submit it to any foundation that seems like it might have an interest in supporting programs for children with special needs." That sounded simple enough, but in actuality it was a monu- mentally time-consuming and tedious chore, made even more difficult by our lack of experience.

Nevertheless, we jumped into the process headfirst, confident that someone with deep pockets would quickly respond to what we thought was a wonderful proposition. Uh-uh. Didn't happen that way. After spending all of our nights and evenings together for several weeks,

Robynn and I began sending out proposals. Then we waited . . . and waited . . . and waited. Finally, the first response came back. A simple, polite, one-page rejection.

Ahh . . . no big deal. We have a dozen lines in the water.

Then the second response came. Then the third . . . and the fourth . . . and the fifth. All rejections. Within a few more weeks, every one of our submissions had been rejected, leaving us not only crestfallen but bewildered. This was such a worthwhile project—why couldn't anyone see its viability? What were we doing wrong?

Compounding my frustration was the fact that the pursuit of this dream was exacting a considerable toll on my personal and professional lives. I spent all of my free time either writing grant proposals or immersed in how-to books about writing proposals. I did not attend a single football coaching clinic the entire winter. I hardly ever went to the weight room to see what sort of progress my players were making. At home I was equally preoccupied. One Saturday afternoon, irritated by the sight of my two sons staring vacantly at the television set, I decided it was time to get everyone out of the house for a day of fun and exercise. We dressed the boys in their snowsuits and took them sledding at a nearby park. While Darcy and I stood at the bottom of the hill watching them, though, my mind began to wander.

"Thinking about Space Camp again, aren't you?"

"Huh?"

Darcy kicked at the snow. "Mike, you're really distancing yourself from everyone. You know that, don't you?"

She was absolutely right. For the first time in my life, I was truly obsessed with something, and it had nothing to do with my family or coaching. That's all I had ever wanted to be: a teacher, a husband, a father, a football coach. That had always been enough for me, but now I had a chance to do something else, something that, in my eyes, anyway, seemed important. It wasn't about me—it really wasn't. I looked at my students, and I looked at my own sons, and I thought, *This isn't right. Why can't these kids have a chance to be like Shawn and Ryan? My boys can do anything they want, be anything they want: astronauts, teachers, doctors, artists, football players. Anything! Nothing is beyond their reach.*

Space Camp wasn't the entire answer. Life isn't that simple. But I saw it as a potentially transcendent experience, something our students could attempt, and if they were successful, something that might alter the way they looked at themselves. It could build their self-esteem, give them pride and courage, make them realize they hadn't scratched the surface of their own potential.

Darcy didn't fully understand or approve of any of this. She came from a family of football players and coaches, and our mutual love for that sport was one of the things that had brought us together. We had a good life, a life that in her eyes was sufficient, and she had a right to be angry, resentful, because my mission, my obsession, was diverting time and energy from my boys and my family. It was changing me. But I had made a leap, and now there was no turning back. I counted on Darcy and the boys to tolerate my madness, and they did. In fact, they did much more than that—they became part of the program. As Darcy watched me struggle with the proposals, she started asking questions, and then she started organizing material for me, and making suggestions about how to tweak and fine-tune the proposals. I never asked her for help, never forced her to share my obsession. I simply tried to make it clear that her help was wanted and appreciated, and she responded. In the back of her mind, though, I'm sure Darcy was thinking, *Okay, get it out of your system. Take the kids to Space Camp, and then I want my life back.* Neither one of us had any idea then that it would never leave my system.

AS THE REJECTIONS poured in, frustration was replaced by something closer to panic. We were running out of time and options. It seemed as though every rejection letter was worded the same way: "Thank you for your interest; unfortunately, we are not providing funding in that area at the present time. We wish you the best."

As winter gave way to spring it became increasingly difficult to maintain a facade of optimism and progress. Each day the students would come into school and ask, "Coach, get any answers back?" I'd smile and shake my head. "Not yet. But don't worry . . . it'll happen soon." Parents were stopping by my classroom, calling me at home, asking for updates. They weren't trying to be intrusive; they were just excited. Rather than squelch that enthusiasm, I lied, or at least embellished. I said everything was fine, we were sending out proposals, getting positive feedback from representatives of various foundations, and that it was only a matter of time before we hit the jackpot. In truth, the whole venture was in danger of being flushed down the toilet. We had received more than seventy rejection letters—*seventy!*—and there was no reason to believe a letter of approval was coming any time soon.

Eventually I consulted Dr. Bondurant. "We're failing miserably," I told him. "And I have no idea what we're doing wrong."

Dr. Bondurant suggested we meet with a friend of his, Dr. Robert Muth, a former professor at Michigan State University who specialized in crafting exquisite and compelling grant proposals.

"He doesn't live too far from you, and I'm sure he'll be happy to give you some advice," Lynn said. "I'll set it up."

A few weeks later, on a Sunday afternoon, I drove to Dr. Muth's home in Rockford, Michigan, about fifteen miles north of Grand Rapids. His wife answered the door and invited me in.

"Yes, he's expecting you," she said. "He's in the den."

I could hear the sound of a basketball game. Dr. Muth was relaxing in front of a television, watching the Michigan State–Michigan game.

"Sit down," he said, not taking his eyes off the TV. "I'd like to watch this until halftime—you don't mind, do you?"

"Not at all."

"You a basketball fan?" he asked.

"Sort of, but I'm more of a football guy."

He shrugged. "That's okay. What team do you like?"

I swallowed hard. I had played college football at Indiana State University, but God knows I'd have given my right arm for a chance to play at the University of Michigan. I just wasn't talented enough. I'd spent practically my whole life in Michigan and had always been a fan of the Wolverines. Knowing full well that it wasn't what he wanted to hear, I said, "Sir, I have to tell you . . . I love the University of Michigan."

Dr. Muth flashed me a hard look. "Hey! Those are dirty words! You're in a Spartan house!"

"Sorry."

He chuckled. "Nah, I'm just kidding." He paused, gestured toward the screen. "But I have to tell you, the Spartans are kicking your butt right now."

And so they were. We watched until halftime, then Dr. Muth turned off the television. "Lynn tells me you're having trouble with your grant proposal. Let's see what you've got."

So I handed him one of our proposals. Dr. Muth was in his sixties by this time and not in the best of health, but he still had an air of dignity and intellect about him. Having just come from church, he was wearing a crisp white shirt, tie, and dress pants; his jacket was draped over the arm of a chair. With his glasses resting on the end of his nose, he looked intently at our proposal, reading . . . reading . . . reading. For several minutes he didn't say anything, didn't ask any questions. Then, suddenly and dispassionately, he crumpled the proposal into a ball and tossed it into a wastebasket.

"This," he said, "is a piece of garbage."

Too flabbergasted to respond, I just sat there and stared at the trash can.

"Come on," Dr. Muth said. "Let's go downstairs.

I followed him to the basement, where he proceeded to hand me a tape recorder and a stack of books about grant writing. "Talk into this thing," he said. "Tell it what you want to do. And then start reading."

He walked to the bottom of the stairs and yelled to his wife. "Honey, get this man a pop . . . he's gonna be here for a while!" Then he walked upstairs, shut the door, and went back to the basketball game, leaving me there all alone, completely lost, thinking, *What is this all about?!* I called Robynn on the basement phone and said, "You won't believe this guy. He's got me sitting in his basement with a pile of books and a tape recorder. He hates my proposal, he hates Wolverines, and I'm pretty sure he hates me, too."

Typically, Robynn just laughed. "Do what he tells you to do," she said. "We have nothing to lose."

True enough, so I called my wife and said I'd probably be late for dinner. I spent the next several hours poring over Dr. Muth's books, and reciting our objectives into the tape recorder. I took dozens of pages of notes. When it came time to leave he looked at what I had written and said, with a sniff, "Well, it's a start, I guess. But you have a long way to go. I want you back here tomorrow . . . and bring Robynn with you."

Although a bit on the brusque side, he seemed genuinely interested in helping us. Over the next few weeks we met several times, with Dr. Muth dissecting every word we wrote. The problem, he explained, was not in the concept; it was in the execution. A proposal is not an essay. It's a sales tool, and without adhering to a specific format, it has no chance of succeeding. As we began to make progress, he became more enthusiastic, not unlike a teacher. He worked closely with us, helped us define and narrow our mission, and, most important of all, target the foundations most likely to respond positively.

Our best shot, we all agreed, was the Kellogg Foundation, which was based in Michigan and presumably more inclined to support programs in its own region. Dr. Muth used his considerable clout to arrange a meeting with representatives of the Kellogg Foundation, so that we could make a personal pitch. We submitted all of the appropriate paperwork a few weeks in advance, and then drove to the meeting. Unfortunately, Dr. Muth wasn't feeling well that day, so he wasn't able to accompany us. No matter—Robynn and I were confident that we had done our homework and, with Dr. Muth's enormous help and guidance, had constructed a nearly perfect proposal.

"You'll be fine," Dr. Muth had said. "You're as prepared as you can possibly be."

He was correct. Our presentation to the Kellogg Foundation's executive board went smoothly. They asked us several questions and seemed satisfied with our responses. Then they dismissed us and asked us to wait outside. Twenty minutes passed as Robynn and I paced the halls, looking at photos on the wall, gazing absently out the windows. I felt like a defendant waiting for the jury to come back.

Finally the door opened. "Mr. Kersjes, Mrs. McKinney . . . you may come in now."

The silence and blank faces told us all we needed to know. I barely listened as the director explained that funds were limited at this time and they had already made a commitment to support various missionary efforts in Africa.

"We'll follow this up with a formal letter, and we do wish you well," he said. "But we can't help you right now. I'm sorry."

Churches in Africa. Hard to find fault with that.

Robynn and I drove home in silence. When I dropped her off, she stepped onto the sidewalk and began to walk away. Then she turned and doubled back, tapped on the window. I rolled it down.

"What do we tell the kids?" she asked.

I gripped the wheel, inhaled deeply. This wasn't easy. "We'll tell them the foundation hasn't made a decision yet, and that we should hear something soon."

Clearly bemused, Robynn said, "Oh?"

"If we go back into that classroom with beaten looks on our faces, it's all over," I said. "Let's stall for a few weeks."

"Okay . . . then what?"

I had no answer. I could only hope that one would present itself.

10

When Dr. Muth heard of Kellogg's rejection, he was nearly as disappointed as we were, but he assured us that our proposal was now strong, and advised us to keep plugging away. To take my mind off our financial woes, I dived into curriculum preparation, but this only served to heighten my anxiety. It wasn't just traveling to Alabama that was expensive, it was preparing and training the students. We'd need crystallization kits, model rockets, pool time at the local YMCA (for microgravity simulation training that would be similar to what they would experience at Space Camp). The list was endless, and we hadn't a dime to pay for any of it.

After spring break I sensed a decline in interest whenever I brought up the subject of Space Camp. The kids would nod, maybe ask a question or two, but generally it seemed as though they were losing faith. I couldn't blame them. After all, there was no tangible evidence that we would ever make the trip.

Robynn and I knew their disappointment would be profound, and that it surely would manifest itself in every aspect of their lives. Already they were acting out in school, getting in more fights, missing more classes, bickering more than usual with one another. So, in early May, when I received a phone call from a secretary in Dan Trierweiler's office, I was naturally concerned. She said that Dan wanted to meet with Robynn and me at the Twenty-eighth Street Burger King on Friday afternoon.

"Around five o'clock," she said. "Is that all right?"

"Of course. No problem," I said. When I hung up the phone my mind began to race. Robynn had recently visited the kids at their job sites and, thankfully, hadn't detected any serious problems. Obviously, though, we had missed something. That day we grilled the students.

"Steve, were you playing stand-up comic with the microphone or something?"

"Uh-uh, Coach. I didn't do anything."

Ben, predictably, rushed to Steve's defense. "I've been with him, Coach. He's been good. Honest!"

Somehow, there was little comfort in Ben standing up for Steve. If I wanted the truth, there was only one place to go: Marion Mills. Marion, like Andrea Burke, wanted so badly to be liked by her teachers that she could not resist tattling on her classmates. If they'd been misbehaving at Burger King, she'd be eager to report the news.

"Marion, what's really going on there?"

She beamed, thrilled at simply having some attention directed her way. "Nothing that I've seen, Coach. Everyone's been good. Really!"

They appeared to be telling the truth, which was perplexing. Dan was an extremely busy guy, and it wasn't like him to ask for a meeting over something trivial.

"Maybe he doesn't want any of our kids working at McDonald's," Robynn suggested. That seemed kind of harsh, but then, Dan was a competitive guy. Perhaps he wanted to discuss some sort of exclusivity clause. But I doubted it. The fact that some of our students worked at Burger King and others worked at McDonald's hardly seemed worthy of Dan Trierweiler's concern. No . . . we'd have to wait until Friday to solve the mystery.

"I'LL START OUT by apologizing," Robynn said. We were weaving through rush hour traffic, on our way to Twenty-eighth Street.

"For what?" I asked.

"I don't know. Whatever it is they might have done. Let's just say, 'We're sorry . . . please don't fire the kids.' "

I laughed, but there was more than a grain of logic in her suggestion. If our students were to lose their jobs, for whatever reason, it would reflect poorly on our program, and certainly affect funding and resources in years to come. This was a delicate matter.

Robynn and I checked in with the manager when we arrived, took a seat in the back of the restaurant, and waited for Dan. He walked in precisely at five o'clock. At six foot five and nearly two hundred fifty pounds, he couldn't help but make a dramatic entrance. Dan had been an athlete, and he continued to live an active, almost Hemingwayesque life: salmon fishing in Alaska, big-game hunting in Africa, that sort of thing. He had neatly groomed silver hair, a perpetual tan, and usually wore expensive three-piece suits. Incongruously, he had a soft, gentle voice. Accompanying him on this day was Stuart Ray, his top assistant, and the contact for our vocational program.

"Stuart's been telling me a lot about your kids," Dan began. "I hear—"

Robynn jumped to her feet and cut him off in midsentence. "Whatever they've done, whatever they've broken, we'll fix it."

Startled, Dan hesitated and gave Robynn a wary look. "That's not what I mean. Stuart has been telling me about your program, and what you're doing at school, and—"

This time it was my turn. "They're talking too much, right? They aren't focusing on their jobs? Disturbing the customers? Look, sometimes they have trouble keeping their mouths shut, but believe me, we'll make sure they're better in the future."

"Dammit!" Dan said. He pounded his fist on the table, nearly spilling my Coke in the process. "Listen to me! Your kids are fine. They're great. It's you guys who are the problem."

Almost in unison, Robynn and I said, "What?"

"What I hear," he continued, "is that you guys suck at writing grant proposals."

Now I was not only confused, I was offended. "Where did you hear that?"

Dan pointed over my shoulder. "From them." I turned around, and there were Steve Bennett and Ben Schmidt, pretending to mop the floor, but really trying to eavesdrop, and Marion Mills, lingering over a nearby table that already had been bused to perfection. "All I want to know is how much money you need to take these kids to Space Camp," Dan said.

Robynn and I exchanged a glance. *Was this really happening?* What we didn't know at the time was that our students had been talking to

Stuart Ray about Space Camp, and had told him, in unflinching detail, just how badly our fund-raising efforts had floundered. "About fifty thousand dollars," I said.

Dan pursed his lips and nodded. "You've got it. I'll give you the money."

I nearly fell off my seat. "You're kidding? Just like that? Why?"

"Because I know how hard you're working, and I know how hard your kids are working." He looked at Ben and Steve and Marion, who by now were crowded around our table. "I like underdogs," he added. "I want to see you win."

With that, Dan Trierweiler excused himself. As I watched him go I couldn't help but think that fate had intervened, that maybe it was our destiny to take these kids to Space Camp. How else to explain a football coach being rescued by an angel built like a linebacker?

ON THE DRIVE home I was so excited that I could barely keep my car on the road. I roared up the driveway, ran into the house, picked up the stack of rejection letters, and threw them into the air. It was an act of pure joy; unfortunately, it scared the heck out of Shawn and Ryan, who huddled together against the refrigerator, convinced that their father had lost his mind.

"*Mom!*" Shawn screamed. "Something's wrong with Dad!"

Darcy entered the room, saw that it was snowing rejection letters, and shook her head. "What now, Mike?"

"*We're going to Space Camp!*"

"Yeah, right."

I rushed over, grabbed her by the shoulders, and gave her a big kiss. "No, you don't understand. I'm serious. Dan Trierweiler is giving us the money. All of it! Fifty thousand dollars! *Can you believe it?!*"

She couldn't, any more than I could. It was beyond anything I might have imagined, a gift so generous and unexpected that it was nearly impossible to comprehend. And yet . . . it had happened. I was sure of that. It had only seemed like a dream. "We can go forward with our plans now, Darcy," I said. "These kids are really going to Space Camp."

Realizing now that I wasn't delusional, she put her arms around my neck and smiled. "Good for you, Mike."

PREDICTABLY, AS WORD spread, the school's administration began expressing an interest in throwing its support behind our program, if only for the sake of publicity. So, on June 2, just a couple weeks before summer break, a press conference was held at Forest Hills Northern. Representatives of the local newspapers and television stations were in attendance, as were our students and their parents, and several administrators. Mike Washburn was there, along with Tom Keller and Denise Boitano. The star of the show, of course, was Dan Trierweiler, who presented us with an initial payment of ten thousand dollars. (Dan was no fool. He wasn't going to give us all the money at once; rather, he would parcel it out over the course of the next eight to ten months. That way, the money that hadn't yet been turned over would not only continue to collect interest, but would also serve as an incentive for us to keep working hard.)

To add a little atmosphere to the event, Robynn and I dressed in blue flight suits, which had been supplied by Space Camp. Ordinarily, we wouldn't have gotten the suits until the summer, when we were scheduled to attend the teacher training program in Huntsville, but when Deborah Barnhart heard about our good fortune, and the attendant press conference, she immediately delivered the suits. After all, this was a great photo opportunity for Space Camp, as well.

My only concern as we gathered that morning was the possibility that some of the students might not be on their best behavior, and thus instigate a bit of embarrassing mischief for the benefit of the local media. I stressed this point before the press conference began, and the kids seemed to get the message. They stood quietly, proudly, as Mike Washburn introduced the important players and made a few remarks. Then Dan Trierweiler stepped to the microphone, explained his reasons for backing the project, and held up a check for ten thousand dollars. Cameras clicked and whirred, flashbulbs popped, and everyone applauded. After Robynn and I were interviewed by a group of reporters, the press conference seemed to be on the verge of dissolving. The students were off to the side, chatting with their parents, behaving impeccably. Again, I was amazed at our good fortune.

Alas, on this most extraordinary of days, there was one more hurdle to clear. The media wanted a comment from one of the students.

I faced the class. "Who'd like to say something?"

The words had barely escaped my lips when Steve Bennett elbowed his way out of the crowd. "How about me, Coach?"

Oh, God . . . please . . . not now.

As Steve was pulled into place for a staged photo alongside Dan Trier-weiler, I mumbled under my breath, "Don't swear . . . don't fart . . . don't belch . . . don't make any weird noises. Please, Steve . . . don't do *anything.*"

But this was too good an opportunity to pass up. Steve stood on his tiptoes and threw an arm around Dan's shoulder. The cameras flashed again. Then a reporter asked Steve if he had anything he'd like to say.

Steve thought for a moment. A wide smile creased his face. "Yeah," he said. "This guy here is going to be working for me someday! Right, Dan?"

Dan Trierweiler looked down at Steve, expressionless at first, then began to laugh. "What a sense of humor! You must have a few kids like that, eh, Mike?"

Ohhhh . . . you have no idea.

PART

TWO

11

Space Camp was conceived in 1982 as an extension of the U.S. Space & Rocket Center, which was developed primarily by Ed Buckbee and the brilliant German scientist Wernher von Braun. The premise and promise of Space Camp was that it would be a highly unique and interactive learning environment, a place where unusually bright and ambitious children could learn not only about space and rocketry, but also math and science and technology. Huntsville, Alabama, was chosen as the home of the U.S. Space & Rocket Center (and thus Space Camp) for some fairly practical reasons, the most obvious of which was the fact that the Redstone Arsenal was already there. Robert Goddard's groundbreaking work on liquid propulsion rockets had been achieved at Redstone, as had the development of the Saturn V rocket. So it seemed a natural fit.

Space Camp, as Robynn and I learned, is not only the name of a facility and a concept, but also an umbrella term for a variety of different programs, each approximately six days in length. Space Camp, for example, is intended for the youngest students, those in grades four through six. Space Academy is for students in grades six through eight. The oldest students, those in grades nine through twelve (such as ours), are enrolled in Advanced Space Academy.

Although Advanced Space Academy naturally demands the most from its students, especially in terms of intellectual and academic dexterity, all of the camps are designed to give students a sense of what it's like to be an astronaut, so they share a great deal in terms of format and schedule. Students generally arrive on a Sunday and depart the following Friday. Working in teams of twenty, they go through a full week of intense training, of actually simulating the work of the various professionals who make a space shuttle mission possible, both on the spacecraft and in Mission Control. Each student is assigned a role, such as pilot or commander (just what they sound like), payload specialist (someone who conducts experiments in a space lab), mission specialist (someone assigned extravehicular duties), or flight director (someone who works in Mission Control and is, really, in charge of the mission). While one title might sound more prestigious than another, there really is no position that is more demanding, or more important, than any other; teamwork is the hallmark of Space Camp.

There is no denying that Space Camp is a rigorous educational experience, but it's also a competitive experience. There is scoring and there is judging; there are winners and losers . . . or, at least, winners and non-winners. The most prestigious award is Best Mission, presented at the end of the week to the team that receives the highest score on its simulated shuttle missions. Awards are also presented for Best Team Patch (each team designs a patch that represents the goals and objectives of the mission) and Best Space Station Presentation (each team designs a miniature space station or lunar base and presents it to a panel of judges). There is also a *Jeopardy*-like competition called Space Bowl. The final award, and the only individual honor, is the Right Stuff Award, presented to the student who not only performs his duties extraordinarily well but also demonstrates exemplary leadership skills and initiative, and is respectful and compassionate toward his teammates, rivals, and counselors. In other words, someone who exhibits the traits of a true astronaut.

The award that everyone wants to win is Best Mission, for the shuttle mission, after all, is the centerpiece of the Space Camp experience. While there is time for recreation and other competitive endeavors, students spend the majority of their time at Space Camp either training for shuttle missions or conducting simulated missions. The missions themselves, which are subject to a time limit (two hours when we made our first trip in 1989), are enormously grueling and stressful. Each team must follow a detailed flight script, from takeoff to landing. Along the way the students are required to simulate many of the tasks undertaken on a real shuttle mission. For example, at a specific time in each flight, the solid rocket booster must separate from the shuttle. For that to happen the crew must take the appropriate steps, trigger the right switches, and do it at precisely the right moment. Similarly, later in the mission, the shuttle is supposed to dock with a space station, and that, too, re quires the following of a specific set of commands and the subsequent throwing of switches—all within a short window of time. This would be difficult enough under the best of circumstances, but the staff at Space Camp makes each mission more challenging through the addition of anomalies. Docking with a space station becomes exponentially more difficult when you've just been told that a fire has broken out in the cockpit. The trick is to know which anomalies must be solved immediately (in other words, which anomalies are so serious that they could result in a mission being aborted or lives being lost) and which can be ignored for a few minutes.

Preparation is the key. Those students who pay attention in class, who take their training seriously, tend to perform better during the simulated missions. Moreover, because our students would be participating in two separate missions, they knew that they would be required to understand more than one position. That, naturally, placed pressure on them to follow the entire script during training, and not merely the parts of the script that pertained to their own particular job.

The judging of each mission is highly subjective, with counselors grading the students on a scale of one to ten in a variety of different categories, including teamwork, problem-solving, successful experimentation in space lab, performance in extravehicular activities, and performance in the cockpit and Mission Control. The highest score possible on any single mission is one hundred. Competitive water activities are also factored into the overall judging of Best Mission. In 1989 that meant jumping into a pool (to simulate microgravity) and using plastic nodes and rods to build a tetrahedron, a pyramidlike geometric figure commonly used in space structures such as solar panels. With a clock running, of course.

It's an intense, exhausting week, which isn't to say the students don't have fun; they do. But in many cases they're being asked to work harder than they've ever worked in their lives. They're up at six each morning and they aren't finished working until ten or eleven at night. The result is students who typically leave Space Camp exhausted, but proud of what they've accomplished.

IN THE SUMMER of 1988 Robynn and I attended a teacher training program at Space Camp, the format of which was virtually indistinguishable from that which our students would be facing. There were several reasons for this trip. First of all, we wanted to collect material and information that we could present to our principal and the Board of Education as justification for a daily, one-hour space and science class to be taught by Robynn and me, and taken by all of our students in the upcoming school year. The material had to be sufficiently challenging and compatible with state curriculum standards to merit accreditation. Second, and perhaps most important, we had to educate ourselves so that we wouldn't seem scared to death when we began training the students. We wanted to repeatedly walk the students through a week at Space Camp, so that by the time they arrived in Huntsville, some nine months later, they'd feel as if they had already been there. That meant teaching them astronomy and space history, drilling them on the thousands of acronyms that are the backbone of conversation during a shuttle mission (for example: EVA for extravehicular activity, RTLS for return to launch site), and rehearsing as many scripts as we could possibly find. It also meant making modifications for students with dyslexia and visual impairments.

The third reason for our enrollment in the teacher training program was that Deborah Barnhart strongly encouraged it. In fact, she waived our tuition fee, which was a pretty clear indication of just how much she had at stake in this experiment. We had visited the camp once before, but this time we'd be immersed in the experience. It was an opportunity for us to learn and practice and study, and for the administration at Space Camp to watch us in action. Robynn and I knew that if we botched the job . . . if we acted like complete jerks or otherwise failed to take the program seriously . . . Space Camp would surely withdraw its support, and rightfully so.

THE TEACHER TRAINING program proved to be an enlightening experience. For starters, I realized that even though I considered myself to be somewhat knowledgeable about space and rocketry, I was woefully ignorant in comparison to the other teachers involved in the program. Robynn and I were assigned to a twenty-person team that included teachers from Texas, California, and Illinois, a pleasant, interesting, diverse group of people whose commonality was an absolute passion for space and rocketry. I was a space buff; these people were space *nuts*. Consequently, we had different agendas. Most of the people in our group were deadly serious about not only learning but *winning*. Space Camp was important to them as a competitive endeavor. Was it important to me? At that point in time? Not really. I didn't care about winning Best Mission or the Right Stuff Award. I just wanted to know what Space Camp was all about. I wanted to soak up as much information as possible and take it all back to our kids. Winning was not important because it wasn't the function or the goal of the trip. A few people on our team accused Robynn and me of not taking the program seriously enough, but we did. We were just focused on a different objective, and that might have been interpreted as complacency. I thought we did pretty well considering our lack of training and expertise. At the same time, I have to admit that I did not stay up late at night studying for the next day's competition; I preferred to use my time taking notes that I thought would be useful to my students.

More than anything else, the teacher training program illustrated rather dramatically just how challenging Space Camp would be for the special education students of Forest Hills Northern High School. On our very first day of training, as I looked at the console in Mission Control, with all its lights, buttons, and switches, and listened to the sirens and whistles, I couldn't help but think of how difficult it was to concentrate in that room. Even an emotionally healthy adult could be easily distracted. Exposing a special ed student with Tourette's syndrome or Down's syndrome or attention deficit disorder to this scenario was tantamount to throwing gasoline on a raging fire. I could just see Steve Bennett crossing the threshold of that room with the dilated look of an inveterate gambler walking into a casino and shouting, "Jackpot!"

That, of course, was beyond our control. All we could do was teach the kids, rehearse scripts with them, simulate as closely as possible the experience of Space Camp. As the week wore on it became apparent that one of the most important and fundamental skills required for success at Space Camp was a thorough understanding of all acronyms used during shuttle missions. Since there wasn't time for translation in the heat of competition, it was vital that students were proficient in the jargon of space travel. It wasn't enough to be merely functional; as is the case when you hope to be conversant in any language, fluency was required.

After a few days of listening to directions issued in code, and finding it nearly impossible to keep up with the pace, I felt a wave of panic wash over me. *My God! If I can't handle this, how am I going to be confident enough to sell it to the kids?* Suddenly I became obsessed with space knowledge in general and acronyms in particular. I had trouble focusing on my own duties as a camper; I couldn't sleep.

And so it was that around midnight on the third day I found myself sitting in the bar of the Huntsville Marriott, nursing a beer and struggling unsuccessfully to devise a way to make this mountain of information scalable for our students. For inspiration I reflected on a recent trip to the University of Michigan, where I had worked as a counselor and coach at the Wolverines' football camp. This had been in late June, shortly after the end of the school year, when Robynn and I were getting inundated with material from a variety of sources: Space Camp, Lynn Bondurant, the library. After the announcement that Dan Trierweiler had promised to fund our expedition, people became quite gracious about donating material, which was wonderful, but a bit overwhelming, as well. I had boxes and boxes of stuff piling up at my home, and the more I received, the more intimidated I became. How on earth was I going to chip away at this stack and turn it into something the kids could digest? There was so much of it, and it was all so . . . *dense*.

Preoccupied with these thoughts one afternoon outside Michigan's practice stadium, I barely noticed that my son Shawn, a camp ballboy, was overmatched by the sack of footballs he was carrying. But someone else noticed: Bo Schembechler. Bo was an icon at the University of Michigan, a legendary football coach whose skill and accomplishments were revered throughout the state, and indeed by anyone who has ever loved college football. Bo was nearing the end of his career by this time (he would retire after the 1989 season), but his personality remained larger than life. Bo liked to ride around the campus in a golf cart during camp, talking to kids, giving motivational speeches, making sure counselors and coaches were putting in a full day's work. Nothing irritated Bo more than to see a coach slacking off. He demanded that every kid get his money's worth, which was one of the things I loved about him. The kids came first to Bo. And his camp was not a place for torture, for mindless, militaristic drilling and hitting. It was a place where kids learned the game of football, where they went to become better players.

As Shawn and I were walking back to the field house after a defensive line drill, I heard Bo's distinctive voice over the hum of a golf cart: "Hey, boy! Pick up that bag!" I stiffened, suddenly alert and slightly embarrassed at having allowed myself to be so distracted. Bo hated it when anyone dragged a bag of footballs, because invariably the bag would develop a tiny hole, which would then grow larger, and pretty soon balls would start trickling out. Bo saw that as wasteful and lazy, and it drove him nuts.

"Come on, Shawn," I said. "Give me the bag." I slung it over my shoulder just as Bo pulled up alongside us, driving slowly. Bo and I knew each other fairly well, mainly because a former high school player of mine, Kerry Smith, had gone on to play at Michigan. And I'd been coaching at his camp for a while.

"What's wrong, Kersjes?" he asked. "You look kind of tired . . . and distant."

I nodded. "Yeah, I guess so. See, Bo, my partner and I have started this program at school. We're taking our special ed kids to Space Camp—"

"Hey!" he interrupted. "That's terrific. Sounds like a great idea."

"Thanks. Unfortunately, I'm drowning in all this material they're sending me. You have to be a genius to figure out all the math and science."

Bo hit the brakes. The cart squealed to a halt. "What's your definition of a genius?" he grunted.

I thought for a moment. "A genius is someone who is very intellectual, very smart, gets a grasp of things quickly."

Bo shook his head disdainfully. "That's not a genius."

"It's not?"

"Nope. A genius is someone who takes something that's complicated and makes it simple." He gave me a long, hard look. "Now, isn't that what you're trying to do?"

He didn't even stick around to hear my response, just drove off and left me standing there with my son and a big sack of footballs.

I was thinking about Bo as I sat in the Marriott bar, replaying that conversation over and over in my head. He was right. That was precisely what I was trying to do: take something complicated and make it simple. But how best to accomplish that task with the material I was gathering that week? None of the kids in our class had ever studied, let alone mastered, a foreign language, and in essence that's what we were going to ask them to do. How could I make it simple? How could I make it interesting? How could I make it *fun*?

It hit me as I was doodling on a napkin, jotting down acronyms and translations: *Why not make it a game?*

Okay . . . what type of game?

How about a board game?

You know . . . that just might work.

Before long I had napkins spread out all over the bar, representing a game board. Then I stuck a chair in the middle of the dance floor to represent a space station (it was late by now and I was just about the only customer left in the bar). I began literally walking through the mission, talking out loud and writing down various acronyms and anomalies, using another chair as my game piece. A roll of the dice would dictate how many spaces each piece was moved. On each space would be some type of direction; warning cards and anomalies would be placed in a stack in the middle of the board.

This went on until a crew came in and began cleaning up the bar. I looked at my watch. It was four-thirty in the morning! I didn't want to leave, though, because I was stuck. I had figured out how to get the shuttle to the space station within the framework of the game's rules, but I couldn't figure out how to handle reentry into the Earth's atmosphere. I needed problems, anomalies—maybe solar flares or quasars. Something like that. It was all in my mind, a game board the kids could use, almost as a cheat sheet . . . I just couldn't quite finish it. My brain had turned to mush. So I used the hotel phone to call Robynn.

"Do you know what time it is?" she growled.

"Doesn't matter. Come down to the dance floor of the Marriott."

"I'm too tired to dance."

"No, no, no. I have to show you something."

Within ten minutes Robynn showed up wearing sweats and slippers. Her annoyance quickly dissipated and was replaced by excitement. Together we spent another hour in the bar, completing a board game that would become not only an efficient learning tool for our students but a viable retail product called Solar Wind Toys. Eventually we manufactured and marketed more than ten thousand of the games to students all over the country. We didn't have the finished product available for our kids in 1988–89, but we did have a prototype, and it did exactly what Bo had suggested: It transformed the complicated into the simple.

Funny thing, though . . . I still didn't feel like a genius.

12

We began the school year with only nineteen students in our class, one less than we'd need for a complete team at Space Camp. As fate would have it, in the first months I received a call from the assistant superintendent for special education for the entire Kent Intermediate School District, wondering whether we might consider taking on the responsibility of an additional student. The girl's name was Brooke Fuller, and she had been attending East Grand Rapids High, the same school that had previously been home to Lewis Dayhuff and Marion Mills. Brooke was a bright but troubled girl who suffered from Prader-Willi syndrome, a genetic disorder characterized by severe hypotonia and feeding difficulties in early infancy, followed in later childhood by excessive eating and, usually, gradual development of morbid obesity. Dwarfism is common among people with Prader-Willi, and indeed Brooke was not only overweight, but extremely short. She also wore thick glasses.

Teenagers with Prader-Willi, of course, suffer terribly at the hands of their classmates. For them, school is like something out of *Lord of the Flies*, a horrific and savage place where they spend most of their time either being tormented or hiding from their tormenters. Making matters worse for Brooke was the fact that she came from a fairly affluent family (at East Grand Rapids, an urban school district, this could be a source of misery rather than comfort) and had two accomplished siblings. Brooke's sister played on the varsity tennis team, and her brother was a football player. They were both smart kids, too. Brooke, on the other hand, didn't play sports and had only a few friends. She was an outcast, tortured by an illness that other kids didn't even recognize as an illness. To them, she was simply short and fat.

Food was the center of Brooke's world. She was compelled to eat, and to overeat, and so her parents not only monitored her diet, restricting salt and fat intake, but also placed locks on the cabinets and refrigerator. She endured a daily ritual of inspections and weigh-ins, which seemed harsh and insensitive when I first heard about it, but after dealing with Brooke for a time I came to discover that it was for her own benefit. She was, quite literally, capable of eating herself to death. For example, one day that fall Brooke was left home alone while her mother went to watch Brooke's sister play a tennis match. Unbeknownst to Mrs. Fuller, Brooke had stashed away some money, and as soon as her mom left, Brooke called a pizza place and put in an order. She figured she had plenty of time to take the delivery and eat the food before her mother and sister returned; she had it all timed out. What Brooke hadn't anticipated was that her mother would come home early because she had forgotten her purse. So, as Mrs. Fuller turned into her driveway, she was treated to the sight of her daughter standing at the front door, taking delivery of a pizza and submarine sandwich. Rather than surrender when she saw her mother approaching, Brooke decided to flee. She paid the pizza guy, grabbed the food, and bolted down the street, shoving fistfuls of pizza into her mouth as she ran. By the time her mother caught up with her, Brooke had put away half the order.

This story was related to me by Brooke's mother, simply as a means of letting me know what we'd be up against. Brooke's problem was well diagnosed. There was no attempt to hide it. Her parents were supportive and compassionate, but serious about combating her illness, and they had come to the conclusion that a change of scenery was in order. The assistant superintendent for special education had agreed, saying, "They have nothing for this girl at East Grand Rapids, Mike. I think your program would be perfect for her." Unfortunately, Denise Boitano, our regional special education coordinator, disagreed.

"Don't take her," she said. "These people are pushing for this for one reason: So their daughter can go to Space Camp. They're using you."

Frankly, I didn't see it that way. After reading her file I was pretty sure that indeed Brooke would be better off in our program. Before she could transfer, Brooke's case had to be evaluated by an Individualized Education Placement Committee (IEPC), and then I had to sign and authorize the recommendation. At the IEPC meeting I heard evaluations and suggestions from social workers, psychologists, family members, doctors, and school administrators. As I listened to the commentary, the descriptions of Brooke and her problems, it seemed to me that she had a lot in common with our students. She was lost and lonely, struggling to find an identity of her own. It wasn't a stretch to envision her in our classroom.

Ultimately, it came down to me. Everyone in the room agreed there was merit to the idea of allowing Brooke to transfer. It was simply a matter of whether I was willing to take her.

"Don't sign the form," Denise urged. "It won't work."

There were no guarantees; but then, that was true of every kid in our class. I thought we had something to offer Brooke: a chance to not only work with her in the classroom but to help improve her self-esteem by allowing her to take part in Space Camp. She'd have a chance to make a fresh start at a new school, to leave behind an environment in which she'd been teased and ridiculed on a daily basis. She'd have a chance to be part of a team, like her brother was in football and her sister was in tennis. Moreover, she'd be reunited with one of her few close friends: Marion Mills. It seemed like a logical fit.

"We'll take her," I said. "Give me the form and I'll sign it."

Denise stormed out of the meeting shortly thereafter, furious that I'd gone against her wishes once again. I didn't think any explanation or apology was necessary. Brooke would be good for the program, and the program would be good for her. What other justification was needed? Did I anticipate a smooth transition for Brooke? Of course not, and in fact within a few weeks of Brooke's arrival Steve Bennett, ever the entrepreneur, tried to exploit her weakness by selling her Twinkies and Ho-Hos out of his locker. Luckily, I could rely on Marion Mills to act as an extra set of eyes. Marion would report back to me whenever she saw Brooke veering from her prescribed diet. Vigilance was required to adequately monitor and assess Brooke's progress, but then, in our class, that hardly made her unusual. Working with these kids, caring about them, was inherently risky business, and I was willing to take chances, to accept the consequences of my actions. God knows I messed up on occasion, but I tried very hard never to make excuses. I wanted to be an example to the students, to let them know, in no uncertain terms, "If you screw up, you're going to pay the price."

In other words, there were repercussions for every action, as I was vividly reminded that same month.

WITH ALL THE time I was devoting to Space Camp, it was inevitable that some of the football players would begin to feel slighted. In all candor, I can't deny that I was somewhat less committed to the sport in the summer of 1988 than I had been in previous years. Football, even at the high school level, was no longer a three-month sport; it had become a year-round activity requiring a substantial commitment from players and coaches alike. We expected our athletes to continue training in the winter and spring months, to work diligently at improving their strength and conditioning. To monitor their progress, in late June we conducted a formal evaluation involving timed sprints and weight lifting. This was a pretty important part of our program, and the kids took it quite seriously; they saw it as an opportunity to compete against their peers and demonstrate to the coaching staff that they were prepared and eager for the upcoming season. An especially impressive performance at the June testing session indicated a level of competitiveness and maturity that the coaching staff could not overlook.

As the defensive coordinator, obviously it was important for me to be deeply involved in this process, but I had been so busy with Space Camp—pursuing funding, gathering research and training material, creating a curriculum—that I simply didn't have time for spring workouts or testing. At the time I didn't really think it was a big deal, or maybe I was too distracted to give it the proper consideration. Either way, the result was a hardening of feelings toward me. One day that summer, just before the start of preseason practice, I stopped by the weight room and received the cold shoulder from some of my defensive players, kids I had known for years.

"What's wrong?" I asked.

At first there was silence. Then one of the players, a senior, spoke up. "Coach, why are you spending so much time with those losers? They can't even make a team here—how are they gonna go to Space Camp?"

Fighting the impulse to jump down the kid's throat—after all, his resentment was not unjustified—I tried to reason with him.

"I don't want to hear that kind of talk," I said calmly. "You guys have had a lot of breaks in your lives. These kids haven't. They need me."

He scoffed at that explanation, which, while true, was somewhat feeble. "And we don't need you? Come on, Coach, you're the defensive coordinator. We're supposed to look up to you, but you're never around."

He was right. But things had changed. I had made a commitment to Space Camp and there was no way that commitment was not going to affect my involvement with the football program.

"You guys know what you have to do in here," I said, looking around the weight room. "And I know what I have to do to prepare our students. You're just going to have to understand that I can't be in here quite as much as I was before."

Eventually they would develop a degree of understanding, even empathy, but it would take time, and there would be discomfort along the way . . . for them as well as for me.

A week before the start of the season I scouted our first opponent, Paw Paw High School, in an exhibition scrimmage. We had a very good team, a team loaded with big strong kids, several of whom would go on to play college football. We were rated high in all the preseason polls and thought there was a realistic chance that in late November we'd be playing for a state championship at the Silverdome in Pontiac, Michigan. Paw Paw, on the other hand, was small and slow and not expected to accomplish much that fall, and the team exhibited nothing in its scrimmage to refute that assessment. Conservative to the point of being soporific—*dive right . . . dive left*—the players appeared to be a team that would be overwhelmed against Forest Hills Northern. In fact, as I watched Paw Paw play, I thought, *We'll kill this team.* Supremely confident that we would waltz through opening night, I brought home a scouting report that depicted Paw Paw as an undersized, overmatched team.

Man, was I wrong.

The following Friday night we traveled to Paw Paw, several busloads of fans in tow, for the first leg of what was supposed to be a long, determined march toward the state playoffs. As it always is on opening night, the atmosphere was electric, so much hope and optimism in the air. Paw Paw received the kickoff, and on its first offensive series, instead of running "dive right," "dive left," lined up in . . . *an unbalanced wishbone!* My jaw dropped. The wishbone is one of the most aggressive and challenging offensive formations in football, and Paw Paw hadn't even offered a glimpse of it in its scrimmage. This was a sneak attack, a gridiron version of guerrilla warfare. By the time the ball was snapped, my heart was racing. We were completely unprepared to defend against the wishbone, and if this team was even remotely proficient at it, we were in big trouble. I could only hope that our superior athleticism would be an overriding factor.

It wasn't.

Paw Paw picked up eight yards on the first play from scrimmage, twelve on the second. Before long the team was in our end zone and leading 7–0. There was another trick, too. Paw Paw had on its roster a superb kicker, a kid who apparently had missed the scrimmage I'd seen because he was playing soccer. This kid drilled two field goals in the first half, including one from forty-seven yards, and repeatedly buried us deep in our territory with beautiful punts, rainmakers that dropped out of the sky only after the coverage had blanketed our receivers and then bounced neatly out of bounds just a few yards from the end zone. We went into the locker room beaten and bewildered, trailing by a score of 13–0. Although we made some adjustments in the second half, it was too little too late. With a raucous crowd screaming its lungs out, and our kids in a state of shock, Paw Paw rolled to a 24–0 victory. Granted, it was Paw Paw's field and their team got a few calls that probably should have gone in our favor, but that's the nature of high school football, especially when you're playing on the road. The bottom line was this: We weren't prepared.

I felt personally responsible for that loss, and our players weren't inclined to let me off the hook. There were comments in the locker room after the game and throughout the next week—indeed, throughout the rest of the season—attributing our dismal performance to my inadequate scouting report and my lack of visibility during the spring and summer.

"Maybe if you'd been around a little more, Coach, we would have been ready for the wishbone," more than one player suggested. "You're always preaching team . . . well, what kind of team member are you?"

I took the criticism to heart, for it was rooted in truth. That's what hurt the most. Paw Paw's coach did a great job, and the players executed perfectly from the opening kickoff. Although at a disadvantage in terms of size, their kids were actually pretty athletic, and they played with uncommon spirit and heart. In sum, they deserved to win the game. Still . . . if we had known they were going to run an unbalanced wishbone offense, there's no doubt it would have been a different game, a more competitive game, and perhaps a game with a different outcome. Whose fault was that? I had scouted Paw Paw, and even though there wasn't any sign that this team was capable of running a wishbone, I should have been better prepared. That was my job: to provide our defensive players with every tool necessary for victory, including information about what to expect from their opponents. I could have made a few more phone calls, done a little more research into Paw Paw's background. I could have made sure that we were prepared for every possible offensive wrinkle, including the wishbone, rather than presuming weakness and ineptitude on the part of our opponent. No amount of rationalizing could debunk the evidence: Responsibility for this loss rested primarily on my shoulders. And it would turn out to be a loss that cost us dearly.

13

Our dismal performance against Paw Paw was not exactly met with compassion and understanding. Supposedly one of the best football teams in the state, we were now in the unenviable position of having to win the rest of the games on our schedule just to have a shot at the playoffs. Our fans, especially the players' parents, were apoplectic, in part because they knew that missing the playoffs would mean diminished media coverage and, consequently, fewer opportunities for their kids to be recognized as scholarship material. Yes, it was only high school football, but there was a lot at stake.

I could handle the criticism from parents and fans. I could even handle it coming from my own family and friends. What really disturbed me was the fact that some of the football players began taking out their frustrations on our special ed students. Kids can be cruel, of course—that's no shock to anyone who has survived high school—but it bothered me terribly to see my own players exhibiting such casual disregard for their fellow students . . . students who had already suffered enough in their lives. I understood why the players were jealous of the time I had spent with my students, and I regretted having been insufficiently prepared for that first game, but that did not excuse their behavior. They were using my students to exact some sort of retribution against me, and it made me sick.

I don't mean to imply that the entire team reacted this way. The taunting and teasing and bullying was limited to a handful of players, but the damage they inflicted was widespread and severe. Athletes, after

all, are among the most revered students in any school, and their behavior, their conduct, is often modeled by other students. Within the
hallways of any school, the pack mentality thrives. When a group of
football players at a place like Forest Hills Northern decides that it's
acceptable to harass less fortunate students . . . well, life quickly becomes miserable for those students.

Ben Schmidt was a frequent target, which really was reprehensible,
considering the boy's capacity for kindness and affection (a common
characteristic of kids with Down's syndrome). Ben wanted nothing more
than to be liked and accepted, and so he did almost anything that was
asked of him. A problem area for Ben, and for most of the students in
our class, was the confluence of four wings, a big open space that was
like the Grand Central Station of Forest Hills Northern. The cool kids—
the jocks and the smart kids and the social elite—would hang out on
the heating registers in this spot in their free time, chatting, flirting,
trying to be seen and noticed; needless to say, our kids went out of their
way to avoid this area. For them it was nothing less than a danger zone,
where provocation and insult were virtually guaranteed.

Unfortunately, their lockers were located nearby, so it was impossible
to escape it entirely. One morning, a few days after the loss to Paw Paw,
a bunch of guys coaxed Ben to come over and join them. Like a puppy,
Ben rushed in with a big smile on his face and sat down. They talked
with him for a while, made him feel like part of the gang, and then did
something so mean, so calculated, that to this day it still makes me
angry. They pointed to a few girls who were collecting books from their
lockers, getting ready for class, and suggested he give them all a big hug.

"Go on, Ben," one of them said. "They think you're cute."

So, naturally, Ben jumped up and waddled over to the lockers and
began throwing his arms around the unsuspecting girls. To the great
amusement of the sadists who had orchestrated this show, and to Ben's
surprise, the girls reacted with shrieks of revulsion. I happened upon
the scene as Ben lurched between two girls, each of them screaming as
if he were some sort of monster.

"Get this creature away from me!" one of them said.

And then, from the peanut gallery: "Go get her, Quasimodo!"

I stepped into the middle of the commotion and pulled Ben close.
His breathing was labored, his heart fluttering, and yet he hadn't

stopped smiling. The poor kid still didn't really understand what had happened. He knew only that everyone was laughing and having fun, and he was part of it.

"What's going on?" I said to a couple of football players who were clearly involved.

"Ah, we're just having some fun, Coach."

"Yeah? At whose expense?"

One of the boys rolled his eyes. "Oh, come on, Coach. Look at him. He doesn't mind. He doesn't even know what he's doing."

The insensitivity, the failure to recognize that this was another human being worthy of respect and dignity, floored me, despite the fact that I had seen it countless times during my career.

"That may be," I said. "But you're embarrassing him. And you know what? You're embarrassing me, and you're embarrassing yourselves."

They shrugged and walked away, unfazed by anything I had said or by the humiliation they had heaped upon Ben. And so it went for the next several weeks, even as our football team recovered and put together a nice winning streak. The weaknesses and flaws of our students were routinely exploited and attacked; interestingly, as word of the Space Camp program spread, and publicity increased, the hostility escalated. It was almost as if by aspiring to something, by refusing to be the bottom feeders everyone assumed they were, our students were upsetting the natural order of things, and that irritated some of the mainstream students; maybe it even frightened them.

Rebecca Shriver was another of our students who seemed to have a bull's-eye on her back. Rebecca was a fighter. Her parents were divorced and she lived unhappily with her mother and her stepfather. Having given up on the possibility of her parents ever reconciling, it was Rebecca's dream to someday move in with her father, a nice enough man who usually came to parent-teacher conferences and seemed to have Rebecca's best interests at heart. Rebecca would often show up at school in the morning with dark circles rimming her eyes, evidence that she'd spent the previous night fighting with her mother and stepfather.

Rebecca also wore a lot of makeup and old, baggy clothes, neither of which could hide the fact that she was an extremely big-busted girl, an endowment that, in her case, was something of a curse. She couldn't walk down the hall without hearing a rude comment. Rebecca had a pretty good sense of humor, so she was quick to respond to the insults, but if the exchange continued, Rebecca's resolve invariably weakened. She wasn't quite astute enough, or quick enough, to trade insults for long, and pretty soon the frustration would drive her back to the security of our classroom, where she could let the tears flow freely.

Robynn and I expected the hostility toward our students to diminish as the weeks went by, but it didn't. It continued to intensify. For a while our kids even had trouble getting into their lockers because someone, or some group, kept sealing them tight with Super Glue. It happened nearly every day—one of our students would walk up to his locker, spin the proper combination, lift up on the handle, and . . . nothing. Wouldn't budge. So he'd try again . . . and again. Pretty soon he'd be kicking the door, punching it, cursing out loud, while all around him students were laughing at his misfortune. *What a riot!*

After a while the resentment bubbled to the surface. Steve Bennett walked in one day and said, "Coach, if this doesn't stop pretty soon, we're going to fight back."

"Relax, Steve," I said. "We can't afford to have anybody getting into trouble right now." That was the teacher speaking. Inside I was thinking, *I don't blame you one bit!*

As we got deeper into autumn I detected a subtle transformation among our students, a shift in attitude that comes when a group of individuals begins to form a team. Our kids had officially begun training and studying for Space Camp, so even as the rest of the school was mocking them and belittling them, they were united in a common goal, and that made them stronger. Oh, there were still times when they baited each other. Scott Goudy would refer to Marion Mills as "Baldy" (which was kind of funny, considering Scott's alopecia had rendered him nearly as challenged in that department as Marion's radiation therapy had rendered her), and he rarely addressed Stephanie Reinks as anything other than "Alice" or "Gump." Steve Bennett fought bitterly and almost daily with a girl named Karen Treffiletti, because each had a dynamic personality and wanted to be considered the class leader. So it would be grossly inaccurate to suggest that our class of aspiring astronauts had become a sea of tranquility. As before, they could be brutal to each other. But the incidents of brutality became less frequent; more important was their response when the cruelty emanated from outside the classroom. They tolerated the jabs and jibes from their own class-mates reasonably well, but when other students picked on them, they became furious. In Scott Goudy's eyes, it was acceptable for him to refer to Stephanie as "Alice," but when the epithet was hurled in the hallway by one of the mainstream students, he was offended.

This development was at once encouraging and disconcerting. The Space Camp program, and the attendant publicity, had placed these kids in an unfamiliar position: They were in the spotlight. By giving our students an opportunity to achieve something special, Robynn and I had unwittingly put them in an arena in which they were more likely than ever to receive abuse. Many of our students were insecure and quick-tempered, which naturally increased the likelihood that a verbal confrontation in the hallways might escalate into the sort of ugly phys-ical altercation that would result in a dissolution of the entire program. We addressed this concern by meeting with the students and their par-ents and explaining to them that there was no margin for error. Not only would they be required to show up for school every day (truancy was a huge problem with our kids), they would have to learn to con-trol their tempers. They could not explode in class. They couldn't lash out at their teachers or classmates. They would have to be strong enough to walk away from a potential fight. The last point was the most challenging, for while our kids rarely looked for trouble, it often came to them. And when backed into a corner, they fought like badgers.

"You are going to have to be on your best behavior," we told them. "And your parents are going to have to support us. Anyone who can't adhere to this policy will be dismissed from the program."

Robynn and I felt a tremendous amount of pressure. Having received money from Burger King and been the subject of some very nice cov-erage in the local press, we sure as heck didn't want this to blow up and leave the story with a sad ending. So we did a lot of damage control and counseling. At the same time, we noticed that the students were not only trying to exhibit more maturity and self-control, but also look-ing out for each other. Sometimes the support took the form of overt interference, such as the time Steve came to Ben's rescue in the cafe-teria. Ben had a weakness for ranch salad dressing. He'd put it on ev-erything: french fries, hot dogs, pizza . . . you name it. Sometimes he'd drink it right out of the bottle, guzzling so much of it that he'd end up in the bathroom, throwing up. On the days when they ate in the cafeteria, Steve often sat with Ben and made sure he ate sensibly and didn't overdose on ranch dressing. One day, though, Ben was invited to sit with some other kids, and of course they treated him like a circus geek, giving him extra ranch dressing and cheering wildly as he inhaled the stuff. Steve heard the commotion and quickly intervened.

"Why are you doing this?" Steve said as he pulled Ben away and wiped his face with a napkin. "This isn't funny."

More fascinating was the way our students applied pressure to each other. Rather than laughing at Steve's symphony of flatulence, the kids started admonishing him. "Cut it out," they'd say. "You'll get in trouble."

Even Lewis, who had never cared about anyone, who seemed to be an island, suddenly had classmates watching out for him. When he tried to provoke a fight or sneak a cigarette or otherwise seek out trouble (which was just about every day), the other kids would remind him of the consequences. They'd get right in his face and say, "Don't blow this for us! Keep your temper under control." A year earlier, even six months earlier, they wouldn't have bothered. They would not have cared whether Lewis got in trouble or not, or whether he got his head kicked in by another student. Now they had a different attitude: *"Don't you dare ruin this!"* There were nineteen other kids willing to step in front of Lewis and prevent him from throwing a punch, or, if that didn't work, to run into our class and say, "Coach! Lewis is about to get in another fight!" In its most fundamental sense, this was teamwork, and I'd never seen it from our kids before.

THE TURNING POINT in the lives of our students—the incident that signaled a cease-fire in the war between them and the rest of the school—occurred in late October. I was walking through the gym on my way to the locker room at the end of the school day when I saw three guys clustered in a corner, apparently arguing with someone. As I got closer I could see that it wasn't really an argument—they had backed a girl up against a wall and were screaming at her, cursing at her, laughing at her. I didn't know who the victim was at first, because she was barely visible, but as I drew near I heard one of the boys say,

"You're gonna be an astronaut, huh? That's a joke! How are you gonna get that fat butt of yours into a space suit?"

The other boys laughed as Stephanie choked out the words, "Screw you!" They were closing in around her, tightening their circle.

"What's going on?" I said, and the boys immediately stepped back and fell silent. Stephanie was almost on the floor, crouched low, coiled up like a snake, ready to strike. There were tears streaming down her face. She wasn't just upset; she was furious. I held out a hand and she came to me, muttering under her breath something about how she was going to kill them. I gave her a hug and then gently nudged her to the side.

Her tormenters were familiar to me only by face and reputation. They were dirt-bags . . . everyday, garden-variety punks. Now they were frozen in their tracks. Still fuming, I grabbed one of them by the shirt collar and held him tight, but before I had a chance to speak, or to do something really stupid, I heard a noise coming from the other side of the gym, near the entrance to the weight room.

"What's up, Coach?"

I looked over and saw a large group of football players veering away from the weight room and marching single file in our direction. They were clearly unhappy, but also aware that I wasn't exactly in any trouble. As they formed a semicircle around us, I loosened my grip and took a deep breath. "Look," I said, trying to make eye contact with as many of the players as I could. "Today is the day that this nonsense stops! Today is the day you guys are going to help us become a team." There was no response, so I kept talking. "I'm asking you guys to become big brothers for these kids. I'm asking you to be more open to them in the cafeteria. I'm asking you to be friendly in the hallway. I'm asking you to recognize our kids as human beings, and if you do that, other kids will follow suit."

I looked at the three stooges who had been harassing Stephanie and added, "Most of them, anyway." The players chuckled at that. Then they began to nod in agreement. They tightened the semicircle just a bit.

"You want us to kick their butts?" one of the players asked, setting off something of a feeding frenzy.

I shrugged my shoulders and started to walk away with Stephanie. I knew my players were smart enough not to engage in mass assault in the gym, but there was no harm in letting these creeps experience a few scary moments. "I don't care what you do with them," I said. "I just wish I was eighteen years old again."

Stephanie and I walked away, leaving roughly two tons of menacing football flesh and three hapless, terrified punks in our wake. That was the last time anyone at Forest Hills Northern picked on any of our kids.

14

As much as possible we tried to incorporate experiential ("hands-on") education into our training program. Students with learning disabilities benefit from visual clues, so before breaking down a mission and discussing it in detail, we utilized cut-and-paste kits from the Space & Rocket Center to construct miniature space shuttles. That way, rather than merely reading about a mission in abstract terms, we could use the model for illustration. For example, instead of saying, "At this point the external tank separates," we would hold up the model and say, "This is the external tank—right here." The kids would instantly understand what was happening, and more important, they'd remember the information.

Similarly, we used the board game that Robynn and I had designed to inject a little competitive fun into the process of memorizing acronyms. We transferred manuscripts to computer discs so the kids could read scripts of simulated missions on the computer, which not only simplified the learning process, but also helped them become more comfortable with computers, which would be crucial to their performance at Space Camp. We wanted them to understand that computers were their friends, not their enemies. The majority of our students were impoverished, so they didn't have computers at home, and since they were labeled as learning disabled, they hadn't spent much time in the school's computer lab. There was a natural apprehension about technology that had to be overcome; without a significant degree of desensitization, it wasn't hard to imagine our students walking into Mission Control at

Space Camp and reacting with panic. Not only would they be frightened, they'd be angry at us for not properly preparing them.

And rightfully so. In this environment they'd be surrounded by "propeller heads," techno-savvy kids who had grown up with computers in their bedrooms, who by the time they were in kindergarten knew an Apple wasn't just something you ate; kids who liked to pass their spare time by browsing through the Encyclopedia Britannica. These were kids who didn't need a lot of advance preparation for Space Camp, and they didn't get it. When Robynn and I went through the teacher training program I repeatedly asked other teachers about their preparatory programs. Usually they'd just shrug and say, "We don't have one." Then they'd paint a verbal picture of their typical student: someone gifted and talented, intellectually nimble and adventurous . . . and almost always from a wealthy family.

"How about you?" they'd ask. "What are your kids like?"

"Uhhhhh . . . pretty much the same as yours."

"Oh yeah?"

"Actually, no. I'm a special education teacher."

At that point the conversation usually came to an abrupt end.

The simple fact was this: Our students could not rely on natural ability. In order to compete at Space Camp . . . in order to be, by any definition of the word, "successful" . . . they would have to work extraordinarily hard; they would have to train their minds and bodies. We were fortunate to have some help in the pursuit of this goal, from people who made it clear that while our students were certainly underdogs, they weren't quite the outcasts they had been in previous months and years. There was, for example, the science teacher who let us use the chemistry lab on weekends, and the government teacher who encouraged his students to assist our kids with script interpretation and the memorization of acronyms. Some of these volunteers became involved with our kids in very personal ways, which was at once surprising and moving. There was a girl named Helen, for example, who was one of the sweetest and most popular girls in the school. Smart and pretty and athletic, she was the type of girl who in the past might not have noticed that our kids even existed. But now she was helping them study, working with them as a peer and a friend.

One day Helen brought a cosmetic bag into class, dumped its contents onto a desk, and hosted a cosmetology clinic. We had several girls in our class who applied makeup as if every day were Halloween. Knowing this, Helen offered her services, but in a way that was neither cutting nor condescending.

She did this on several occasions. Once I walked into the room and saw her fixing Stephanie's hair. "Looks like a rat's nest," I joked. That was the kind of relationship I had with the kids—we teased each other and no feelings were hurt. Stephanie, in fact, just laughed. But Helen didn't see the humor.

"You know, Coach," she said. "That's not very nice."

I felt the blood rush to my face. It was strange, and more than a little embarrassing, to be corrected in the same way that I had so often corrected others.

"I'm sorry," I said.

Stephanie gave me a wink, while Helen smiled and went back to work.

BY LATE OCTOBER the Forest Hills Northern football team had, to put it mildly, experienced a reversal of fortune. The opening-night loss to Paw Paw had nearly faded from memory, bleached by a string of impressive performances that left us with a 7–1 record. With each successive week we improved just a little bit, gained some confidence, played more like the team we were supposed to be. The computerized rankings compiled by the Michigan State Public High School Athletic Association were published every Monday morning, after the weekend's games, and each week we collected a few more points, inched a little higher in the polls. Earlier in the season I had found the expectations of fans to be unrealistic and self-serving; I couldn't stand being cornered in a grocery store or shopping mall or restaurant and being asked, pointedly and unsympathetically, "Gonna win the rest of them . . . right, Coach?"

Now, though, my mood had brightened considerably, for suddenly it seemed that we really were going to win the rest of them. If that happened, we might make the postseason playoffs after all, but the odds still were not in our favor. We were a Class C school at the time, and there were many Class C schools in our region. Several years later the playoff format would be revamped so that four Class C teams from our region would qualify for postseason play; however, in the fall of 1988, only the top two teams in the rankings advanced to the playoffs. For everyone else, the season was over. Heading into the last game of the regular season, there were three teams ranked ahead of us, including Paw Paw, the team that had beaten us on opening night.

In sports there are few things more frustrating than not having control over your own destiny, but such was the scenario we faced. We could do no more than play our best and hope that the planets were favorably aligned. As it happened, our final game, on the last Friday night in October, was against our sister school, Forest Hills Central. It was a perfect night for a high school football game: crisp, clear, a big fluorescent moon overhead, and a stadium full of fans filling the air with cheers. Most of the kids from my special education class were in the stands, screaming their lungs out in an unabashed display of school spirit that would have been inconceivable a year earlier, before the advent of the Space Camp program. Now they were doing what "normal" kids did. They were going to football games. They were studying. They were even eating in the cafeteria. That alone was cause for celebration.

We won that game, as we should have, and finished the regular season with an 8–1 record. After losing our opener, we had gone on an eight-game winning streak and become, without a doubt, one of the best Class C teams in the state of Michigan. Now there was nothing we could do but await the outcome of the rest of the weekend's games. At least one, and probably two, of the three teams ranked ahead of us had to lose in order for our season to be extended. As the fans flooded the field and the seniors embraced each other, knowing that perhaps they had played their last football game, I felt a lump rising in my throat.

Please, God, give us one more game with these guys.

There was no party afterward. The players went home and the coaches came to my house. We sat around and tried to figure out every possible permutation, every conceivable record. Because the rankings were determined by computer and based not exclusively on won-lost records, we could only make an educated guess as to what might happen. And since two of the other teams were playing on Saturday, it was almost pointless to fret about it now. Nevertheless, that's exactly what we did.

As it happened, each of the three teams ahead of us won its last game. Our season ended not with a dramatic, last-second drive for a touchdown—it ended not on the field, but at home, with a Sunday afternoon phone call from a member of the playoff committee.

The final rankings were in. We were done.

During morning announcements before school on Monday, all football players were asked to turn in their gear. I don't know how many times that day I heard someone say, "If only we'd won that first game." It wasn't said in a malicious way, but still . . . there was no getting around it: We had missed the playoffs because of a single poor performance, and I was the architect of that performance. At the end of the day, as the seniors filed into the locker room and handed over their equipment, some with tears in their eyes, I couldn't help but feel responsible. This was one of the best football teams Forest Hills Northern had ever produced. We had won the league championship. If not for one bad night, we might have had a chance for a state title.

If only I hadn't screwed up.

The kids in our class knew exactly how I felt, just as they knew better than to joke around with me on Fridays, when I had my game face on. One after another they approached me during the day and said, quietly and sincerely, "Sorry you didn't make it, Coach." They tried to comfort me, but for a few days I was practically inconsolable, so profound was the sense of loss. I don't mean to sound melodramatic—after all, I'd been coaching football for eleven years and I understood pretty clearly that losing a football game or missing the playoffs was not the end of the world. What concerned me most was the possibility there would be some type of fallout that would affect our students and the Space Camp program; that some of the football players, seeking to affix blame for their misfortune on me, and, by extension, my students, would revert to the ugly behavior of earlier months.

Instead, a wondrous thing happened: Life simply went on. Within a week most of the football players had exchanged uniforms. They were wrestling, swimming, skiing, playing basketball. One of the nice things about high school athletics is that a lot of kids play more than one sport. The seasons overlap, blending seamlessly into one another, so there isn't time to be sad or bitter. Most of our players immediately shifted their focus to another sport, another game, another competition. And they weren't alone. I, too, had something on which to focus.

ONE WEEK AFTER football season ended, on a Saturday morning, we went for a swim. At Space Camp, as we had done in our teacher training program, the kids would have to work together under conditions that simulated microgravity. They'd be asked to jump in a pool and construct a tetrahedron as quickly as possible. Our training during the previous two months had been largely academic, with an emphasis on history and science. We'd rehearsed dozens of scripts, memorized hundreds of acronyms, but Space Camp was not merely an intellectual experience. In order to compete effectively the students would have to be able to swim. And not merely dog paddle or float. I knew from experience that constructing a tetrahedron underwater, with a clock ticking, was a rigorous exercise requiring not only teamwork, confidence, and skill but a level of physical fitness that most of our kids could only imagine. To reach that level we'd have to go into training.

Only a few students were proficient swimmers. Ben Schmidt was one. He'd been swimming since he was old enough to walk, so even though his presence at pools and public beaches sometimes agitated life-guards (who couldn't believe that a kid with Down's syndrome wouldn't immediately sink to the bottom like a rock), Ben was actually quite capable of taking care of himself. Or so we had been told. Scott Goudy was also a good swimmer, so good, in fact, that he later joined the swim team. For the most part, though, our kids were landlubbers, so we had our work cut out for us.

Not having a pool at Forest Hills Northern, we had to rent time at the local YMCA. The kids showed up bright and early, along with a few football players who had volunteered to serve as swimming instructors (thereby squashing, once and for all, any concern that they might have some sort of vendetta against our students). I went into one locker room with the boys, Robynn went into another with the girls. After changing we lined the kids up by the side of the pool and talked about goals and objectives. They shivered and rubbed the sleep from their eyes as I explained that this would be nothing more than an introductory session.

"There's no reason to be nervous," I said. "We'll take it slow. All we want to do today is see how well each of you can swim."

As most of them nodded, Lewis Dayhuff stepped forward and dipped a toe into the water.

"Damn, that's cold! You sure we have to do this, Coach?"

"No, Lewis, you don't have to do it—as long as you don't mind forfeiting your spot on this team."

"Okay," Lewis said. "I'm cool."

Our intention was to do nothing more than an evaluation in this session. We wanted the kids to do a couple laps. They didn't have to look like Mark Spitz—they simply had to make it from one end of the pool to the other, and then back again, thereby proving that they weren't likely to drown when we got to Space Camp. So, after much teasing and stalling, we finally got everyone into the water. Before we began doing laps, though, there was a disturbing noise from somewhere outside the building, a loud *boom!* that shook the walls of the YMCA. And then, just seconds later, the building was plunged into darkness.

Later we would find out that the blackout was caused by an auto accident—someone had collided with a telephone pole and knocked out a transformer that supplied electricity to the entire neighborhood. At this moment, however, with only a sliver of natural lighting available, I wasn't concerned with the source of the problem; I was concerned only with getting every student out of the pool alive. This was a teacher's nightmare: to have twenty special education students in a pool, and to have no way of monitoring their movement or activities.

Robynn and I stood next to each other on the deck, practically paralyzed with panic.

"We have to get them out of there!" she said.

"I know. But how?"

"Let's do a head count," she said.

That was as good an idea as any. "All right, listen up!" I yelled. "Everybody out of the pool." Fortunately, almost all of the kids had been hanging on to the edge of the deck, so all they had to do was pull themselves up out of the water. After a minute or two I began calling out names:

"Steve?"

"Here!"

"Stephanie?"

"Here!"

"Scott?"

"Here!"

"Pat?"

"Here!"

"Rebecca?"

"Here!

"Lewis?"

"Here!"

"Ben?"

Nothing.

"Ben?!"

Again . . . nothing.

"Ben!"

Suddenly the kids started yelling, panicking, scared to death that something had happened to Ben. My chest tightened. Ben was supposed to be a good swimmer, but he was easily excited, and it wasn't hard to envision him becoming disoriented in the dark, maybe hitting his head or hyperventilating, and disappearing beneath the surface.

"Ben!" The kids were calling his name, too. Still, there was no response. So, with my heart pounding in my temples, I dived into the water, with Robynn right behind me. We took turns scraping the bottom of the pool, looking for poor, lifeless Ben. Each time we came to the surface, we called out to each other.

"Anything?"

"No!"

Finally, just as we were about to give up, a familiar voice, lilting and mischievous, drifted down to the water.

"Look out below . . ."

I squinted hard, and through the darkness I could see the pear-shaped form of Ben Schmidt bouncing on the end of the diving board.

"Here I come!"

With a big *sproing!* he launched himself high into the air and then plummeted into the pool, a geyser of water dramatically signaling his return from the dead. As the Y's generator sparked the backup lights, Ben swam to the side, pulled himself up onto the deck, and stood there smiling, as if nothing had happened.

Practically overcome with a mixture of anger and relief, I managed to sputter out the words, "Ben . . . why didn't you answer? You scared the hell out of us."

"Yeah, Ben!" Stephanie chimed in. "What are you trying to do—give Coach a heart attack?"

Ben's face turned sad. His upper lip began to quiver. He took a few steps in my direction, until we were only inches apart. Slowly he looked up at me, his face still dripping. And just as it seemed he was about to cry, Ben smiled, clapped his hands gleefully, and shouted, "Gotcha, Coach, didn't I?"

With everyone laughing I threw an arm around the back of his head and gave him a squeeze. "Yeah, Ben . . . you sure did."

15

O ne of the visual training tools that worked best was also one of the simplest. After trying for several weeks to teach basic astronomy out of a textbook, and watching the kids' eyes glaze over with boredom, I decided to invite everyone over to my house one evening in the fall. It was a perfect night for stargazing, so we climbed onto the roof and sat there for a while, staring up at the sky, identifying various constellations, discussing the composition of gases that were visible. We did this probably half a dozen times during the autumn months, and it proved to be an enlightening and enriching experience for all of us. The kids would bring astronomy charts and binoculars, lie on their backs, hold the charts up to the sky, and point out as many objects as they could.

"There's Mars!" one of them would say.

"I see Ursa Major!"

"There's the Milky Way!

"Yeah . . . like that's hard to find!"

The sessions were beneficial not only because the kids really did learn something but because they brought us closer together, made us feel more like a team. Being together in school or at work was one thing— there was no choice in that—but spending time together away from the classroom, at night or on the weekends . . . that demonstrated another level of commitment, of caring, and the interaction, while not always smooth, was nonetheless invaluable. They saw each other in a different light. They saw each other as friends. Sometimes the conversation would drift off-topic, and we'd talk about what was happening in their lives: boyfriends, girlfriends, siblings, what movies they wanted to see, what type of music they liked. It really didn't matter, so long as we were all together.

My family got something out of these sessions, as well, for they saw the students in another, more human, context. Darcy's first reaction upon watching us scale a ladder and spread out on the roof of the house was predictable: She was horrified.

"Please, Mike, don't let any of them fall off."

It didn't help that some of our neighbors would stare out their windows in disbelief, thinking, I'm sure, *There goes Kersjes again, taking those wacko kids of his up on the roof. The guy must have lost his mind.* But after watching a few of these tutorials, and listening to the conversations, Darcy softened a bit. One night when we came down from the roof, cold and hungry after two hours out in the night air, Darcy had a platter of sandwiches and some hot chocolate ready and waiting. When Steve Bennett walked into the kitchen, eyed the food, and responded like a dog, emitting a loud, *"Woof! Woof!"* Darcy actually smiled. At the sight of Pat Zerfas hanging off my shoulder like a cockatoo, afraid to let me get more than a few inches away, she melted. In her eyes I could see an awakening, a new awareness that these students required an extraordinary amount of help, and that maybe her husband hadn't been so self-indulgent after all.

IT WAS PART of our ritual that each time we gathered on the roof we would have to listen to Steve Bennett talk about a friend of his who supposedly ran the planetarium at the Grand Rapids Museum of Science. Given Steve's propensity for stretching the truth and doing almost anything to get a reaction—given his fascination with what could be loosely interpreted as "performance art"—it was understandable that no one paid much attention to him. We all figured it was just another story, and that eventually he'd grow tired of repeating it. So it surprised me somewhat when Steve approached me at school one day in November, after another dry astronomy class, and said, in all seriousness, "Coach, you know I really know this guy at the planetarium. If you want, I can set us up. He'll do a special presentation for us. Whatever we want."

There was something in Steve's voice and demeanor that gave me pause. He wasn't as jittery as usual. He was calm, yet serious. There were no nervous ticks, no mice jumping out of his pockets.

"You're not kidding, are you?" I said.

Steve shook his head. "Uh-uh."

"All right, give me the guy's number. I'll think about it."

That night, after dinner, I pulled the number from my wallet. Even as I dialed, I could hear a tiny skeptical voice saying, *"Oh, I don't know if this is such a good idea. This guy is probably a security guard or a janitor."*

Well, guess what? Steve had been telling the truth. Somehow he had indeed struck up a friendship with the director of the planetarium, and the guy had been waiting several months for us to take him up on his offer. He'd read about our program in the newspaper, seen us on the local news, and was eager to help in any way possible.

"How much will it cost?" I asked. "We're on kind of a tight budget."

"Not a penny," he said. "It's on the house. Just let me know when you'd like to come over and we'll arrange a private showing tailored to your needs."

This was almost too good to be true, but then, serendipity had played a major role in this entire venture, so why should it be any different now? We set a date for late November, and I called all of the parents to let them know of our continued good fortune. Steve Bennett—class clown, court jester, teller of tall tales—was now a man to be taken seriously.

WE AGREED TO meet at the planetarium on a Tuesday night, around dinnertime. Most of the kids were dropped off by their parents, but a few—Stephanie, Steve, Lewis—needed rides. Robynn and I took care of them. Thinking it was likely to be an exciting and educational evening I decided to bring Shawn and Ryan, and they were not disappointed. This guy put on a great show for us, like an IMAX ride through the galaxy. I think the students absorbed more information in that one night than they had in all of our astronomy classes and stargazing sessions combined. They were totally into it, openly enthusiastic in a way I'd rarely seen. They shouted out the names of constellations and planets, identified things they remembered from class. They whooped and cheered at the special effects, and when the show ended they stood and applauded. The night, it seemed, was an unqualified success.

Several parents had requested that we drive their kids home after the presentation, and Robynn and I had happily agreed. She took one group, I took another. Ryan and Shawn, who naturally had been completely blown away by the planetarium show, and were now suffering from a combination of motion sickness and exhaustion, sat in the middle row of our minivan, along with Stephanie. Steve sat in the front seat, while Lewis, Scott Goudy, and Andrea Burke sat in the third row. Like an expert chauffeur, I began circling the greater Grand Rapids metropolitan area. I'd been to Steve's house, so I knew where he lived, and I was roughly aware of the location of Lewis's foster home. Next came Scott and Stephanie, each of whom provided expert directions along the shortest route to their homes, so that I could get Ryan and Shawn home and in bed as quickly as possible. That left only Andrea. After Scott had jumped out of the car and waved good-bye, I turned to Andrea and said, "Okay, how do I get to your house?"

She stared at me blankly.

"Andrea?"

Her lip began to tremble. Suddenly the tears flowed down her cheeks.

"I . . . I . . . I . . . don't know," she sobbed.

Andrea was the most sheltered student in the class, a girl prone to crying over absolutely nothing, so I'd grown accustomed to her fragility. Still, this was amazing.

"Honey, you don't know where you live?"

She shook her head furiously, pathetically. Andrea was sixteen years old and didn't know her own address. It didn't seem possible.

"Okay," I said, trying to be calm. "Don't worry. We'll find your house."

"I want to go home!" Andrea shouted. She was bawling now. My sons, bless their hearts, moved closer to her and patted her on the back.

"Don't worry," Ryan said. "I know how to get to my home. Maybe I can find yours."

I smiled. *Nice logic, son.*

So, there we were, wandering aimlessly through the darkness of a suburban neighborhood, me and my two little boys and a distraught teenage girl. I knew that Andrea lived in the Forest Hills Northern school district, so the only thing to do, the only option, was to drive around slowly and hope that something jumped out at her, some landmark that she would recognize. Or . . .

"By any chance, do you know your phone number?" I asked with very little optimism.

Andrea stopped crying. "Uh-huh."

I hit the brakes. "Andrea . . . why didn't you say so?"

"You didn't ask."

Ryan and Shawn laughed. We drove out of the subdivision and looked for the nearest convenience store. I bought a Coke and used the change to call Andrea's house on the store's pay phone.

One ring . . . two rings . . . three . . . four . . . five . . .

I got back in the car. "Andrea, your folks aren't home."

"I know. They went out to dinner."

God . . . give me strength!

By now it was nearly ten o'clock. Ryan and Shawn were slumping down in their seats, their tired little bodies supported only by their seat belts. I gripped the steering wheel tightly and pulled back out onto the street. I had come to the conclusion that there was no way we were going to find this particular needle in this particular haystack, so the best solution was to take Andrea back to our house and wait until her parents returned. That way, at least, I could put the boys to bed. Just as I was about to turn onto the interstate, however, Andrea shouted from the back seat . . .

"I recognize that house!"

"Which house?"

"The brick one—right there!"

So happy I wanted to cry, I pulled the minivan over to the side of the road. "Is that your house, Andrea?"

Please say yes.

"No."

This girl is going to kill me.

"Well, then, whose house is it?"

"I don't know . . . but I've seen it before."

I rubbed my forehead. Shawn and Ryan groaned. "Andrea . . . we've been by this same spot three or four times tonight. Maybe that's why you recognize it."

She shook her head. "Uh-uh. I think one of my mom's friends lives here."

At this point I was nearly desperate enough to walk up to the front door, ring the doorbell, and ask if anyone recognized Andrea. But not quite. If she was wrong, and the odds were heavily in favor of that being the case, I could only imagine the response. A balding, six-foot-two, 230-pound middle-aged man trying to dispose of a sad-eyed teenage girl.

"Honey! Hannibal Lecter is at the door! Call the cops!"

We drove back into the subdivision one more time, and lo and behold, Andrea suddenly found her way home.

"Turn here!" she said breathlessly. "Now here . . . Take a left . . . and a right . . ."

She was so excited that she was starting to wheeze, and I was concerned she might hyperventilate and pass out before she got home.

"There it is!" she cried. "My house!"

I pulled into the driveway. By now her parents had returned and the lights were all on. They met us at the door and Andrea rushed into their arms, sobbing uncontrollably. I apologized for being late and for nearly losing their daughter, although what I really wanted to say was, *"How in the hell can you send this girl out at night without giving her directions home? What is wrong with you?"*

When we got back to our house Darcy was waiting. Agitated by the fact that we were more than a little late getting home, on a school night, no less, she gave me a cold stare as I walked into the kitchen. Ryan and Shawn finally broke the ice.

"Mom, you wouldn't believe it," Ryan said. "Dad had to drive this girl all over the place."

"Oh?"

"Yeah," Shawn added with a giggle. "She didn't know where she lived."

Darcy's frown dissolved into a smile. "These kids really are a handful, aren't they?"

"Sometimes," I said.

"You sure they're going to be all right at Space Camp?"

That was a good and fair question, for it was hard to imagine that a girl who couldn't remember her own address was going to be of much use in such a competitive, demanding environment.

"You want to know the truth? I have no idea what to expect. But I'll tell you this: We could sure use your help down there."

This was as good a time as any to recruit Darcy to the cause. To her credit, she'd been far more receptive to the whole venture in recent weeks, but my biggest concern was having enough adults nearby in Huntsville in the event that a problem arose. Robynn and I couldn't do it on our own. We needed assistance from our aides, and from anyone else who wanted to lend a hand.

"What would I do?" Darcy asked.

"Give them encouragement and support. Help us keep things in order on the plane and in the airports. Be kind of a surrogate mom. Believe me, they'll appreciate it." I smiled. "So will I."

I expected a flat rejection. Darcy's life was busy enough, what with a job and two little boys, and me hardly home at all. Now I was asking her to give compassion and support to a group of kids who were largely responsible for my absence and preoccupation. On top of all that, Darcy hated to fly. What I was asking was patently ridiculous. Not to mention selfish.

She looked at me, then looked at the boys, then said something that surprised me as much as anything I had heard in the ten years that we'd been married.

"Okay, I'll do it."

AS FALL GAVE way to winter, and the novelty of the program wore off, I could sense the training beginning to take its toll. Yes, the students were absorbing historical and scientific material, memorizing acronyms and learning flight scripts. They were also becoming stale. Boredom is a potential problem with any educational endeavor, but it's especially likely with special-needs students, whose tolerance for inactivity and repetition is often quite low. That's why we tried to infuse the training with interactive experiences, field trips . . . anything to break up the routine. And, on occasion, we just had to get out of the classroom and do something as a group that was completely unrelated to Space Camp.

Like bowling.

This was Robynn's idea, and it wasn't a bad one at all. Take the kids to a bowling alley, where virtually everything is indestructible and no one cares how much noise you make. The perfect outing for special ed students. For one student in particular, it was like Christmas coming early. In addition to his passion for cars, Pat Zerfas also was a fanatic about bowling. Pat was quiet in class, drifting in and out of an autistic fog, never bothering anyone, but when he did engage in conversation, the topic was usually one of these two things. On the morning of our bowling excursion, as I stood outside my room talking to another teacher, Pat suddenly appeared at my side. He tapped me on the shoulder.

"One second, Pat."

He tapped me again.

"Pat . . . I'll be with you soon."

Another tap.

"Pat! Go back in the room and take your seat. This is not appropriate."

He didn't move, just stood there with a tight-lipped smile on his face. "You know, I'm really a good bowler, Coach."

The other teacher laughed, and so did I.

"That's good, Pat."

The truth? I had no idea whether Pat knew a bowling ball from a basketball. Our kids often told stories, embellished aspects of their personal lives to the extent that it was impossible to know where fact ended and fiction began. Most of them had difficult lives, and so they routinely reinvented themselves. Pat was no different. He said he was in a bowling league and two or three times a week he would come into class and boast about having rolled a two hundred . . . or two twenty-five. Most of the time I barely paid any attention. I'd just give him a high five or a slap on the back and send him on his way.

"Whatever you say, Pat." And he'd smile that goofy little smile, like a first grader who's just presented the teacher with an apple, and shuffle back to his desk.

One of the great things about the Space Camp program was that it allowed us to see the kids as something other than just students with problems. We saw them in another context, and at times it was enlightening. While the rest of us rented equipment from the bowling alley, Pat showed up with his own shoes and neatly polished ball. Before warming up he strapped on a high-tech wrist guard, one of the surest signs that a bowler is serious about his game. As Pat stepped on the alley and cradled his ball, I turned to Robynn.

"What's this all about?" she asked.

"Just part of his fantasy . . . I think."

Pat took two smooth, graceful steps and released the ball. It barely made a sound as it left his hand and slid down the alley, arcing neatly from the right side of the lane into the pocket. The pins exploded upon contact and were instantly cleared away.

Strike!

As Robynn and I stared in disbelief, Pat turned and walked back to his seat without celebrating, as if this were the most natural thing in the world.

"Pat!" I said. "You really do know how to bowl."

"Uh-huh. Told you."

For the next two hours Pat put on a bowling clinic. He picked up impossible splits, ran off six, seven strikes at a time. His first game was a two thirty-six. His lowest was a one ninety-five. The kid was like a bowling version of Dustin Hoffman in *Rain Man*. He even tried to give lessons to the rest of us. I hadn't bowled in a few years, but I thought I'd have no problem picking it up again. Wrong. I was tossing gutter balls all over the place. So Pat and I reversed roles. He became the teacher and I became the student.

"Coach, that three-step approach went out a long time ago. That's for old people. Use the two-step."

"Thanks, Pat."

"Try some powder on your hands, Coach."

"That's okay, Pat, I'm fine."

"Don't be nervous, Coach."

"I'm not nervous!"

My shoes were sticking, my wrist was sore, and my back was killing me. The kids, most of whom were having better luck than I was, thought all of this was hilarious. My highest score that day was around one hundred forty—my lowest was a ninety-five. Even Stephanie, who had never bowled and whose approach involved crouching at the top of the lane and pushing the ball with two hands, outscored me in that game. All in all, it was a thoroughly humiliating experience, one the kids would never let me forget. Weeks, even months, later they'd come into school in the morning and say, "Want to go bowling, Coach?"

"Not today. Thanks for asking, though."

Although it had nothing to do with school or Space Camp, it was one of the best days we had as a team, a day filled with camaraderie, friendship, laughter. And for a change, they were laughing *with* each other, rather than *at* each other. That event marked a turning point in the development of our team. The students began hanging out together after school and on weekends, even when they didn't have to. They went to the mall together. They went to the movies. They bonded . . . like any other group of high school kids.

16

E ven though the students had become intensely committed to the training program, and in many cases seemed practically obsessed with the idea of attending Space Camp, there were times when it looked as though we might suffer casualties.

Rebecca Shriver was among the first. Exhausted by the constant bickering with her mother and stepfather, she campaigned daily for the right to live with her dad. When that opportunity came—when her mother grew so tired of Rebecca's anger and resentment that she agreed to relinquish custody to her ex-husband—Rebecca was suddenly confronted with the most difficult decision of her young life. She loved her father dearly and had said for years that all she wanted was to move in with him; maybe then everything would be all right. At the very least, the fighting would stop and she could live quietly and peacefully.

But the timing was unfortunate. For the first time Rebecca was actually enjoying school, doing well in class, and working hard to achieve a goal. Space Camp had become one of the most important things in her life, and now she was being asked to abandon that goal. Moving in with her father, who did not live in Grand Rapids, meant moving to a new school district. It meant Rebecca would have to transfer out of Forest Hills Northern; it meant she wouldn't be going to Space Camp.

I explained all of this to Rebecca one tearful morning in January 1989, when she told me of the developments in her family life. "You have a big choice to make," I said. "And I can't make it for you."

"What if my dad moves into a new apartment—in this school district? Then I wouldn't have to transfer, right?"

She was grasping at straws, searching for some way to make the new arrangement work without sacrificing Space Camp. Rebecca's father had been to several parent-teacher conferences, and he'd been unfailingly polite, lucid, supportive. I had no doubt that he had his daughter's best interests at heart. Nevertheless, it seemed a stretch to expect that he would move out of his home to accommodate Rebecca. In fact, I suspected that she hadn't even broached the subject with him.

"I don't think you can count on that," I said. "When you're making this decision, you have to assume that if you move out of your house, you'll have to give up Space Camp. Personally, I'd hate to see that, not only because you've worked so hard and I think you deserve a chance to go but because we need you." Rebecca sniffed and nodded. I took her hand in mine. "But it has to be your decision."

I was walking a very fine line here, as I often did with our kids. Many of them were so needy, and so lacking in familial support, that it was tempting to make decisions on their behalf that I really wasn't qualified to make. In this case I wanted nothing more than to see Rebecca complete the program and make the trip to Space Camp, for she had blossomed as much as anyone in the class during the preceding months. At the same time, I was well aware of what her home life was like, and how desperately unhappy she had become. When I asked myself, "What's best for this kid?" the apparent answer was, "To be with her father."

Rebecca went back and forth on this issue for the better part of two months, one day swearing she was moving out because her stepfather was hassling her again, the next day insisting she'd be okay and that she couldn't give up Space Camp. In the end Rebecca displayed what I thought was a considerable level of maturity and toughness: She opted to complete the school year in her mother's home. Later, she moved in with her father. To this day I still don't know if that was the right decision, but I do know this: I'm glad she stayed.

IF ONE STUDENT in the program was most problematic, it was Lewis Dayhuff. Even as he assimilated into the school and learned to keep a reasonable leash on his raging temper, Lewis was never more than an insult or an accidental bump away from being suspended, expelled, or arrested. At one hundred forty pounds, with auburn hair and the hollow eyes and sunken cheekbones that come with malnutrition and exhaustion, Lewis hardly looked like the violent type. Upon closer inspection, though, you could see the vasculature in his narrow arms, ropelike veins that popped and bulged, the by-product of hard labor at a tender age. If you crossed Lewis, if you made him angry, you'd see those same veins rising on his throat and at his temples. And Lewis was angry a lot of the time.

He had been born into a white-trash family near Grand Rapids and spent the first seven or eight years of his life in the squalor of a rundown trailer park. His parents were drunks who fought often and worked rarely, so it was inevitable that Lewis and his little brother would end up as wards of the state. They were a package deal, and usually they proved to be more than a foster family could handle. By the time he reached Forest Hills Northern, Lewis had attended eight different schools and lived in more than two dozen homes. He had moved so frequently and accumulated such a long and complicated rap sheet that trying to make sense of his case was enough to induce a migraine.

When I first met Lewis I could tell almost immediately that he was a deeply scarred young man; there was tremendous hurt inside him, and he was quick to lash out at others over seemingly minor transgressions. Despite his relatively diminutive stature, Lewis was a fighter—in the most primitive sense of the word. To have his nose bloodied or broken was a small thing to Lewis, a temporary discomfort that could not possibly compare to what he'd already experienced. Lewis was not a bully—he was a legitimately hard kid . . . a city kid. I had grown up in the heart of Grand Rapids, so I knew a city kid, a street kid, when I saw one. Lewis was cut from that mold, and so he naturally stood out in the hallways of a suburban school like Forest Hills Northern. Lewis would tease other kids, sometimes in a very harsh and vulgar way, and expect them to shrug it off; or, perhaps, he was trying to provoke a confrontation. Certainly when another student exhibited even the slightest disrespect toward Lewis, he wasted no time responding with an expletive-laced tirade and a challenge to fight. That this was something of a double standard never occurred to Lewis.

"You can't talk to people that way," I'd say to him.

With a blank stare he'd respond, "Why not?"

"Because it's wrong."

He'd shrug, say, "So what?" and walk away.

There were times when it seemed that Lewis was a true sociopath, destined to perpetrate a string of violent acts or crimes escalating in seriousness and culminating in a long-term sentence to a state penitentiary. He'd already had some minor brushes with the law before he arrived in our classroom, and his behavior was sufficiently hostile and confrontational that more trouble appeared inevitable. To be honest, if not for Space Camp, and the fact that he was making legitimate contributions to the training program—contributions that reflected a glimmer of hope—I'm not sure I would have kept Lewis in my classroom. He was simply too problematic, too much work . . . too far gone.

And yet, like most of our students—indeed, like most kids in general—Lewis was not without positive attributes. The innate ability to love and care, to be compassionate, had been all but beaten out of him. He exuded anger and false confidence, walked around twenty-four hours a day with a chip on his shoulder, utterly apathetic about anyone and everything, with a few notable exceptions. When the subject turned to his little brother, Lewis became a different person, bright-eyed and protective and almost fatherly. I believe Lewis would gladly have stood in front of an oncoming bus for his brother—his devotion was that deep.

Lewis's other great passion in life was art. He was a gifted illustrator, as talented as any student I had ever seen. Not only could he draw, he could write. Lewis would produce incredible illustrated stories, with richly developed characters and densely woven plots. Like any true artist, Lewis revealed his deepest feelings through his work, which made the stories not only entertaining and impressive, but truly disturbing. Sometimes Lewis would get involved in some type of altercation early in the morning, and later I'd see him sitting at his desk, head down, scribbling furiously, oblivious to everything around him. Before the end of the day he'd drop the material on my desk and rush off. Implicit was the understanding that I would read the story, examine the cartoon, and glean from it precisely what Lewis had felt that day. In this way he expressed himself fully, openly, freely.

Most of his stuff was pretty dark: sad, evil, profane characters leading miserable, violent lives. Although Lewis obviously loved to draw, to create, you could see immense hatred in what he produced. Not surprisingly, he took only a few art classes in the entire time he was at our school. The teachers were too rigid, too conservative, and not likely to sympathize with Lewis's skewed view of the world. Nevertheless, I tried to nudge him in that direction.

"Why not take an art class this quarter, Lewis?"

"Nah . . . no challenge."

If Lewis had spoken so boldly of any other subject, I'd have considered it false bravado, but in this case he was right. As an artist, he was beyond anything the school had to offer. What he lacked, of course, was commitment, self-discipline . . . the ability to see beyond the boundaries of his own little world. Bitterness fueled his creativity, and if it gave him an edge, it also seemed likely to ruin any chance he had of making something of his life.

Not that Lewis didn't have good reason to be pissed at the world. His current foster parents operated a farm in East Grand Rapids, where Lewis and his brother were essentially unpaid labor. The way their foster parents saw it, exploitation was not an issue. Mucking out the barn, grooming and feeding the animals, repairing fences—these were reasonable chores to be performed in exchange for providing three square meals and a roof over the boys' heads. Never mind that Lewis was sometimes too exhausted from working to get up for school, or that the parents probably were in violation of child labor laws. Lewis hated his foster parents and resented the way they treated him, but after so many years of abuse, he had come to expect it.

By February 1989, as our trip to Space Camp drew near, I could sense a heightening of tensions between Lewis and his foster parents. He talked openly about how much work he was doing, and how there wasn't time to do any homework or study for Space Camp. The foster parents, I learned, were using Space Camp as leverage, telling Lewis that if he didn't work harder, longer—and keep his mouth shut about it—they would remove him from our program. In other words, they were blackmailing him. I encouraged Lewis to be strong, to get through the year, and then we'd see about getting him reassigned, but I could tell he had another plan in mind.

One cold, rainy night the phone rang in our house. All of my students had my home phone number and permission to call whenever they wanted. They were pretty good about not calling late at night unless something very bad had happened. As I rolled over in bed and picked up the phone, I looked at the clock. It was eleven forty-five.

"Hello?"

"Hey, Coach. It's Lewis."

His voice was shaking. I could tell he was standing out in the rain.

"What's up?"

"I did something bad. I'm in trouble."

"Okay . . . talk to me."

Lewis proceeded to explain that in a fit of anger he'd stolen a radio from his foster parents and run away. He didn't even want the radio. He just wanted to hurt them.

"I need you to come and pick me up," he said. "Take me to child protective."

I slapped the phone against my pillow in frustration. Lewis had done a lot of stupid, irrational things, but this was near the top of the list. "What were you thinking of?" I asked.

"I was thinking that they're jerks and they don't deserve to have a radio. Now, are you gonna come and get me or not?"

He sounded as though he might start crying, and while I did feel sorry for him, I couldn't bail him out. Not this time. Not this way.

"Lewis, listen to me. You're going to have to atone for this. Go back home, return the radio, and tell them what you've done. I'll call your foster father in the morning and we'll set up a meeting."

There was a long pause as Lewis breathed deeply into the phone. "I can't do that."

"Son . . . you don't have a choice."

A FEW DAYS later we gathered in a counseling room at the high school—me, Robynn, and the various social services and law enforcement personnel who owned a piece of Lewis Dayhuff: his foster parents, his social worker, his probation officer. The foster father reeked of liquor and was overtly antagonistic.

"They're rotten kids," he slurred. "Him and his brother. They don't follow any of our rules and they don't appreciate anything we do for them."

Trying to control my temper, I asked the foster father for a suggestion as to how to handle the situation. With a throbbing, tubercular cough, he leaned forward in his seat. "Personally, I'd like to see the little bastard thrown in jail." He paused, looked at me. "But I'll settle for having him thrown out of this Space Camp thing."

"That's wrong and you know it."

"No!" he shouted. "What I know is this: We had an agreement. If he was a good boy, he'd get to go to Space Camp. If he broke rules, he wouldn't. Well . . . I think ripping me off counts as a deal breaker." He leaned back, laughed, and folded his arms across his thick chest.

At this point, I figured, Lewis was on his way out, so I had nothing to lose by being candid. Anyway, I couldn't just sit there and listen to the sanctimonious ranting of a drunk.

"Let's be honest here," I said. "You've been abusing this kid."

"Ah, bull—"

"Shut up!" He seemed to sober up for a moment, a look of astonishment crossing his face. Clearly this was a man who wasn't accustomed to being told what to do. Unlike Lewis, he was a bully. "This kid and his brother are just slaves to you. They work on your farm all day, shoveling shit out of your barns for hours on end, until they're so tired they can barely stand up. Lewis gets no sleep. I don't even know if you feed him."

"He eats just fine."

"I'll bet . . ."

He waved me off. "Ahhhh . . . you don't understand."

"I understand that if anyone here is a thief, it's you. You're stealing from these kids and you're taking advantage of them." I stopped and turned to address the social worker, a grim woman who had obviously been hardened by years of thankless, depressing work. "I don't condone what Lewis has done, but I am not kicking him out of Space Camp. Please . . . give him one more chance."

She shook her head. "Lewis does burn bridges," she said condescendingly. The probation officer nodded in agreement. It seemed as though no one else in the room cared about this boy in the least, not even those people who had been assigned to protect him and help him.

"My God!" I exclaimed. "This kid has been from foster home to foster home, like a stray cat. No one has ever given him any direction, other than to say what a rotten kid he is. This guy"—I pointed to the foster father—"has him working to death. And you"—I pointed to the social worker—"you're supposed to be coming in here and evaluating his progress in school. When was the last time you were here? I haven't seen you in months. Where have you been?"

The woman averted her eyes.

"Maybe if everyone had been paying a little more attention, this incident wouldn't have happened. If you ask me, Lewis Dayhuff is the one who's been victimized. He's had no love, no support, no family . . . nothing! I'd be misdirected, too."

They were all quiet now. I could only hope that I was making some sense.

"I'm not taking this kid off my caseload," I said. "I'm not letting him out of this building and I'm not kicking him out of the Space Camp program. If you want him, you'll have to take him. You won't have my cooperation."

It took all of five minutes for the social worker and probation officer to agree that the best solution, for now anyway, was to leave Lewis in my class. As the meeting broke up and we walked out into the hall, the foster father shot me a dirty look. He was a mean-spirited man, and I knew it was possible that he would try to take out his frustrations on Lewis and his little brother. So I caught up to him and said, quietly, calmly, "If you lay a finger on either one of those kids, I'll have them out of your house so fast your head will spin. Then let's see you run that ranch."

He grunted and walked away. Lewis, meanwhile, was waiting in my room for the outcome of the meeting.

"What's the word, Coach?" he asked, as if expecting more bad news.

"The word is . . . *behave!*"

Lewis smiled. "I'm in?"

"Yeah, Lewis, you're in. For now."

17

The clock is no friend to a student with special needs. The ticking and humming, the sweep of the second hand—to a special education student these are more than indications of the passing of time. They are glaring reminders of his inadequacy, of his inability to effectively process information, like everyone else in school. The clock is always there for him, peering over his shoulder, heckling, chiding, berating.

"Come on, you moron! Hurry up!"

Robynn and I were accustomed to dealing with the shortcomings of our students and tailoring programs to meet their needs. More often than not this involved giving them additional time to complete assignments and projects and tests. At Space Camp, though, the kids would be expected to adhere to the same rigid standards as every other camper. When they entered the shuttle for their first simulated mission, the clock would begin ticking. Two hours later the mission would be over, whether our team had successfully completed all requirements or not. There was nothing fluid about it. In fact, almost everything they were going to do at Space Camp would be measured against the clock. That our students did not have the intellectual, emotional, familial, or financial resources of, say, students from an elite New England prep school or a magnet school in Manhattan mattered not in the least. The game had a beginning, a middle, and an end, and the boundaries were the same for all contestants.

In the beginning of our training we did not use a clock or a stopwatch, because we knew the kids would get nervous. Instead, we memorized acronyms, studied astronomy and rocket propulsion, and the history of space and science. We read countless scripts, exchanging positions on a daily basis so that each student would be comfortable in every chair. Our focus was on understanding procedure, regardless of time. We could see the results. The kids were absorbing material, working well together, and getting pumped up about the trip. There was just one problem: They weren't really ready. Until they proved they could accomplish the same level of work with a clock running, they weren't prepared for Space Camp. With that in mind, we decided to turn up the heat—perhaps just a bit too quickly.

In addition to timing portions of our script readings, we began working with crystallization kits. Similar to those used by mission specialists at Space Camp, the kits were virtually foolproof, provided you followed directions precisely. Each kit included several individually wrapped packets of chemicals that had to be mixed in specific amounts at specific intervals. If you missed a step, measured incorrectly, or tried to rush the process, the crystals would not grow properly and the experiment would fail.

As much as anything else, it was an exercise in discipline and concentration:

Step 1: Add liquid "A" to solid "B"
Step 2: Wait thirty seconds
Step 3: Add liquid "C"
Step 4: Wait two minutes

And so on . . . The crystallization kits were little more than a variation on the old vinegar-and-baking-soda experiment that most kids learn in grade school, which is to say . . . they held the potential for disaster. Okay . . . maybe not *disaster*, but at least great *mess*. This was an experiment that required patience and focus to achieve the desired outcome; and yet, it was not a dangerous experiment, which made it perfect for our kids. I could just imagine the headlines if they were permitted to work with something more volatile:

TEACHER BLOWS UP SCHOOL!

No thanks. The crystallization kits were challenging enough.

So, one day we divided the class into three groups. One large group practiced reading scripts while another large group constructed plastic tetrahedrons on the floor of the classroom. The remaining group consisted of two students: Pat Zerfas and Rob Johnson. I walked them down to the chemistry lab, which was free that period, and explained that they were going to be conducting a crystallization experiment similar to the ones they'd encounter at Space Camp.

"You're going to have to watch the clock and follow the directions word for word. Is that clear?"

They nodded.

"One of you should probably be in charge of the experiment, and the other person should be the observer. You know what an observer is, Rob?"

"Someone who observes."

I rolled my eyes. "Right. And in this case the observer also records the information on paper."

"Oh. Pat . . . you can be the observer."

That was fine with Pat, who wanted nothing so much as to please Rob, one of the stronger personalities in our class. Educably mentally impaired, but street-smart and athletic, Rob was good at hiding his limitations. He was a varsity wrestler whose fondness for practical jokes— placing a thumbtack on a seat, tying someone's belt loop to a chair— kept other students on edge, for they knew that crossing Rob was likely to provoke a sneak attack, one that would almost surely result in their being embarrassed. A fringe benefit of being Rob's sidekick was that Pat rarely was the target of Rob's odd sense of humor.

"At Space Camp," I said, "you'll be expected to fax the results of your experiments to Mission Control. We'll make it simple here. When you're done, just walk the results over to me. Is that clear?"

"No problem, Coach."

Since the chemistry lab wasn't far from our room, I planned to circulate among the groups and monitor everyone's progress. Rob and Pat seemed to be doing just fine in the beginning. They worked calmly, intently, read instructions out loud, and measured each ingredient carefully. I sensed no reason to be alarmed.

"You guys okay if I run down to the room for a few minutes?"

"Sure," Rob said, without even making eye contact. "This is easy."

"Yeah," Pat repeated. "Easy."

Although I felt some trepidation about leaving the two boys unsupervised, I knew that their development depended on a degree of trust. If they couldn't complete a simple crystallization experiment here, in the chemistry lab, how could they possibly hope to succeed in the pressurized atmosphere of Space Camp? Anyway, what could possibly go wrong in the five minutes that it would take me to check in on the other groups?

As it turned out . . . plenty.

THE VOICES, STRAINED and combative, and easily audible from far down the hall, signaled trouble.

"What are you doing?"

"Never mind! Find a mop or something!"

"Where?"

"How should I know?!"

As I entered the room, I was shocked to see a multicolored river of crystals flowing out of a bucket like molten lava out of a volcano. Pat and Rob were on their knees, desperately trying to clean up the mess, or at least contain it, but it seemed to have a mind of its own. They pawed at it with wads of paper towels, scooped it up by the handful, but still it expanded, bursting into new and more vibrant colors with each passing moment.

"Good God! What's going on here?!" I yelled.

Pat looked up, his face splattered with purple and green dye. "Sorry, Coach. Rob thought we needed more sodium. The experiment wasn't moving fast enough."

The chemical reaction—the formation of crystals—was supposed to occur in two minutes. Apparently, Rob had started to panic at around the one-minute mark. His response was tantamount to putting a frozen pizza in the oven and setting the temperature at five hundred degrees: *There! Just crank this sucker up and we'll get the experiment back on track!* So now there were crystals everywhere: in the bucket, on the floor, in the sink . . . even on their clothes and arms. And it was hardening fast, forming ribbons of coral on everything it touched.

"What do we do, Coach?"

Before I could answer, in walked the chemistry teacher. He removed his glasses, rubbed his chin, and said, with a tone of bemusement, "Hmmmmm . . . interesting way to make rock candy."

"Very funny," I said. "This isn't rock candy. You know what this is."

He laughed. "Yeah, it's a mess . . . Rob, how much sodium did you use?"

Rob peered up from his position on the floor and smiled sheepishly. "The whole box."

"What?! You're supposed to get twenty experiments out of that box! What were you thinking?"

The answer, of course, was that they weren't thinking. Later on, after the chemistry lab had been cleaned up, I gathered the entire class and asked them what they had learned that day. Ben Schmidt immediately thrust his hand in the air.

"Uhhhhh . . . don't let Rob pour in the chemicals?"

Everyone cracked up, with the exception of Rob, who had a slightly different take on the fiasco.

"I think the lesson is, don't watch somebody else do something and expect it to be done on time."

Huh? I had no idea what he was talking about, whether that was a shot at Pat for not taking a more active role, or at me for expecting them to complete the assignment on time, and without my help.

"I'm not sure I understand what you mean, Rob."

He frowned. "You said we had to follow the clock, right?"

"Yes."

"Well, I didn't think we were going to make it."

"Rob," I said. "You had twenty-five minutes to complete the experiment, not two minutes. There was plenty of time left."

Rob muttered something under his breath as the other kids laughed. Fortunately this was just a scrimmage, because we were going to need a lot more practice before game time.

EVEN MORE DISTRESSING was our first attempt to compete against the clock while building tetrahedrons underwater. The fact that it occurred in a pool notwithstanding, this was truly the dry run from hell. The kids had gotten pretty accomplished at constructing these things on land. In fact, they had demonstrated a degree of competitiveness I hadn't detected before. Working in groups of four, they sometimes resorted to name calling or outright sabotage. More than once I saw Steve, when his team was behind, sneak over and kick one of the nodes belonging to another team, so they'd have to waste time chasing it down. Similarly, Rob Johnson would unscrew pieces of his competitors' tetrahedrons when they weren't looking. Not exactly sportsmanlike behavior, but in a weird way I found it encouraging. At least they wanted to win. At least they cared.

Of course, on land, constructing a tetrahedron wasn't all that difficult a task. It was merely a matter of inserting plastic rods into plastic nodes and connecting the various pieces—like a big geometric Tinker Toy, each side approximately three feet in length. We had even timed the kids on a few occasions, just to apply some pressure, and they had responded admirably. In the water, though, everything would change. There would be less dexterity, less visibility, more resistance. They'd have to hold their breath while working. On land, a mistake meant nothing. If you dropped a node or a rod, there was no place for it to go. In the water, however, it would sink to the bottom. (Similarly, in space, it would fly off into the void, never to be retrieved.)

As the kids began swimming laps to get warmed up, Robynn and I removed the nodes and rods from a big duffel bag and placed them in two separate piles on the drain shelf of the pool.

"All right!" I shouted. "Everybody out. Play time is over. Let's get to work."

This time we divided the class into two groups of ten, since that's the way they'd be divided at Space Camp. There, too, they'd be tested in twelve feet of water, an intimidating depth for even an accomplished swimmer, and few of our students fell into that category. At the YMCA we had to settle for nine feet of water. It may sound like a subtle difference, but it's enough to play tricks on the mind.

As they stood on the deck, I gave them a little pep talk, told them to work as a team—or two separate teams, in this case—to be patient and confident and meticulous. They nodded assuredly, as if it were no big deal at all. Then Robynn blew a whistle and they jumped back into the water. Within seconds it was apparent that we had completely misjudged their ability and preparedness. On neither team was there even a hint of cooperation or leadership. Constructing a tetrahedron underwater is difficult, but it's not impossible. It simply requires teamwork. If the team members work in pairs—with one person holding a node while the other inserts a rod into the proper receptacle on the node—the process can go quite smoothly. Here, though, the kids were flailing about, each person acting as an individual disconnected from the effort of the team. Predictably, it wasn't long before nodes and rods began sinking to the bottom of the pool, followed by fighting and bickering among teammates. The kids were screaming and cursing at each other, refusing to take responsibility for their own mistakes. Some of the girls were crying.

Robynn and I tried to take control, to steer them back on track, but it was hopeless. This was as ugly as any session we had experienced since the beginning of our training program. It was the worst, actually, because it came at a time when I thought we had already crossed a significant threshold: the one separating individuals from teammates. I really had anticipated a smooth transition from land to water. I thought the kids would dive right in, build perfect tetrahedrons, pat each other on the back, and then we could concentrate on the more demanding intellectual aspects of the program. But here they were, splashing and fumbling about, fighting with each other, and generally behaving in a manner reflective of a Marx Brothers movie. To a casual, uninformed observer, I'm sure it would have been a comical sight; to me it was merely painful.

I nudged Robynn. "Blow the whistle. This is going nowhere."

As the shrill chirp of the whistle reverberated through the pool, the kids stopped and treaded water, instantly aware that they were in trouble.

"What's wrong, Coach?" Scott Goudy asked.

"Do you really have to ask?"

He didn't respond. None of them did.

"Pick up the nodes and rods, put them back in the duffel bag, and go take a shower," I said. "We're done here."

From deep in one of the groups, Rob Johnson shouted, "Good idea. This is a waste of time anyway. Most of these idiots can't even swim."

"Screw you!" Scott replied.

And with that they were screaming again, fighting among themselves with an intensity and an insensitivity I hadn't seen in months. Slowly they broke away from one another and swam to the side of the pool. Most of them chose not to speak to Robynn or me as they walked to the locker room, but a few did. With a big goofy grin on his face, Ben Schmidt said, "Can't we try again, Coach? We can do better."

"Not today, Ben."

And from Pat Zerfas, this: "Maybe we should just stick to bowling."

"Enough with the bowling, Pat!"

"Sorry."

LATER, ON THE ride home, Robynn and I reviewed what had happened, but were at a loss to explain its cause. We knew only that we had a big problem. Less than twenty-four hours after our arrival at Space Camp these kids were going to be changing into swimsuits and building tetrahedrons. A performance as dismal as the one we saw on this day would surely result in a complete meltdown. The primary purpose of the tetrahedron exercise was to evaluate the students' ability to work as a team. Watching them today, I thought, their score would be . . . well . . . *zero*. It was that bad.

"Maybe it's time to get back to basics," Robynn suggested.

"What do you mean?"

"Have them work in smaller groups . . . and turn off the clock."

Although I hated the idea of taking a step backward, especially with only a few months left before Space Camp, I knew Robynn was right. This way, at least, the kids would get accustomed to working in the water, and with only two people on a team, they'd be less inclined to argue. I had taken too much for granted. Just because the kids could build a tetrahedron on land did not mean those skills would easily transfer to water. As a coach, I should have known that. Practice makes perfect, after all, and a fundamental tenet of practice is that at some point you have to simulate the conditions of a game. You don't win football games without endless practice and preparation, and it was unrealistic to think we'd build a perfect tetrahedron on our first attempt in the pool.

It reminded me of something I had once heard another coach say to a group of players at an All-Star Game. We were on the practice field, and some of the players were just going through the motions, not really taking the upcoming game seriously. Each of them wore a brand-new, snow-white commemorative T-shirt, emblematic of their status as the best players in the state of Michigan.

"You all look great in those T-shirts," the coach said. "But you know what? Right now, that's all you are: T-shirt All-Americans. Let's see how you look when we put the pads on, because that's when it counts."

Trite, I know, but it was absolutely true. And our students were the same way. They were T-shirt All-Americans on land; however, when we entered the water, we became scrubs. Hard as it was to witness, that debacle was necessary. It reminded all of us that we weren't nearly as well prepared as we thought we were. We still had a lot of work to do, and a shrinking window of time in which to accomplish it.

18

In the two weeks following the tetrahedron disaster a malaise settled in over our program. The kids were listless, unfocused, apathetic. One Saturday morning we attempted a complete shuttle mission with the clock running. Everyone was assigned a part, just as they would be at Space Camp. One group was in Mission Control, another group in the shuttle, and another conducting experiments.

Within minutes after liftoff it was clear that the mission was doomed. The kids were barely interacting. They mumbled their lines, almost as if they didn't want to be heard. Words and phrases that had rolled off their tongues in previous months were now jumbled and unintelligible. "Anomaly" became "nomma." "Accelerate" became "axil." Suddenly they couldn't even talk.

When Robynn and I saw what was happening, we stopped the mission.

"What's going on?" I asked. "What happened to five months of training?"

At first, no one responded. Then Steve Bennett offered an explanation. "What's the use, Coach? We screwed up in the pool, we'll screw up here."

So that was it. A single bad episode had left them so utterly despondent that they had decided to quit. A part of me wanted to curse at them, to read them the riot act as I might have done with my football team, but then I remembered: *These kids are different.* Because of their various disabilities, and also because of the tremendous pressure they were facing, they carried everything—disappointment, happiness, anger—closer to the heart. That's the way it is with kids who have special needs. They're uniquely wired. While most of us recover quickly from minor setbacks, these kids take their problems to bed each night, feeding and nurturing them until they become insurmountable.

With the kids looking beaten and bewildered, I searched for the right words. It was important to choose them carefully. As I often did in these types of situations, I turned to sports for a suitable analogy.

"You know, even our football team has bad moments. We don't have a great practice session every day." Their faces remained blank. I was getting nowhere. "Think about your parents. Some nights they come home happy, right? Because they've had a good day at work. The next day they're grumpy because they got yelled at by the boss."

A few of them nodded in agreement. "This is the same thing. You guys had a bad day . . ."

"Really bad," Ben added.

"Horrible," said Stephanie.

And, from Steve Bennett, the exclamation mark: "We sucked!"

Everyone laughed. That was good. The mood was lightening.

"Okay," I said. "You sucked. *We* sucked. Ms. McKinney and I have to take responsibility for this, too. And we will. We're going to help you get ready for this trip, but you have to have faith in us and confidence in yourselves. You can't quit. And you can't get down on each other. If we succeed, we succeed as a team, and if we fail, we fail as a team. Is that clear?"

This time all of them nodded.

"Good. Now . . . turn off the computers and put away all the gear."

"Why?" they asked.

I pulled a Frisbee out of my desk drawer. "Because we're going to go outside for a while . . . have some fun."

"Uhhhh . . . Coach?"

"Yes?"

"It's thirty degrees outside."

"I know. Bundle up."

As they filed out of the room, I stopped Scott Goudy. "Hang back for a minute, Scott."

"Sure."

After everyone else was gone, I had a very frank, adult conversation with Scott. The truth was, I felt that in many ways he was the most disappointing member of our team. Scott was perhaps the smartest student in the class, and one of the few kids who was comfortable with his body. He had the potential to be a true leader, someone the other students would follow and look to for advice. So far, though, he had coasted along on natural ability, happy to do his own work and quick to criticize the slipshod work of his classmates. When he had difficulty understanding Ben's slurred speech, or when Stephanie stammered over a challenging word, Scott became agitated, and that made everyone uncomfortable.

"You need to lighten up," I suggested. "Don't be so harsh with these guys. You know you're the best reader in the class."

"Right."

"Well, everyone else knows that, too. You don't have to make them feel bad about it. Try not to put other people down. You have to be more patient. You have to listen."

"But it's hard, Coach."

"I know it's hard. It's supposed to be hard. No one ever said being a leader was easy."

He frowned. "Who said I was a leader?"

"I'm saying it now. Without you, we don't have a chance down there. On every team someone has to set an example, and I'm depending on you to be that person."

"All right," Scott said. "I'll try."

THROUGHOUT THE YEAR I kept in close contact with Lynn Bondurant, in part because he had been such a strong advocate for our program that I felt he deserved to know how we were doing, and in part because I respected his opinion. When I told him that we seemed to have reached a plateau in our training, he offered a suggestion.

"You need someone from the space program to come and see you, maybe talk with your students."

A wonderful notion, but I couldn't imagine who would volunteer for such a mission.

"How about Jack Lousma?" Dr. Bondurant said.

I was dumbstruck. Jack Lousma's pedigree was impeccable. A colonel and fighter pilot in the U.S. Marine Corps, he had gone on to become one of the first men to fly the space shuttle. He had also spent seventy-two days on the space station *Skylab*. Although he had long since exchanged his space suit for the grays and blues of the corporate world (he was an engineering consultant), Jack remained one of the true heroes of the U.S. space program.

"You're kidding, right?" I said.

"Not at all. Jack is a good man, and he loves kids. I think he'd be very interested in what you're doing. Let me give his wife a call—she handles all of Jack's business affairs—and see if we can put something together."

After Lynn had greased the skids a bit, I drove to Jack's home in Ann Arbor with my son Ryan. Jack was on the road, which wasn't unusual, but his wife, Gratia, was happy to take a meeting. Before proposing our idea to her husband, she wanted a full explanation of the program. That was fine with me. She was the gatekeeper, and she was merely doing her job. Moreover, she managed to do it in a thoroughly disarming way. Gratia, you might say, was a very gracious woman. She welcomed us into her home, immediately offered my son some cookies, and then treated us as guests, rather than as solicitors. She apologized for her husband's absence, which wasn't even remotely necessary, and then invited me to make a pitch.

"Tell me what kind of exciting things you're doing with these kids," she said. "I want to hear all about it."

As I explained the program and why I thought it would be wonderful for our kids to meet a real astronaut, Gratia scribbled furiously in a notebook. She asked a lot of smart questions and seemed genuinely intrigued by the conversation. Afterward she thanked us for making the trip, tousled Ryan's hair, and said she'd be in touch. And I knew she meant it.

That week I told the students what had happened, that I'd met with the wife of a famous astronaut and that he might be coming to visit. They didn't know Jack Lousma, but as I shared the highlights of his résumé, their eyes lit up.

"You really think he might want to meet us?" Stephanie asked. "That would be so cool."

"Will he wear his space suit?" Ben wondered aloud.

For the most part they were enthusiastic, which was precisely the reaction I had hoped to provoke. There were, however, a few detractors, just as there had been more than a year earlier, when I first broached the subject of Space Camp. Including Lewis Dayhuff.

"Right," Lewis said sarcastically. "Like an astronaut is going to want to spend time with a bunch of idiots like us."

Sometimes the kids would belittle themselves in this way purely for effect, to elicit sympathy or anger. As any special education teacher knows, you can't respond to every epithet, not without losing your mind. Sometimes it's best to just ignore the self-flagellation. This seemed to be one of those occasions. The important thing was not to soothe their damaged egos, but to reignite the fire within them, to get them excited all over again. It was almost impossible for them to comprehend that an astronaut would want to get involved with children other than his own, especially children who had a history of academic, emotional, and social problems.

"I can't make any promises," I said, trying hard to be both optimistic and realistic. "But I did go to Ann Arbor and I did have a very nice meeting with Mr. Lousma's wife. All I can tell you is that they are extremely interested in this program, and that means they're interested in you."

Whether it was because they were excited about the possibility of meeting a real astronaut, or simply because they were more resilient than we had suspected, the kids began to come around. For a while the clock was removed from all aspects of training and preparation. Instead, we focused on prioritizing. We reiterated, for example, that during their missions they would be confronted with a variety of anomalies, and they were going to have to decide which anomalies required the most immediate attention. *Do you take care of a gravely ill pilot or do you fix that little computer glitch? Ask yourselves: Which of the two problems is most likely to bring the mission to an abrupt end?*

Some problems, too, appeared more serious than they really were. They were designed to induce panic, to throw the entire mission into a state of chaos, when in reality there existed a simple solution. The most glaring example of this was something known as the "Christmas Tree," wherein the shuttle's panel of warning lights would begin blinking hysterically, presenting a harried and frantic crew with the daunting task of solving thirty-two anomalies at once. Of course, this wasn't really possible—by the time you were through, the mission would be over. However, the student who had studied and prepared, and paid attention during classes at Space Camp, would have known that the Christmas Tree was actually just a trick—by throwing a single electrical switch, he or she could stop the panel from blinking.

By concentrating on mastering the elements of the mission, rather than the time it took to achieve this mastery, we made significant progress. A similar approach was effective in the pool. To get their confidence back, we had them work in groups of two or three. There were at least a dozen pieces to each tetrahedron, so we decided at first to concentrate on just building the base. Then we worked on building the sides. Then we worked on putting the sections together. A few weeks after that first miserable effort at the YMCA pool, we staged another competition, but with a slight wrinkle: the kids were divided into four groups, rather than two groups, and we did not use a clock.

"We just want to observe you working as a team," Robynn said by way of explanation. "We want to see who's demonstrating leadership, who has a good attitude. Remember—at Space Camp, you'll be graded on teamwork."

We knew the kids would naturally view this as a competitive situation. Even though the clock wasn't running, each team would want to be the first to complete its tetrahedron. And knowing that they were competing only against each other, and not against a clock, they would be less likely to panic.

Or so we hoped.

As it turned out, our suspicions were correct. The groups interacted well and worked extremely hard; at the same time they never lost sight of the fact that they were sharing the pool with three other teams. You could see them looking over their shoulders, assessing the competition, but rather than allowing that pressure to eat away at their confidence and composure, they used it as motivation. They encouraged each other, helped each other. Finally, after approximately four minutes (I was keeping an estimate on my watch, without telling the kids), the first group finished. Scott Goudy, Steve Bennett, Ben Schmidt, and Andrea Burke exploded out of the water, yelling and holding a tetrahedron overhead. They swam to the side of the pool and compared it to the model we had placed on the deck as an example. It was perfect!

"All right!" they shouted, as they exchanged high fives and slapped each other on the back. Some of the other kids were angry, because it was obvious that the winning team had been stacked with the strongest swimmers, but the tension quickly dissolved.

"You all did great," I said. "We're on the right track. Now let's split up the teams and try again."

After distributing the better swimmers evenly among the other teams, we repeated the exercise three more times. No group came close to matching the speed of the first group, but at least we were making progress. Granted, we'd have to improve significantly before Space Camp, where most teams would need less than three minutes, and perhaps as little as two minutes, to build a tetrahedron, but considering how badly things had gone a few weeks earlier, I couldn't help but be encouraged.

REMEMBERING THE GALVANIZING effect that a little publicity had had on the kids the previous year, when we first announced our intention to go to Space Camp, Robynn suggested an update.

"Let's call Jack Lousma and see if we can get him to commit to a date," she said. "And why don't we invite Congressman Henry, too?"

"What do you have in mind?" I asked.

"Put Jack in the pool with the kids and have them build tetrahedrons together."

Brilliant! The students would love it, the parents and administration would be impressed, and the media would eat it up. Coincidentally, Robynn's sister worked for Unistrut, the company that manufactured the equipment we were using to build tetrahedrons. So they generously agreed to get involved in the promotion of our program by donating T-shirts and additional nodes and rods. From there, everything fell into place. Jack Lousma needed no convincing. His wife had told him all about the program and my visit, and he was happy to help out. And, just by chance, Paul Henry was scheduled to be in Grand Rapids that same day, so he, too, was quick to commit.

We held the event at the YMCA on a Monday morning in early March 1989, just two months before we would leave for Space Camp

We had contacted the various media outlets in the area, and hoped that the turnout would be as impressive as it had been for Dan Trierweiler's check presentation. Well, it far surpassed our expectations. Reporters from all three local television stations showed up, as well as from a half dozen radio outlets, the Grand Rapids and Kalamazoo newspapers, and even the *Detroit News*. Apparently, we were now in the big leagues.

When we arrived at the YMCA, the kids went into the locker room to get changed. Robynn and I waited outside for a few minutes to greet some of our visitors. One of the first to show up was Denise Boitano. Just in case I was laboring under the illusion that she had somehow shifted allegiance, Denise strolled right up to me and said, quietly but firmly, "Mike, I hope these kids know how to behave today."

One side of my brain formed this response: *"Why you miserable little witch . . ."* while the other side, the side experiencing an anxiety attack, said, *"Yeah . . . me, too."* All that came out, however, was, "I'm sure they'll be just fine, Denise. Thank you for coming."

Jack Lousma walked in with Congressman Henry. Both were members of the Republican Party, and Jack had even once run for the U.S. Senate, so they'd known each other for some time. As you might expect from a Marine Corps colonel and former astronaut, Jack cut an impressive figure. Now in his late fifties, he still appeared fit and athletic. More than six feet tall, with thinning hair, wide shoulders, and a sturdy chin, Jack looked a little like former U.S. President Gerald Ford. He had an easy smile and an air of authority and confidence about him, the kind that I can only presume comes with having been a fighter pilot . . . or from flying a space shuttle.

"How do you do, sir?" I said, extending a sweaty hand. I was as nervous as I had been since we embarked on this journey, not only because I was meeting an astronaut but because the stakes on this day were quite high. It was like a big exhibition game, with jobs on the line. If we did well, we would score major points with the parents and administrators and others in the audience who had been backing us, people like Dan Trierweiler, who wanted to see us succeed. And to the skeptics, like Denise Boitano, we could collectively thumb our nose.

"I'm doing very well, thank you," Jack said. He looked around at the reporters and television cameras, at the parents who were waiting anxiously in the bleachers. "This is quite a thing you have going here, Mike. I'm happy to be a part of it."

I laughed nervously. "I hope you feel the same way an hour from now."

"I'm sure I will."

By now our kids were seated in the bleachers. They were unusually quiet, focused, serious. There was no farting from Steve, no laughter from Ben, no cursing from Lewis, no crying from Andrea. As Jack excused himself and headed off to get changed, I noticed Robynn walking out of the locker room. She appeared dazed, which at first concerned me, until I realized what had happened. She was walking out of the *men's* locker room!

"I can't believe I just did that," she said. "I'm so nervous."

I stifled a laugh. "What happened?"

"What do you think happened? I was starting to get undressed when some guy walked by and said, 'Ma'am, I believe you're in the wrong locker room.' I said, 'I don't think so.' But then I saw the urinals . . . and . . . oh my God!"

I laughed out loud and threw an arm around Robynn's shoulder. "Get a grip, McKinney."

She nodded. "I'd better get changed."

"Me, too."

Jack talked briefly to the audience, explained why he was interested in the program, and said that he would be helping the kids with an exercise that was similar to one used by NASA in training astronauts. Then he invited the kids to ask questions. A flood of adrenaline hit my stomach, and for a moment I felt queasy. This was an open forum, an invitation to our students to say almost anything that was on their minds. There was, of course, the possibility that one of them would say something controversial, something inflammatory, and that the comments would be aired that night on the local news and printed the next day in newspapers all across the state. But this was their moment, another test of their maturity and progress.

I held my breath, then exhaled as Rebecca Shriver raised her hand. *Whew! At least it's not Steve asking the first question.*

"I was just wondering . . ." Rebecca began.

"Yes," Jack said with a smile.

"Ummmm . . . did you get sick in space?"

A ripple of laughter spread through the audience. It was a funny question, but actually a good question, too. A fair question.

"No," Jack said. "I didn't. But it's not uncommon for astronauts to experience motion sickness. It does happen."

Another hand went up. *Oh, God . . . Steve!*

"How do you go to the bathroom in space?"

More titters from the audience, and a knowing nod from Jack Lousma, who was clearly accustomed to answering such scatological inquiries. We had been over this in class, but hearing me discuss the specifics of bodily functions in zero gravity was not the same as hearing it from someone who had firsthand knowledge.

"In the shuttle," Jack said, without a hint of embarrassment, "you sit on a toilet and a vacuum sucks the feces and urine into a dehydration system, where it's converted into a powder. Oh . . . and you have to be strapped in."

There were many more questions and more elegant, straightforward responses, but the best was saved for last.

"What's it feel like to be launched into space?"

Jack hesitated before answering, then chose his words carefully, words that captured the violence and beauty of space travel.

"It feels like somebody is sitting on your chest. You're thrust back into your seat, and there's tremendous pressure against your body. But then, suddenly, you're in space, and you can see the whole country, the whole planet, just as though you're looking at a map or a globe. The wonder of it all . . ." He hesitated, blinked, as if seeing it in his mind's eye all over again. "It's absolutely overwhelming."

As the crowd sat silently, in awe, Jack segued neatly into the next portion of the program. "Okay," he said, rubbing his hands together. "Let's get in the water and see what these guys can do."

As the kids jumped into the pool and began swimming laps to warm up, Jack grabbed one of the baseball-sized nodes and began playing with it, rolling it over in his hands, examining it closely. He seemed perplexed.

"Something wrong?" I asked.

He held up the node for me to inspect. "Yeah. Where's the nail polish?"

"Nail polish?"

Jack smiled. "Uh-huh. At NASA, all the nodes are marked with waterproof nail polish so you'll know exactly where to insert the rods. It's kind of like a cheat sheet."

I was astounded. Each node was covered with dozens of holes, like a wiffle ball, so matching the right rod to the right hole was no easy task. But I guess I hadn't realized until that very moment just how difficult it really was. I mean, if astronauts couldn't do it . . .

"We don't use nail polish, Jack."

"You don't, huh?"

"No."

"And your kids can do this?"

"Yes, sir."

He rubbed the node some more, tossed it into the air and caught it. "Well, this is going to be interesting."

We divided the class into four groups. Robynn took two groups to one end of the pool, while Jack and I took two groups to the other end of the pool. When Jack gave the command—"Ready . . . set . . . go!"— the kids dived underwater and began working like crazy. Within four minutes the first group, with Jack helping out, had constructed a tetrahedron. For nearly a half hour Jack gracefully orchestrated the session, moving from group to group, offering advice and encouragement to just about every kid in the class.

Afterward, as the kids draped themselves in towels and huddled with their parents, the press moved in on Jack and fired questions at him. Before answering, he grabbed Ben Schmidt by the arm and pulled him close (Jack had taken a real liking to Ben, which wasn't hard to do). "This kid is like a fish," Jack said. "I've never seen anyone who could hold their breath so long." Ben beamed, and I could tell right then that in Jack Lousma we had found another advocate. This was not a publicity stunt to Jack; he believed in us.

"What do you think about these kids?" one of the reporters asked Jack.

"I think they're an amazing group," he responded.

"Really?" the reporter said, sounding somewhat skeptical. "Why do you say that?"

Jack picked up one of the nodes. "We have some pretty smart guys at NASA, and yet we mark these with nail polish so we'll know how to put the pieces together." He paused, gave Ben a pat on the back. "These kids do it blind . . . while treading water. That shows how well they work together as a team. If you ask me, they're ready for Space Camp right now."

Not quite. But we were getting close.

19

I t's easy to be cynical and skeptical about the media, and God knows in my years as a football coach I've seen some shoddy and self-serving reporting; I've seen grown men take advantage of kids who have never had microphones thrust in their faces. I've heard them ask questions that simply shouldn't be asked of a fifteen-year-old.

At the same time, I can understand and even appreciate the role of the media, which is not merely to inform and enlighten, or even to act as a watchdog (although all of these things are true), but also to entertain, titillate, shock—in short, to create a product that will be of interest to consumers and advertisers. All claims to the contrary notwithstanding, newspapers and radio and television stations are primarily businesses, and like any business they want to turn a profit. So, when it comes to coverage, the sensational and the sappy often take precedence over the substantive. The old adage about newsroom prioritization rings true: "If it bleeds, it leads!"

In the wake of our performance at the YMCA pool, we became media darlings, and although both Robynn and I worried about the possibility of exploitation, we also understood that if the media could use our students to increase ratings, then we could use the media to help our cause. It was indeed a two-way street. Each time a story about the students appeared in the newspaper, it served as validation for our program, and for the money being spent by people like Dan Trierweiler. Moreover, it provided an enormous boost to the often fragile egos of the students themselves. These were kids who rarely received any attention at all, and when they did, it usually was in a negative context. All things considered, the benefits of media coverage seemed to far outweigh the drawbacks.

Not that I didn't put on a little bit of a sweat show each time the cameras began to roll. With our students, there was always the potential for misbehavior, or at least behavior that the viewing public might consider unusual, so before each press conference and interview I had a knot in my stomach. Such was the case in late February, when a reporter from Channel 13, one of the local network television affiliates, asked if she could bring a camera into our class and record our reactions and conversations as we watched a space shuttle launch. As always, I had to get clearance from the principal, and while that might have been difficult a year earlier, it was now simply a matter of asking. While Tom Keller was hardly a fan of mine, he was smart enough to see that the community and the media had rallied behind our program, and there was nothing to be gained by standing in our way.

The parents all signed off on it too, which may not sound like a big deal, but in the case of many of our students, it was no small accomplishment. While some of the students were fortunate to come from loving, supportive homes, many did not. They were raised in apathetic, sometimes abusive environments. Interestingly, though, the preparation for Space Camp seemed to have a healing effect on some of these families. Parent and child were drawn together in ways we had never seen. Fathers and mothers who routinely skipped parent-teacher conferences began showing up for special events at school, including the shuttle launch. Maybe it was because they were seeing their children in a different light; maybe it was because they now had reason to believe in their children all over again; maybe it was something less noble, like the need to grab a piece of the spotlight now being cast on their children. Whatever the reason, Space Camp brought these families together, created a closeness, or at least an opportunity for closeness, and that was encouraging. I'd been teaching special-needs students long enough to know that few of them would live happily ever after. But this reminded me: Some of them did indeed have a chance.

Several parents came to school on the morning of the launch. They sat in our room with their children and listened with a combination of amusement and respect as the kids, many of whom had rarely displayed any scientific aptitude whatsoever, provided color commentary to the televised broadcast. They defined acronyms as they were broadcast over the air; they identified components of the shuttle. As the countdown progressed, my nervousness subsided. The students were conducting themselves in a mature way, and yet they were clearly excited and enthusiastic. Of course, there was still a chance that something might go wrong, particularly with the launch itself. A little less than three years had passed since the Space Shuttle *Challenger* had blown up on national television, providing a tragic and vivid reminder that while space exploration had become infinitely more advanced than it was in the days of John Glenn and Neil Armstrong, it was not without its risks. Even now, in 1989, each time a shuttle took flight, I held my breath and prayed for the safety of the crew.

"T-minus thirty seconds," said the voice on the television, emanating from Mission Control. The class fell completely silent.

"T-minus twenty seconds . . ."

The anxiety in the room proved to be too much for Steve Bennett. He had a captive audience, a window of opportunity, and, best of all (for him, anyway), a television camera recording every word. "Oh, man," he sighed. "I'll bet those guys are ready to shit their pants right about now, huh?"

A couple of the girls immediately yelled, *"Steeeve!"* I chose to ignore him, because attention was precisely what he craved. This was typical of the kind of stunt pulled by Steve. There were times when he just couldn't help himself. He didn't intend any harm; he simply wanted to make people laugh. And, I have to admit, sometimes I had to leave the room after one of Steve's outbursts so that I could laugh in private, and thus not appear to have condoned his actions. He was a smart, funny kid who just didn't know when to turn it off; who sometimes wasn't capable of throwing the right switch.

At any rate, interest was deflected away from Steve within a few seconds after he delivered his wisecrack. The launch pad burst into flame, and as the kids applauded and whistled and cheered, the shuttle rose swiftly and smoothly into orbit. The mission went off without a hitch, as did the story filed by the reporter from Channel 13 (a thoughtful young woman who actually became so enamored of the students that she spent a couple days with us at Space Camp). It was a story free of any references to Steve's poor choice of words . . . a story without condescension. As I watched the piece air that evening, I thought, *Well, what do you know? They got it right.*

AROUND THIS SAME time we began to delve heavily into rocketry and propulsion. In keeping with our strategy of experiential education, we obtained from Lynn Bondurant dozens of kits for constructing paper airplanes. Most of them were quite simple—all that was required was a pair of scissors and some paste. But we also used a more elaborate kit called White Wings, which featured intricately designed replicas of some of the most famous airplanes in history—from the Wright Brothers' first plane to Charles Lindbergh's *Spirit of St. Louis*, to an F-14 fighter. When built exactly according to specifications, these models were not only strikingly authentic in appearance, but they could fly with remarkable stability and grace.

Late one afternoon, as I was introducing the White Wings kits to the class (to encourage teamwork, and to get as much mileage as possible out of the kits, my plan was to have the kids work in pairs), Grant Plunkett approached my desk. Looking, as usual, like Eeyore, with his head hanging and his hands buried deep in his pockets, Grant mumbled something under his breath.

"I like . . . mmmmm . . . uhhhh . . . kind of . . ."

"What's that, Grant?"

"I said . . . mmmmm . . . uhhhh . . . brbble . . . good at it."

Talking with Grant could be frustrating, since he was not only educably mentally retarded, but prone to retreating into himself and ignoring the world around him. When he did interact, it was usually in the form of a criticism or complaint. So relentlessly bleak was Grant's outlook on life that the other students went out of their way to avoid him. Although he occasionally hung out with Rob Johnson and Pat Zerfas, Grant was basically a loner.

"Please, Grant," I said. "Slow down, speak clearly, and tell me what's on your mind."

He lifted his head slightly. "I like doing this stuff."

That surprised me. I didn't think Grant liked *anything.* "You mean models? Airplanes?"

He nodded.

"Have you ever done this before?" I asked.

"Uh-huh. I'm pretty good at it, too." He picked up one of the kits, looked it over longingly, and then placed it back on my desk.

"Would you like one of these, Grant?"

He nodded again, and then he did something remarkable, something I'd almost never seen him do. He smiled. "Can I take it home with me?"

"Wouldn't you rather have a partner?" I asked.

Grant shook his head vigorously. "I'll help someone later, but I want to take one home, first."

I looked at the kit. The directions alone would take Grant the better part of a night to read. I envisioned him opening the box, fumbling with the various pieces, struggling with the instructions, and giving up. At best, I envisioned him bringing in a horribly mutilated plane, something that looked like it had already crashed. On the other hand, I figured there was nothing to lose. This kid generally did not talk at all. He was unreachable. I had tried everything with Grant. I had joked with him, teased him . . . I'd been gentle and harsh with him . . . I had tried being his father and his brother and his friend. Absolutely nothing had worked. As far I could tell, he was just a kid collecting dust. So why not give him his own kit? Why not let him try? This was one of the very few times I'd seen Grant get excited about anything. Maybe I'd been wrong. Maybe there was more to Grant than met the eye.

"All right," I said. "If I let you take this home, are you really going to build it?"

"Uh-huh."

"And you'll bring it back into class?"

"Uh-huh."

"You have everything you need at home to put this thing together?"

"Yup."

"Okay, Grant. You can have it."

I handed the kit to him. He took it, but didn't move.

"What's wrong, Grant?"

"Can I have two?"

"No, Grant, you can't have two. But I'll tell you what. If you do a good job with this one, I'll give you another one. Sound fair?"

"Yeah."

So Grant took the kit home, and sure enough, the very next day, he brought the finished product into class. A project that I thought would take him at least a week, if not a month, to complete had been accomplished in just a few hours. Far from the discombobulated mess I anticipated, Grant's plane was . . . well . . . *exquisite*. That's the only way to describe it. Like something off the shelf of a master craftsman, his model was perfectly symmetrical, every line and cut exactly where it was supposed to be. There were no globs of glue or paste, no splintered wings, no shredded fuselage. He'd painted it, too. As Grant walked through the room, proudly displaying his airplane, the rest of the kids in the class gawked in disbelief.

"Where did you learn to do that?" asked Stephanie Reinks.

"I don't know," Grant responded with a shrug. "I just know how to do it."

I was thunderstruck. Never before had I so completely misjudged a kid. I looked at Grant and saw Boo Radley, the misunderstood and hermetic character from *To Kill a Mockingbird*. A big, slow-witted kid who wouldn't hurt a fly, but who simply wasn't capable of communicating with people. What I didn't know was that Grant had the hands, and maybe even the eye, of an artist. Not an artisan—an artist. Oh, I'd seen him in wood shop, so I knew he was capable with a power sander and a saw and could even do some fine finishing work. But this . . . this was something else entirely.

"Grant, who taught you this stuff?" I asked.

"No one. I taught myself."

Suddenly it occurred to me: *This is what Grant does to pass the time.* He went home each night to that depressing house of his, with his poor, sick father, and behind closed doors he retreated into a fantasy world, a world of model airplanes and imaginary pilots and astronauts . . . a world in which he had a measure of control.

"You actually did this all by yourself, Grant?" A stupid question, really, because there was no one else at home to help him.

"Uh-huh."

"Did you get your homework done, too?"

"Uh-huh."

"That's great, Grant. That's fantastic. I'm proud of you."

"Thanks. Can I have another one?"

While a part of me fairly rejoiced over Grant's accomplishment, another part of me felt more than a little ashamed. I had never known what made Grant tick, and in fact I had stopped trying to find out. I'd given up on him, and now I realized what a mistake that had been. This kid had an extraordinary gift, and if not for his own perseverance, it might have gone unrecognized forever. I could take no credit. Grant had been practically invisible throughout the months of training, had seemed to make almost no progress. While most of the students had grown in ways large and small, Grant was stagnant.

"Yeah, Grant . . . you can have another one," I said. "But I want you to do something first."

"What?"

"I'd like you to work with the other students. They could really use your help."

"Okay."

With that Grant shuffled away and began circulating around the room, tutoring kids on the finer points of building paper airplanes. He turned out to be a wonderful teacher, calm and patient and understanding. Not once did he yell or laugh or otherwise insult anyone. He just helped.

Later we took a bunch of bed sheets and pieced them together and drew a map of the United States on the surface. Then we set up the sheets in the gym and staged a competition. The idea was to choose a particular state and then launch your plane with such accuracy that it would land exactly on that state. Planes, of course, were crashing all over the gym. Grant was the lone person who hit the bull's-eye. But there was one catch: He would only fly his classmates' planes. His own plane was perfect, and would surely have flown straight and true, but Grant refused to put it in harm's way.

"I don't want anything to happen to it," he said. "I'll fly theirs instead."

"Okay, Grant," I agreed. "That's fine."

I wasn't about to push him. Grant was helping his classmates; he was being part of the team. He had earned this moment.

20

From simple paper airplanes to sophisticated White Wings, and finally to model rockets—such was the arc of our training in rocketry and propulsion, the final stage of our preparation. There was something frightening about the notion of special education students working with flammable . . . even *explosive* . . . material, but it was unavoidable if we were to properly prepare for Space Camp. The trip to Huntsville was fast approaching, and there the kids would be required to build their own rockets, and to launch them into the southern sky. From the very beginning our strategy had been rooted in desensitization:

They have to swim at Space Camp? Fine, we'll make sure they know how to swim.

They have to understand thousands of acronyms? We'll memorize every last one of them.

They have to endure two intense shuttle missions? We'll simulate ten times that many before we leave.

They have to build and launch rockets? Uhhh . . . let me think about that one.

ROBYNN AND I took a trip to Colorado during spring break to meet with a representative of Estes, the world's most famous and successful manufacturer of model rockets. Estes, in fact, supplied all of the models to the Space & Rocket Center, which is why I thought they might be willing to cut us a deal. Really, all I wanted was a discount on a couple dozen kits for our students, so I thought it was strange that they wanted to meet with us in person. As it turned out, they had bigger plans in mind.

"Have you ever thought about doing a communitywide rocket launch?" asked one of their public relations representatives.

"It crossed my mind, but we just don't have that much money."

"I'll tell you what," he said. "If you guys are willing to take some pictures and put together an article that we can use in our company newsletter, we'll send you two hundred kits—rockets, engines, chutes . . . everything. How's that sound?"

I did the math in my head. Each kit cost approximately twenty dollars, much more for the larger models, like the nearly four-foot replica of the Saturn V that I hoped to include in the deal. So this was an offer of approximately four thousand dollars, plus shipping costs. It was, to say the least, extremely generous. The fact that organizing a communitywide rocket launch would be a huge and potentially problematic undertaking didn't deter us one bit.

"Sounds great," I said. "You've got a deal."

WHILE WAITING FOR the kits to arrive, we used a software program to study basic rocketry and propulsion. We discussed and analyzed the various types of rockets, explained the differences between the Mercury series and the Apollo series, for example. We talked about engines and how they were capable of lifting such a massive piece of machinery beyond the Earth's atmosphere. This wasn't advanced physics; rather, it was a very basic overview of a highly complicated subject. Still, it was more intellectually demanding than almost anything they had encountered in their high school careers. And yet they were unintimidated. They devoured the material . . . couldn't get enough of it.

"This is pretty cool," they'd say. And then they'd add, "When are the rockets coming?"

They came on a Tuesday in late March, approximately six weeks before we were to leave for Space Camp. A custodian knocked on the door of my classroom, poked his head in, and said, "Coach, you'd better come down to the loading dock."

"Why?"

"Because there's a truck parked there and it's marked 'Explosives,' and the driver says he has something for you. Keller's already down there, and I don't think he's too happy."

Of course not, especially since I hadn't told the principal about the community rocket launch (which was probably a mistake). Standing on that loading dock, staring down a truckload of explosives while some fifteen hundred kids attended classes just a few feet away . . . I could only imagine what was going through his mind.

"Scott, Rob . . . you guys come with me," I said. "I need your help."

Tom was waiting when we arrived.

"What in the hell are you doing?" he asked incredulously.

"Don't worry," I said, "we're not building a bomb." He didn't laugh, didn't even smile. So, as quickly as possible I tried to defuse the situation (so to speak). I told Tom we were planning a communitywide rocket launch as part of our Space Camp program, and that this was merely a delivery of a couple hundred rocket kits from Estes. "My idea is to have our kids work with middle school students and elementary school students in putting these things together," I explained. "Then we'll fire them all off."

For some reason Tom seemed to take little comfort in this information. In fact, his expression turned from one of anger to one of befuddlement. "You're going to do this in one day?"

"Yeah . . . great idea, isn't it?"

Tom rolled his eyes, and as he walked away I could hear him mutter under his breath, "Oh yeah, Mike. Just great."

Robynn and I sent out a memo to all of the elementary and middle schools in the district detailing our plan and offering the services of our students. In some circles, naturally, the plan was not warmly embraced: *Special ed students teaching little kids how to build rockets? Who's the genius behind this one?* For the most part, though, the response was positive. Our students worked on their own rockets during the day, and after school (the high school was the first to dismiss its students) some of them would volunteer to work with the younger kids. It was at once amusing and heartwarming to see them in action. Pat, Grant, and Rob worked as a team, and one day I watched them assist a group of third and fourth graders at Orchard Grove Elementary School, which was located in my neighborhood. These three boys, who had so often been a source of frustration to their own teachers, suddenly became teachers themselves, and I could hear them echoing things I had said:

"Take your time."

"Follow directions."

"Come on, kids . . . don't get too excited."

Remarkably, our students, so often tortured by impatience and hyperactivity and attention deficit disorder, presented an air of calm and control. They were so thoughtful, patient, involved. Robynn and I had been concerned that the entire project might backfire, that our students would be so jittery and anxious that they'd frighten or discourage the younger students. But it didn't work that way. Our kids were so laid back and relaxed that they set precisely the proper tone for a learning environment. To me, at least, it was a revelatory experience. Once again I had been reminded of just how much these students were capable of accomplishing—when they were given a chance.

The rockets were not exclusively cut-and-paste models. Some could be snapped together in a day, yes, but even those required a degree of skill, for the engine had to be inserted properly and the fuselage had to be shielded by the right amount of insulation. The parachute had to be neatly folded and packed. From Estes we learned a few tricks of the trade, such as pouring a little talcum powder on the plastic joint between stages, so that the rocket would pop open easily and allow the chute to be released. These were the fundamentals of model rocketry. Some of the kits were far more complicated. They had triple fins, double stages, payload compartments. There were rockets that contained miniature cameras. There were short rockets, long rockets, skinny rockets, fat rockets. Rockets that looked like space shuttles. And, of course, there was a Saturn V, exquisitely crafted by Karen Treffiletti, with the help of her two older brothers, who happened to be members of a rocketry club.

We adopted a laissez-faire approach to the project—we didn't force our students to work with the younger kids, and we didn't force the younger kids to work with us—and it all turned out beautifully. I did not hear a single complaint—not from our kids, and not from any teacher or student at the other schools.

LOGISTICALLY SPEAKING, A community rocket launch is no small endeavor. The fire department had to be informed and available, in the event that one of the rockets ignited a small fire of some type. The local airport had to be notified. We were in close contact with the National

Weather Service, so that we'd know whether rain or snow was anticipated, and how strong the wind would be blowing. We staged several
small test launches, not only to make sure the batteries and starters
worked but to make sure the kids understood the importance of following all safety procedures.

Eventually word leaked out to the local media. Okay, it didn't really
leak. We sent out press releases, and the response was, once again, enthusiastic. Not only would there be a few hundred local students and
parents, our press release explained, but the launch would also feature
a guest appearance by a real astronaut. That's right, Jack Lousma, whose
benevolence continued to astound, had agreed to take part in the rocket
launch. As an added inducement to the broadcast media, we offered to
build a model rocket for each local television station. The rockets, which
looked like space shuttles, would be decorated with the numbers of the
stations, and a reporter from each station would be invited to participate
in the countdown and launch of his rocket.

A week or so before the launch I called Dr. Muth, the man who once
had thrown my grant proposal into a garbage can, but who had later
become one of the strongest advocates of our program. Dr. Muth had
shown up at some of our events, and we had talked many times on the
phone in the previous months. I thought it was only fair to invite him
to the rocket launch, but when I called his home, Dr. Muth's wife explained that he recently had taken ill and was now hospitalized with
pneumonia. The next day I brought a card into school and asked all the
kids to sign it, which they were more than happy to do. As the card
circulated around the room, a voice rose from the back. It belonged to
Karen Treffiletti.

"Coach?" she said.

"Yes, Karen."

"I think we should give Dr. Muth the Saturn V." The room fell quiet
for a moment. The Saturn V was supposed to be the star of the rocket
launch. Impressive in every way, it promised to serve as a punctuation
mark for the accomplishments of our program. That Karen was willing
to part with something that obviously meant a lot to her, something she
had worked hard to create, was only somewhat surprising. Although
she could be a tiger, Karen was also a congenial and caring girl who
took her greatest pleasure in helping others.

"You'd really do that?" I asked.

Karen nodded.

"What about the rest of you?"

Slowly the students began to nod in agreement.

"Okay," I said. "I'm sure it'll mean a lot to him."

That was an understatement. Robynn and I brought the rocket to Dr. Muth in the hospital a few days later. He was pale and weak, his once robust frame now withering away.

"Dr. Muth," I said. "For all the work you've done on our behalf, and for helping us get into Space Camp, the kids would like you to have this."

I propped the Saturn V, now adorned with the signature of every student in the class, on the edge of his bed. Dr. Muth smiled and ran a frail hand along the side of the rocket. With tears welling in his eyes, he whispered, "Thank you. You didn't have to do this."

"I know. It wasn't my idea. The kids insisted."

We excused ourselves a few minutes later, after Dr. Muth had fallen asleep. As it turned out, that was the last time I saw him. We left for Space Camp a few weeks later, and he passed away shortly after we returned. I remember attending his funeral and feeling not so much sadness as gratitude—for I was lucky to have known him, and I was fortunate to have had an opportunity to thank him for all he had done for our program, and for our students . . . kids he didn't really even know, and had no obligation to help. Gruff as he might have sometimes been, Dr. Muth was one of the good guys.

WE HELD THE launch at Forest Hills Northern Middle School, on a Saturday morning in late April; it was a brisk spring day that felt more like late winter. In order to keep things moving, two launch pads were employed. It wasn't advisable to launch more than one rocket simultaneously, but at least this way we wouldn't waste time setting up after each launch. Instead, while one rocket was launched and recovered, we could prepare for the next launch from the second pad.

Our plan was to begin the day with a special launch featuring Jack Lousma. Lewis Dayhuff had volunteered to build a model of the SR-71, a sleek stealth fighter that was used primarily for reconnaissance, and a full-size replica of which was displayed at the Space & Rocket Center.

The SR-71 was one of the most complicated and delicate models in the Estes portfolio, but I figured if anyone was capable of putting it together (aside from Grant Plunkett, of course), it was Lewis. He had an artist's eye and an artist's hands. Unfortunately, he also had the temperament of an artist, so it was certainly possible that he'd end up smashing the kit in frustration. I had told Lewis ahead of time that I was too busy to help him on this project, and he said that he understood. He never talked about it during the days leading up to the launch, did not reveal the progress he was or was not making. But when he arrived on the morning of the launch, Lewis carried with him a finished SR-71. And it was gorgeous. In fact, I'm not sure that even Grant could have done a better job.

"Lewis," I said as I looked at the model. "That's beautiful."

"Thanks."

"No . . . I mean it. It's perfect. In fact, it's too perfect to launch. Let's save it."

Lewis frowned. "Uh-uh. I'm giving it to Jack."

So that's the way the day began, with Lewis Dayhuff and Jack Lousma walking out to the middle of the soccer field, to the launch pad. Trailing behind them, I kept asking Lewis if he was sure the plane was ready to go.

"You packed the chute?"

"Yes, Coach."

"Insulated the fuselage?"

"Uh-huh."

"Talcum powder?"

"Coach!"

A crowd of several hundred parents and students and administrators had gathered by the time we reached the launch pad. Jack took the plane from Lewis, caressed it gently, and said, "Man, you must have put a lot of time into this, huh?"

"I guess so."

"And you're sure you want to launch it?"

Lewis smiled. "Yes, sir."

"Okay, then . . . let's do it."

The two of them placed the SR-71 on the launch pad (the rocket was held in check, vertically, by a thin metal rod), and then each of them, the astronaut and the juvenile delinquent—the kid everyone, including myself, had nearly written off—placed a hand on the ignition switch.

"You start," said Jack.

Lewis nodded. *"Ten! Nine! Eight!"*

The crowd picked up the countdown from there . . .

"Seven! Six! Five!"

I closed my eyes and began to pray. *Please let it fly . . . please let it fly . . .*

"Four! Three! Two!"

Please . . . please . . .

"One!"

Please . . .

"Blast off!"

I opened an eye and saw Jack and Lewis lean into the ignition switch. There was a pause, complete silence as the crowd held its breath, and then . . .

WHOOOOOOOSH! The SR-71 jumped off the launch pad and roared into the sky. It flew high and straight, at one point disappearing completely from sight, as the crowd exhaled, then began clapping and cheering and whistling. After a minute or so the model reappeared, floating beneath a fully deployed parachute. There was more applause, then Jack Lousma gave Lewis a pat on the back.

"Fine job, son," he said.

Lewis shrugged. "Thanks."

It was not Lewis's style to reveal any emotion, except anger, of course. But I could tell he was happy. I could tell he was proud.

THE DAY WAS an unqualified success, despite the fact that we managed to launch only about seventy-five of our nearly two hundred rockets. There simply wasn't time for more than that. A few drifted far off-course, and some were destroyed when either their parachutes failed or insulation was not sufficient. But that was to be expected. That's the way Goddard and von Braun learned about rocketry and propulsion: by thinking, building, *doing*. By failing and trying again. Overall it was a wonderful experience, not only because it was educational but because it was an event that brought a community together. And our kids, so accustomed to being overlooked or ignored or forgotten, were at the center of that event.

The day ended spectacularly, and hilariously, with the launching of the rockets dedicated to the three local television stations. Channel 8 went first. The reporter stepped up, hit the switch, and the space shuttle soared into the sky. *One for one*, I thought. Next up was a reporter from Channel 3. His shuttle, too, lifted off without incident.

Two for two.

Last was Channel 13, which had already demonstrated its support of our program by agreeing to dispatch a reporter to Huntsville when we went to Space Camp. This time the station was represented by a different reporter, a nice guy I knew from his coverage of various sporting events. I explained to him the procedure for launching the rocket, and he stepped forward and placed the shuttle on the pad. Apparently, though, the rod had somehow loosened, probably from the cumulative shock of having been involved in so many launches in one day, and now it was leaning at a slight angle (although we didn't realize it at the time). As the reporter simultaneously provided running commentary and hit the switch, the rocket fired and instantly became a weapon. It left the pad with a *WHOOSH!* . . . and headed straight for the reporter's partner, a cameraman for Channel 13.

That evening on the news, viewers of Channel 13 were treated to the sight of a rocket zeroing in on the camera, as if attacking, and then the camera spinning and tumbling as the hapless cameraman fell to the ground, safe but scared half to death. In the background could be heard the voice of a certain special education teacher screaming, "Check the pad, for God's sake!"

Afterward, as we cleaned up, some of the parents came up to Robynn and me and offered their congratulations and thanks. At the same time, the kids hung out nearby, talking and joking with each other in that kinetic way that teenagers have. I couldn't help noticing that we were all one team now, but two distinct groups: teachers and parents over here . . . students over there. I could tell some of the parents, the ones who had always been so supportive and caring, wanted to rush up to their sons and daughters and grab them and hug them and kiss them, and in fact that is precisely what they were accustomed to doing. They were used to smothering their kids with affection and scooping up the detritus of their mistakes and maladjustments. Now, though, they stood back. They watched. And it seemed to me that maybe that's what this launch was all about: the kids standing on their own two feet, weaning themselves from their parents, and distancing themselves from their teachers.

"You know what?" I said to Robynn.

"What?"

"They're ready."

ANOTHER EVENT THAT illustrated just how far our class had come, and how much the students had evolved and matured, was the Forest Hills Northern spring semiformal, an annual dance sponsored by the junior class. Since Robynn and I had been asked by some of the kids on the planning committee to serve as chaperones for the dance, we naturally tried to recruit some of our special ed students.

A year earlier such an effort would have been pure folly, so convinced were the kids of their own worthlessness, so determined were they to be invisible.

"Why bother?" they would have said. "So we can get picked on?"

Any type of interaction with mainstream students was generally viewed as painful, and thus something to avoid. The cafeteria, gym class, the hallways . . . these gathering places were harsh enough . . . but a dance? Please! For our students to attend a dance would have been an exercise in masochism. That's the way they saw it, anyway, and I can't say their views were completely without merit.

Now, though, things had changed. The Space Camp training program had given them, perhaps for the first time, a measure of confidence and security, and with that came a willingness to drop their guard. When Robynn and I asked if they might like to come to the dance, they reacted not with sarcasm or anger, but with curiosity. They wanted to know whether a date was required, or whether it was acceptable to go solo (it was). They wanted to know how they should dress. They wanted to know what the music would be like. We answered as enthusiastically as possible, but tried not to force the issue. If they wanted to attend the dance, they'd have to make the decision on their own.

Scott Goudy was the first to commit, although this was no great shock since he mixed comfortably with regular ed students and, more important, had a steady girlfriend and an attendant level of responsibility and expectation. More impressive was the news that Mark Tyler had bought a pair of tickets—and his date would be Sheila McHugh, another of the students in our program. Steve Bennett also decided he wanted to go, as did Stephanie Reinks and Marion Mills. By the night of the dance' (held just a couple weeks after the community rocket launch), approximately half of our students had purchased tickets.

Marion and Stephanie were the first to arrive, and I have to admit that my initial reaction, upon seeing them in crisp, bright dresses, with their makeup carefully applied and their hair so neatly coiffed, was complete and utter shock.

Hey, our kids clean up pretty good!

I wasn't alone in this response, for it was obvious as the kids arrived that they surprised themselves, too. Although they saw their classmates every day in school, they did not see them like *this*, and the impact was quite dramatic.

"Wow," Steve Bennett said as he walked into the cafeteria (which had been transformed into a dance hall). His jaw dropped, and then, as if recognizing this was a moment that begged for some sort of performance, he suddenly became Charles Boyer, adopting a French accent and a ludicrously debonaire demeanor.

"Mademoiselle," Steve said, stroking an imaginary mustache and then taking Stephanie's hand in his. *"You look so beautiful."*

Stephanie giggled. It was obvious she enjoyed the attention. "Thank you very much."

Steve then walked over to a stand where flowers were being sold and purchased gifts for both Stephanie and Marion.

"For you two lovely ladies," he said with a deep bow. Then he held out two wet and wilting carnations, which Stephanie and Marion graciously accepted. *"Sweet flowers for sweet girls. Appropriate, no?"*

Scott and his date were among the last students to arrive, which didn't surprise me at all since Scott was habitually tardy, thanks to an ongoing love affair with his most prized possession: a ten-year-old truck he had bought with his own money and restored with his own hands. Scott adored that truck, despite the fact that it was forever breaking down and causing him immeasurable grief. Rather than borrow his father's car or rent a nice set of wheels for the dance, Scott insisted on subjecting his girlfriend to a jittery ride in his pickup. When they walked into the cafeteria, Scott's hands blackened, his face smeared with grease, it was pretty clear the truck had betrayed him again.

"What happened?" I asked.

Scott frowned. "Battery problems."

His hair was matted, his shirt stained with sweat, and he smelled like gasoline. None of which seemed to bother him or his girlfriend in the least. She was a sweet girl, one of the nicest kids in the whole school, as a matter of fact, and I think she found everything about Scott to be endearing—including his devotion to his truck, which really was nothing more than an attempt to be self-sufficient . . . to be a grown-up.

As is usually the case with high school dances, it took a while for the kids to loosen up. Inhibitions typically keep the dance floor clear for most of the first hour or so, and this event was no different. It was Robynn, predictably, who gave the party just the spark it needed; a live wire by any reasonable definition of the term, she also happened to be a seasoned veteran of summer stock theater and a seriously accomplished dancer. As such, Robynn lived for occasions such as this.

"Come on," she said, taking me by the arm. "Let's grab a dance and try to get these kids moving."

Now, I'm not bad on my feet, but I'll never be mistaken for Fred Astaire, that's for sure. Fortunately, the music was slow and all I had to do was shuffle back and forth a little. Before long we had company, including Steve Bennett, who elbowed me in the side as he glided past with a girl on his arm and said, with a wink and a smile, "See, I can do this, Coach."

As the band segued into a song made famous by the Carpenters, "We've Only Just Begun," I spotted Stephanie and Marion sitting together at the edge of the dance floor. While they laughed and chatted, a skinny, blond-haired boy approached from the rear. I recognized him immediately: He was a member of the football team. Though he lacked talent and size (he was perhaps five feet nine and weighed less than one hundred fifty pounds), this kid gave up nothing in the courage department, which was evident not only on the football field, but at this very moment, as the object of his affection, Stephanie Reinks, unfolded her legs and stood up . . . and up . . . and up . . . until, like a mountain, she towered above him.

Unfazed, he took her hand in his and the two of them walked slowly, silently, to the middle of the dance floor, the oddest but cutest couple in the world. Smiling so hard that it looked as though her face might actually break, Stephanie leaned forward and rested her head on the boy's shoulder; he gently placed an arm around her waist, and the two of them began to sway as the band played on . . .

PART

THREE

21

The scene at the airport in Grand Rapids on Sunday morning can best be described as "barely controlled chaos." Darcy was accompanying us on the trip to Huntsville, and she was now experiencing considerable anxiety and guilt. It wasn't so much that there was cause for concern over the well-being of Shawn and Ryan—the boys were staying with Darcy's sister, whom they knew and liked, and who was, quite frankly, a world-class baby-sitter. It was simply that Darcy had never been away from our children for any length of time. The fact that she abhorred flying only added to her nervousness. I must admit, I wasn't crazy about leaving them behind either, and looking at Robynn, hugging her kids, it was obvious she was experiencing a similar level of ambivalence.

Cold as this may sound, though, separation anxiety was a luxury we could not afford to indulge. There simply wasn't enough time. Our focus, by this point, was a different set of kids—the students—and as they streamed through the airport doors, with their parents and siblings in tow, and in some cases with enough luggage to see them through a month, rather than a week, on the road, I was struck by the enormity of this undertaking. And the attendant responsibility.

Steve Bennett was among the first to show up, his pockets stuffed with the usual assortment of toys and gizmos.

"Hey, Coach," he said, before pulling out a kazoo and blowing it loudly enough to disturb just about everyone in the ticketing area. I rubbed my ears and held out an open hand.

"Give it to me."

"Why?" Steve asked, smiling.

"You know exactly why. None of that stuff is going on the plane. Now hand it over . . . or give it to your parents."

Steve pressed the kazoo into my palm, laughed, and walked away. I turned to Robynn and said, "Geez, I hope he doesn't pull any stunts like that on the plane."

Meanwhile, several of the kids were going camera-crazy, snapping off one photo after another. Pictures of their parents, pictures of their friends . . . pictures of the baggage handlers, for God's sake! *Click-click-click-click.*

"Guys, please . . . save your film," I said. "We're not even out of the airport yet."

I understood what was happening, that they were just trying to work off some of their nervous energy, and so I was reluctant to come down too hard on them.

For several of the parents it was an extremely emotional scene. Granted, we had some disinterested and even some bad parents among our group, mothers and fathers who really didn't give a damn what happened to their kids. But we also had some good parents, people who loved and supported their children regardless of the hell they were occasionally put through. While it's difficult being a teacher of special education students, it's even harder to be the parent of one. If these parents had a flaw, it was that they often smothered their children with affection and protection, thus making it almost impossible for the kids to stand on their own two feet.

One after another the parents approached Robynn and me. Some of them just wanted to say "thanks" or to offer words of encouragement. Others had questions, or they needed reassuring that their children, their precious cargo, would be all right. Brooke Fuller's mother wanted to make sure that her daughter would have access to a safe and sensible menu, one that wouldn't exacerbate the symptoms of Prader-Willi syndrome.

"Yes," I said. "It's all set."

"Are you sure?"

"I'm positive."

"And you'll keep an eye on her?"

"Of course."

"Because, you know, I'm really worried."

What could I say? I understood her concerns, and I sympathized with her. But the truth was, there was no way to guarantee that Brooke wouldn't encounter temptation, and in fact be overcome by it. There would be no padlocks on the refrigerators at Space Camp. To a great extent, Brooke, like all of the other kids, would be on her own. At Space Camp she would be held accountable for her own actions, perhaps for the first time in her life.

Nearly every parent, or set of parents, also presented me with a small bag containing the prescription medication that their children needed to cope with life on a daily basis. It's not unusual for special-needs students to be reliant on pharmaceutical help for their various afflictions, and I was certainly aware of the fact that many of our students were medicated. Typically, though, the kids would go to the nurse's office during the day to take their medication, so I'd never been directly involved in the process. I really did not understand the magnitude of their dependence until that morning, as I stood near the ticket counter and accepted dozens of tiny bottles, and literally hundreds of pills. Pills to help Marion Mills in her fight with leukemia; pills to help Steve Bennett deal with Tourette's. Ben Schmidt had pills for his chronic runny nose and eyes. There was a river of Ritalin, one of the most commonly prescribed drugs for kids suffering from attention deficit disorder, and just about everyone had some type of medication for motion sickness.

Throwing the bottles into a big carry-on duffel bag, I felt like a pharmacist . . . or, worse, a drug dealer. Some of the kids—a minority—were visibly upset as they watched the exchange of medication take place. They had wanted to go off their medication for the week, had said, in effect, "Coach, I don't need this stuff." Invariably, though, their parents had stepped in and said, "Oh yes, you do." I was inclined to side with the parents.

Most of the kids, to their credit, were well aware of what might have happened if they were to have suddenly stopped taking their medication. "Coach," they'd say. "Please make sure I get my meds, or I'll be worthless down there."

The weight of that bag could not be measured in mere pounds, for

Robynn and I had made a very difficult decision regarding the distribution of its contents. Rather than turning over the medication to the nursing staff upon arriving at Space Camp, as the rules dictated, we would be in charge of doling it out each day. This was, of course, a very fine ethical line we straddled, and perhaps crossed, but as I explained to Robynn, "If these kids have to run back and forth to sick bay so that they can get their pills from the nurse, they won't have any time for camp. They'll get distracted, and some of them will be so embarrassed that they won't even take their meds. It'll be a disaster."

So, kind of secretly, at the airport, we told the parents that we would be responsible for distributing medication to their children. To my surprise, they didn't seem to mind at all. When I think back on this now, I can't help but feel a bit ashamed. We took a huge risk, and probably a foolish one at that, but our motives were pure. We didn't want the kids missing out on anything; we didn't want them to feel any additional pressure. That this plan could have resulted in catastrophe only crossed my mind for a moment, before I blocked it out, rationalized it in this way: *If a kid has a problem and ends up in sick bay, he's probably not going to open up to some nurse he's never met. He's far more likely to be honest with me or Robynn. Then, if there's a real problem, I can take the kid to sick bay, meet with a nurse or a doctor, call the kid's parents, and make sure he gets the proper treatment.* I honestly believed that we were doing the right thing. Aside from their parents, no one knew these kids better than me and Robynn. We didn't need a nurse to be the gatekeeper on their medication.

BEFORE BOARDING THE plane, we passed out tickets and gave the kids their seat assignments. A predictable amount of grousing and grumbling ensued, but thankfully it did not escalate into the sort of leather-lunged assaults we had so often seen and heard in our classroom. The reason was simple: They were too nervous to be angry. If they were unhappy with their seats, it was only because they wanted to be close to me . . . or to Robynn . . . or to Darcy. In the tense moments before their first trip on an airplane, these kids, who so often wore a facade of toughness, of self-reliance, wanted nothing so much as the comfort and security that comes with being in proximity to an adult. This was even true of Lewis Dayhuff, the only student who had no one to hug or even bid him farewell as he walked down the jetway. Lewis's foster parents had simply dropped him off in front of the airport. More so than any other student in the class, Lewis was alone, and as I watched him wander around the terminal, looking at his classmates, his teammates, surrounded by their families (dysfunctional or otherwise), my heart ached. What a lousy hand this kid had been dealt. That he was here at all, about to leave for Space Camp, was a small miracle, testament more to his own strength of will than anything we had done for him. Lewis was truly a survivor.

About the only kid who didn't seem concerned about his seat assignment was Steve Bennett. Having grown up in an affluent family, Steve was the lone member of our group who was something of a globetrotter. He was no stranger to air travel, a point driven home within minutes after he boarded the plane. As the other kids nervously fiddled with their safety belts and armrests, Steve wandered about the cabin, chatting with the flight attendants, asking them if there was any room in first class, bragging about his destination.

"You know . . . we're going to Space Camp," Steve announced. The flight attendants, professionals all, just smiled and responded with, "Really? That's very nice. Please take your seat." Steve complied, but not before poking his head into the cockpit. "Hey, Mr. Pilot!" he shouted. "Looks a little like the space shuttle in here, huh?"

The pilots, too, were calm and cool, unflappable even when a kid with Tourette's syndrome invaded their space. They gave Steve a quick tour of the cockpit, laughed at a few of his jokes, and sent him back to his seat, a happy and satisfied customer.

Before takeoff, as the flight attendants recited the usual list of precautions and emergency procedures, the cabin became a very serious place. Most adults ignore this presentation, preferring instead to nap or read a newspaper. Our kids, however, hung on every word.

"Don't go too fast," Stephanie said at one point. "I don't want to miss anything."

Meanwhile, Steve, ever the big brother, repeated the instructions aloud, not to be a pain in the neck, but just to make sure that Ben Schmidt, who was seated next to him, would hear everything. This much was certain: In the event of a crash, our kids would be the most well-prepared passengers on the plane.

The tension in the cabin was palpable as we rolled down the runway.

Some kids smacked their gum and closed their eyes. A few seemed to be praying. To be honest, I took some comfort in their discomfort, because it meant that they were far too preoccupied with their own fear to pull any sorts of pranks. We had talked to the kids in great detail about how they should behave on the flight, and what would and would not be tolerated. This may sound ridiculous, but we actually warned the kids not to make any jokes about hijacking or blowing up the plane. Common sense prevents most people from even considering such an outrageous action, but with our kids, the "edit" button sometimes malfunctioned; the most inappropriate behavior was always a possibility.

"No one will think it's funny," I had said to the class, although my eyes were locked on Steve. "If you tell someone you have a gun in your pocket, just because you want to get a laugh, you won't be sent home. You'll go to jail. Trust me on that one."

Apparently, they got the point, because the first leg of our journey, a short hop from Grand Rapids to Chicago, was uneventful, less so, anyway, than the layover itself, during which half the students immediately ran to a nearby bank of pay phones and tried to call their parents so they could deliver the startling news that indeed they were still alive!

"Guys," I said, incredulously. "That was a twenty-five minute flight. Your parents won't even be home from the airport yet. Why don't you wait until we get to Huntsville?"

Layovers, I have come to realize, are the bane of anyone chaperoning a group of students. In a vast, crowded, public setting, such as O'Hare International Airport, nothing good can happen. There are endless opportunities to lose kids, misplace kids, and for kids to find trouble large and small. Looking at Andrea Burke, I thought, *This girl couldn't get home from the Grand Rapids planetarium. How would she get home from Chicago?* The very thought of one of our kids drifting away from the group and catching the wrong moving walkway made me shudder.

This being our first trip to Space Camp, we naturally kept the students on a short leash, but perhaps not short enough. When Steve, Ben, and Scott failed to return from a bathroom break after more than fifteen minutes (our layover was only scheduled to last forty-five minutes), I became concerned. Maybe someone was sick. Maybe they had decided to go for a little unauthorized stroll. Maybe they had wandered onto the wrong plane!

As I jumped out of my seat and began jogging toward the men's room, Ben Schmidt walked out, smiling as always.

"Ben," I said. "What's going on? I've been worried about you guys. Where are Scott and Steve?"

Ben gestured over his shoulder, toward the bathroom. "They're talking to some guy in there."

"Who?"

Ben shrugged. "I don't know."

I envisioned the worst: Scott and Steve cornered by a security guard after wreaking some sort of havoc in the men's room—maybe Steve plugging the toilets with paper towels or something. I rushed in, and there, standing near a sink, arms folded across his chest, chatting casually, pleasantly, with Steve Bennett and Scott Goudy, was a man I recognized instantly as Steve Fisher, the head basketball coach at the University of Michigan. Fisher had been in the spotlight a lot lately, since his team had just won the NCAA championship, and Steve and Scott had recognized his face from watching the Final Four on television. Most kids would have given the man some privacy, especially in the bathroom. At the most, they would have said hello, maybe asked for an autograph. But not our kids. They had simply walked up and introduced themselves (at what point during the coach's visit to the bathroom this introduction occurred, I didn't know; quite frankly, I didn't want to know).

I stepped in front of Steve and Scott, sort of elbowed them out of the way, and apologized to Fisher for their inconsiderate behavior.

"No problem," the coach said. Fisher had a reputation for being warm and fuzzy, and I saw nothing to refute that assessment. Here he was, stuck in an airport, out on yet another recruiting trip, cornered by a group of overzealous teenagers, and he wasn't the least bit resentful or rude. Quite the opposite, in fact. "These guys were telling me all about your trip to Space Camp," he added. "It sounds just wonderful."

He shook my hand, said good-bye and good luck, and went on his way. I admonished the kids for bothering such a busy man and, more important, for failing to return from the bathroom in a prompt and timely manner. I have to admit, though, that a part of me wanted to applaud their behavior. With the notable exception of Steve Bennett, these kids were painfully introverted around people they did not know. But here they were, chatting up a Big Ten basketball coach, one of the top guys in the game, shooting the breeze as if they were old buddies. That took a lot of confidence, and confidence was something we'd need at Space Camp.

IT WAS SEVERAL hours later, following a flight from Chicago to Atlanta, another layover, and a short hop from Atlanta to Huntsville, that we finally found ourselves flying in above the bright red clay of northern Alabama. I had hoped that our approach would take us past the Space & Rocket Center, but it didn't; however, we did fly right over the Redstone Arsenal, which was an impressive sight in its own right. The students were more attuned to the topography, to the seemingly endless sprawl of farms. These were Midwestern kids, after all. To them, cotton was something found in their clothes. They'd never seen it before it was picked. It was all so new, so fascinating.

As the plane taxied back up the runway to the Northwest Airlines terminal, I looked out the window and noticed some of the airport employees in their sweat-soaked uniforms, and suddenly I remembered something important, something the kids might not find so appealing. Alabama in the springtime was not exactly like Michigan in the springtime. It was hot. In fact, the weather could be positively stultifying. I wondered how they would react to that first blast of tropical air when they stepped off the plane. Would they gasp in disbelief and say, "Oh, man . . . this sucks!" Or would they think it was kind of neat?

Because we had flown in on a small plane, we did not have access to a jetway. Instead, we stopped on the tarmac and disembarked in the open air. As we walked out the door and down a rickety set of stairs, I could see that some of the kids were shocked by the heat and humidity. It had to have been at least ninety degrees, and the air was so thick even the slightest movement prompted a flood of perspiration. I didn't say anything about it. I just told the kids to keep moving. They shuffled along, quietly wilting beneath the afternoon sun. Finally, just before we entered the terminal, Steve Bennett broke the silence.

"Hey, Coach?"

"Yes?"

"Can we go swimming?"

I looked at Robynn. We both laughed. At least it wasn't a complaint, just a request . . . and not an unreasonable one at that.

"Not today, Steve. We've got work to do."

22

A s we waited outside the airport for a bus that would take us to the U.S. Space & Rocket Center, our group began to expand. Students from all over the country seemed to be arriving at the same time, and it wasn't long before our kids were engaged in conversation with the young men and women against whom they would soon be competing. I sensed a level of tension in the air, not only because they were from different backgrounds, different cultures, but probably because they all wanted the same thing: to be named the very best team at Space Camp.

A certain quirkiness is not at all unusual among students at Space Camp. They're not just bright and affluent—in many cases they're unusually gifted, and their deep interest in science and technology lends them an air of eccentricity. Kids who might be perceived as oddballs in the halls of their own schools fit in perfectly at Space Camp, for they are surrounded by students just like themselves. The team from Forest Hills Northern High School—the group wearing the Burger King T-shirts—did not fit the usual mold, and their differences were immediately apparent to the other campers. In fact, some of them seemed downright amazed that we'd even been invited.

"Is he on your team, too?" one boy said, gesturing toward Ben Schmidt.

Steve Bennett, with a chip resting firmly on his shoulder, was quick to respond.

"Yeah, he is. Why?"

"But he has Down's syndrome . . . doesn't he?"

"Uh-huh. So what? You have a problem with that?"

The kid sighed and walked away. As he rejoined his classmates, I heard someone say, "Wonder who's gonna zip up his flight suit for him," followed by callous laughter. I'm sure some of our kids heard this, too (though, thankfully, Ben wasn't one of them), but they didn't react. Not even Steve, who took such pride in playing the role of Ben's protector. Our kids had always been resilient—they had to be in order to get this far in life—but now they were routinely displaying a level of maturity and restraint that I'd never thought possible. As the laughter continued, I saw on the faces of some of our boys—Steve, Scott Goudy, Rob Johnson—a look of, well . . . *condescension*. A look that seemed to say, *"Is that your best line? If so, then this is going to be a pretty good week."* Our kids had heard it all before. Heck, they'd *said* it all before. They gave as good as they got.

"Who's gonna zip up his flight suit?"

To our kids, this wasn't even an insult; it was amateur hour, and it did nothing to intimidate them.

DRIVING INTO THE Space & Rocket Center, we passed a full-size replica of a Mercury rocket, a jaw-dropping spectacle that even today leaves most visitors breathless. But it was the futuristic space habitat that really captured the attention of our team. Not nearly as impressive from the outside as the Mercury, the space habitat was a bulbous gray building that looked like something left over from the set of *2001: A Space Odyssey*, or, perhaps, *Star Wars*. Which is to say . . . it looked vaguely artificial. I guess that's exactly what the kids liked about it, the fact that it seemed to have been lifted from their dreams, their imaginations, and placed right here in front of them. Unlike the Mercury, which was part of history and, therefore, just a little too . . . *real*. Moreover, the space habitat was going to be their home for the next week. They would sleep here, study here, go to the bathroom here. In essence, it was nothing more than a giant bunk—a place where campers could rest between activities. But, man . . . what a cool bunk it was.

"Oh, wow!" Scott Goudy said. "This is way better than it looked in the videos."

Inside, the kids were instructed to pick up their bed linens and team badges, drop off their luggage, then report back for the distribution of reading material. The sound of it—*reading material*—made me uneasy. Our kids had done their training. They were as well prepared as any team. And, yet, I couldn't help wondering how they would react when the reality of the situation settled in—when they realized that they'd be studying and working intensely for the better part of fifteen hours each day. Would they panic? Would they be angry? Most important of all, would they doubt themselves?

Interestingly, and encouragingly, they opened the books and began flipping pages, looking for material they recognized. I detected no apprehension, no fear, no resentment. It was too early to make any bold predictions, but they actually seemed more than just excited. They seemed confident.

The next phase of Space Camp orientation—and the first night was indeed a whirlwind of activity—involved something a bit more enjoyable. At least, that's the way it was intended. We were led to a big room, at the center of which was a huge pile of bright blue NASA flight suits. The kids had seen pictures of the uniforms during training, so they knew roughly what to expect, but seeing them in person, and having a chance to try them on . . . well, suddenly the experience of Space Camp became real.

"Pick out one that you like," one of the counselors said. "Because you'll be wearing it a lot this week."

The kids broke ranks and sprinted to the mound of flight suits. They started pulling them on, throwing them off, searching for just the right uniform. For most of them it didn't take long to find a suit that fit reasonably well, but there were two exceptions. The first was Stephanie Reinks, who had a difficult time because she was so tall and big-boned. Eventually, though, Stephanie found a flight suit that was at least functional, if not exactly a perfect fit. Less fortunate was Grant Plunkett. At nearly 250 pounds, and yet several inches south of the six-foot mark, Grant was every tailor's nightmare. Loose and baggy, the flight suits were designed with practicality and comfort in mind; they were, in a word, forgiving. You didn't have to be built like a model in order to wear one. But Grant proved too much of a challenge. Long after all of his classmates had selected their uniforms, Grant continued to sift through the pile. My heart ached for him. Here he was, the only kid in the entire camp who couldn't find a suit that would fit, and he happened to be a special-needs kid.

When it became apparent that his search was in vain, I walked over to Grant and put a hand on his back. "You know, Grant. The suit doesn't make the man."

He tossed a wrinkled uniform back onto the pile and stood up straight. "I know, Coach. Don't worry about it."

With that, Grant shuffled away and joined the rest of the Burger King team. That night we got him a T-shirt emblazoned with the words "Space Camp," and the next afternoon a generously cut flight suit mysteriously appeared. It was far from an ideal fit, but at least it was usable, and Grant would have it for our missions. Unfortunately, the uniform would not arrive in time for the team photo, which was to be taken Monday morning, but Grant didn't appear to be distraught, or even disappointed. Rather, he took the news in stride, which I thought was rather remarkable for a young man who had usually worn his depression on his sleeve. This was an unfortunate, embarrassing start to the week, and yet he handled it with an admirable amount of grace.

A GROUP ORIENTATION, for all of the approximately two hundred students attending Space Camp that week, was conducted in a large education room shortly before dinner. Here the students were introduced to each other, as well as to their counselors and to some of the camp administrators. They also were given a detailed schedule of the week's activities, and it was, to say the least, ambitious. Each day would begin with a wake-up call at six-thirty A.M., followed by breakfast at seven. By eight o'clock, the students would be fully engaged in classes or competition. On most days they'd be busy until the minute their heads hit the pillow—at around ten-thirty P.M. Our kids were unfazed by the demands of the schedule, for it contained no surprises. We had told them repeatedly that Space Camp would be the most demanding week of their lives, and by the time we left Grand Rapids, they didn't doubt us.

There was, however, one surprise, and it was a whopper. Before dismissing the students from the orientation meeting and sending them on to the cafeteria, one of the counselors announced that there would be a short "entrance test" later that evening.

"Nothing too heavy," he said. "Just some basic questions about science, space, and technology."

The idea behind the quiz, we later learned, was to give the staff some sense of the abilities of the students, to help determine which position on each mission team might be most appropriate for a given student. For example, there would be twenty-five questions on the exam, and it was presumed that the student who scored highest on a team would be the most logical candidate to play the role of pilot, commander, or flight director, simply because he or she obviously already knew a lot about the subject matter. The reasoning was flawed, of course, because there was more to being a pilot or commander or flight director (or any other position) than having the ability to answer trivia questions. I understood what they were trying to do: give the most capable students a chance to accept more responsibility, while preventing less capable students from getting in over their heads. Since the Space Camp staff would be assigning positions, they wanted to have at least a few tools at their disposal in trying to make the right choices. The entrance exam was such a tool. Still, something about it rubbed me the wrong way.

For one thing, we had no idea that it was coming. Either we hadn't been told, or Robynn and I had somehow overlooked it. The cause was less important than the effect: Our students would react to the news of a "pop quiz" with far more anxiety and trepidation than the rest of the students at Space Camp. Special education students tend to get very nervous before taking tests, and when they haven't had sufficient notice before the exam, the results can be disastrous. Panic attacks, mental blocks, even emotional outbursts—all are possible in this scenario. Robynn and I had spent months training these kids, preparing them, walking them through every minute of Space Camp so that nothing would come as a surprise once they were here. And now? Less than an hour after we arrive? A test?!

This was not good. This was not good at all.

"Coach! You never said anything about a test!" Karen Treffiletti shouted as we walked to the cafeteria. Clearly she was upset, as were most of the kids.

"I know, Karen. I'm sorry."

"But you never told us what to study!"

"That's because I don't know what's on the test. I didn't even know there would be a test."

The students were gathered around me, shaking their heads, moaning, whining, complaining.

"How many more tests are there before we get started?" asked Lewis Dayhuff, his tone more than a little sarcastic.

"This is the only one," I said. "Just do the best you can."

Lewis shook his head angrily. "It's not fair."

I knew I had to say something to get the kids back on track. They were right—it wasn't fair. But this was no time for self-pity. They had to be strong. So I cut them no slack.

"You guys have worked hard to get to this point," I began. "You've surprised a lot of people. But you know what? None of that means anything if you quit now. We've taught you everything you need to know. You can handle this test—regardless of what's on it."

They stared at the floor, scuffed their feet, did their best to hang on to their anger. "You want to be treated the same as everyone else here, right?" I continued. "You want to prove they're no better than you. Well, this is where it starts. Right here, right now."

Dinner that night consisted of hamburgers, hot dogs, and french fries, a classic All-American kids meal. And yet, our students ate almost nothing. They picked and poked at their food. While most of the campers chatted nonstop, filling the cafeteria with the noise and exuberance of adolescence, the members of the Burger King team sat stoically and silently at their table, looking as if they were awaiting execution.

"When do we have time to study?" Scott Goudy asked near the end of the meal.

I sighed. "You don't."

"None? Not even an hour or so?"

"Nope. Clean off your plate and let's go."

On the way to the testing room, Ben Schmidt waddled up behind me and threw an arm over my shoulder. "Don't worry, Coach. We'll do good."

I smiled. "I know, Ben."

"This is multiple choice, right?"

"I think so."

Ben's face lit up.

"Give me a pen! I'm good at making circles."

I had never been happier to have Ben as part of our team. He was unflappable, irrepressible, and his attitude was almost always upbeat. I pulled him close. "Thanks, Ben."

While passing out the test sheets, the counselors tried, rather unconvincingly, to make the case that it wasn't really a test. "It's more like a questionnaire," they professed. I had proctored a lot of tests and quizzes and exams in my career, and the atmosphere in this room was no different than it was in June of any school year, when students traditionally took final exams. I saw pencils being chewed, feet tapping rhythmically beneath desks, eyes wandering and darting all around the room.

As with any test, the proctors strolled up and down aisles to keep everyone on his or her best behavior. The only concession granted to our kids, based on their myriad learning disabilities, was permission for Robynn and me to help them with reading. Not that we were allowed to actually read the questions for them (nor would we be allowed to read manuscripts with them during simulated missions), but if one of them had a specific question regarding a difficult word, we could help. For example, one of the questions on the entrance exam asked for a definition of the term "LOS." When Rob Johnson got to that question, he raised a hand. "Coach," he said. "This is an acronym, right?"

I looked at one of the counselors, who nodded, thus giving me permission to provide Rob with that tidbit of information.

"Yes, Rob. It's an acronym."

"Oh, okay," Rob said excitedly. "I know what it means." The correct answer was "Loss of Signal," and Rob did indeed get it right, as did just about everyone else on our team. There were no set rules regarding the involvement of myself or Robynn; it was completely arbitrary. Truthfully, though, the kids asked for very little help. They simply didn't need it.

Thirty minutes after the tests had been distributed, one of the counselors announced, "Time's up." Most of our kids had already turned in their papers. They seemed calm, confident, poised. During the test itself they had neither panicked nor complained, which both surprised and delighted me. They were not good at disguising their emotions. If they had been stumped by the test, the frustration would have registered on their faces, but I had detected not even a trace of concern.

Afterward, as the room emptied and the campers went outside to unwind, I stopped one of the counselors in charge of the exam.

"You're going to grade these tonight, right?"

"As soon as we can, yes."

"When you get the results, can you let us know how we did? As a team?"

He smiled. "No problem."

Robynn and I joined some of the kids on the basketball court. Again, they seemed relaxed, almost pleased with themselves. I had looked at some of the questions and was confident that our kids knew the answers to most of them. It was all material we had covered in our training: *Who was the first man to walk on the moon? What does NASA stand for? Who was the first Russian in space?* Things like that. Very basic, elemental questions about space and science. So I asked the group how they felt about their performance. Most of them just shrugged. A few said they thought the test was pretty easy.

"Really?" I asked. "Anyone think they got every question right?"

Not a single hand went up, which I should have expected, but which worried me nonetheless.

Within an hour the verdict was in. A couple of the counselors pulled me and Robynn aside and said, with blank faces, "We have to tell you something."

Oh, brother, here it comes. The pressure of the test got to them and they all failed. God . . . we should probably just go home right now.

I swallowed hard. "Yes?"

The taller of the two counselors looked at his clipboard. "Out of twenty-five questions, your kids answered an average of eighteen point seven correctly."

Robynn and I exchanged glances. "That's not too bad . . . is it?" she asked.

The counselor looked up from his clipboard. "Actually," he said with a big smile, "that's the highest team average in the entire camp. We consider anything above thirteen or fourteen to be respectable."

I felt my heart beat in my temples. This was incredible. "Uhhhh . . . are you sure everyone took the same test?"

Both counselors laughed. "Yeah, I'm sure," the one with the clipboard said. "Your kids know a lot of stuff. They're going to do just fine here."

Although I had anticipated that we'd have a pretty good week, I was thoroughly unprepared for the shock of hearing that we had just outperformed some of the smartest students in the country. More than that—some of the smartest students in the *world* (groups from France and Costa Rica gave Space Camp an international flavor on this particular week). The news was so startling that at first I couldn't quite believe it. I wondered, *Is this some kind of cruel joke? Is it a trick? Is someone at Space Camp setting a trap to give our kids a false sense of security?* Pathetic, I know . . . and somewhat paranoid. But I really felt that way. Fortunately, Robynn was more firmly rooted in reality.

"Let's not read too much into this," she said. "Let's just accept it and be happy."

So that's what we did. We congratulated the kids, reiterated our confidence in their ability to compete with the best and the brightest, and then told them to get a good night's sleep, because tomorrow the week would begin in earnest.

Tomorrow, the scores would count.

23

My head hit the pillow around eleven-thirty Sunday night, but sleep did not come without a struggle. As I lay in bed with my eyes wide open, listening to the hum of an electric clock, envious of my wife, who dozed peacefully beside me, I could feel the anxiety taking root.

We had walked the kids back to the habitat earlier that evening and helped them get settled in their bunks. Months earlier, while planning this adventure, Robynn and I had toyed with the idea of rooming with our students, but ultimately we'd decided against it. For one thing, of course, we weren't alone on the trip. Having asked our classroom aides and my wife to be part of the entourage, the least we could do was provide adult accommodations at the Marriott. More to the point, though, if Robynn and I had bunked at the space habitat, it would have resulted in monumental embarrassment for our kids. Since none of the other groups shared lodging with their teachers, our presence would only have served to remind everyone that the team from Forest Hills Northern, the kids from Burger King, were not quite . . . *normal*. And that was the last image we wanted to promote.

As progressive and compassionate as we wanted to be, however, we still were more than a little concerned about how the kids would react, how they would behave (or misbehave) in our absence. Yes, they had been more mature in recent weeks and months, and they had conducted themselves admirably since our arrival in Huntsville. Still, all of my years as a special education teacher and coach had instilled within me an apprehension that wasn't easily dismissed. All of the good that we had accomplished could be wiped out in the blink of an eye—or at least in the small amount of time it would take our students to provoke some sort of a dispute with their fellow campers in the space habitat.

We had harped on this subject before leaving Grand Rapids, and reiterated our concern before leaving them Sunday night.

"When the counselor says, 'Lights out,' I want your butts in bed," I had told them. "I want you showered, and I want your teeth brushed."

If that sounds a bit too parental, well, it was nonetheless necessary. Our students were not always diligent about their personal hygiene, a fact that naturally contributed to the animosity directed at them by other students. In the confined atmosphere of Space Camp, such a cavalier attitude would lead to instant rejection, if not outright revulsion. Imagine the horror of having an embarrassed counselor corner you in a quiet moment and say, "Coach, I hate to tell you this, but . . . your kids stink." Nope. We couldn't allow that, and if we had to be a bit callous to make sure it didn't happen, to be certain that no one's sensibilities were offended, then so be it. In this first week, there was no margin for error.

So I tossed and turned, watching the minutes tumble away, thinking about the next day's schedule, wondering how our kids were sleeping, whether they were comfortable on those metal cots in the space habitat, hoping that no one was homesick, or just plain sick . . . hoping they remembered what we had said, and what was at stake . . . thinking, above all else, *Oh, man . . . in a few hours all hell is going to break loose. And there's nothing I can do about it.*

I don't know when I drifted off. I know only that the alarm rang at 5:30 A.M., and by 6:15 I was at the habitat, making sure the boys were up and showered and dressed; Robynn did the same with the girls. Our assistance, our *vigilance*, wasn't really needed. Proving once again how far they had come, the kids were ready to go by the time I arrived. They'd even made their beds!

Because team pictures were to be taken right after breakfast, the dress code on Monday morning was simple: flight suits. And yet, it was both odd and touching to see the way our students, so many of whom usually had little or no regard for their appearance, primping and posing before leaving the bunk. They tugged out wrinkles, brushed away lint and dust, and even used warm, wet wash cloths to dab at old stains. No one at Space Camp that week was prouder of their flight suits than our kids; they wanted to look perfect for the team photo. So fussy were they that several of them actually tucked napkins into their collars during breakfast to avoid spilling anything on their uniforms. A few refused to drink any of the various fruit juices served with the meal, fearing that these would produce the worst stains.

"Guys, come on," I said. "It'll come out in the wash."

They looked at me as if I were the one with the emotional problems: *How can you not understand, Coach?* I did, actually. It was no different than what happens when a kid puts on a football uniform for the first time, or a basketball uniform, or a baseball uniform, or a soccer uniform. Kids are transformed. They see themselves differently, think about themselves differently. I'd witnessed this peculiar phenomenon countless times over the years, but this was the first time I'd seen it in my special education students, and I have to admit it was startling.

The team photo was taken outdoors, in the bottom of a replica of a giant lunar crater. Everyone was on his or her best behavior, even Steve Bennett. The only disappointing thing about that photo, which still hangs in my office, is the fact that Grant Plunkett had to pose without a uniform. So that he wouldn't feel completely ostracized, Robynn and I declined to wear our flight suits for the photo. Instead, like Grant, we wore Space Camp T-shirts. I'm not sure how Grant really felt, but I do know that in that photo, surrounded by his friends and classmates, Grant looks pretty happy.

ALL OF THE campers were immersed without warm-up into the world of space and science on Monday. There were classes on acronyms and script reading and the job associated with each position during shuttle missions—all of which we had covered ad nauseam during the school year. The bulk of the day, however, was devoted to team-building activities in microgravity simulation. In other words . . . it was time to go swimming.

The teams gathered outside by the curb and waited for the buses that would take all of us to the athletic facilities at the University of Alabama-Huntsville. Our kids hung back and kept to themselves. At the front of the line I noticed students from some of the other teams looking over their shoulders, pointing, snickering, obviously cracking jokes. Their disrespect bordered on contempt—they didn't even seem to care whether they were seen or heard, and in fact their insensitivity quickly infected the whole group.

"Let's get the front seats," I heard one kid say. "Let the retards sit in the back."

Another made a snide comment about not wanting to be on the same bus as Ben, and our kids heard it. I could sense the tension rising. I could see it in the eyes of Steve Bennett and Scott Goudy, and especially in the way Lewis Dayhuff withdrew, pulled his arms tight around his body, as if shielding himself. Remarkably, they said nothing at all. Not a word. As the buses pulled up and threw open their doors and the campers began to board, one of the counselors approached me and Robynn.

"I'm sorry," he said sheepishly. "Do you want us to say anything to them?"

I looked at Robynn. She shook her head.

"I don't think so," I said. "Not right now. We actually expected some of this."

The counselor pursed his lips. His face reddened. "You know, if I were one of your kids, I think I'd walk over there and punch someone right in the mouth."

I winced. "Please . . . don't say that. That's how they used to be. That's the way they handled everything. They reacted exactly the way people expected them to react." I watched our team boarding the bus, politely, quietly, respectfully. "But they don't do that anymore. They've matured to the point where they can handle situations like this in an adult manner. The last thing I want to do is encourage them to use their fists to solve their problems. Most of them have been doing that their whole lives."

He nodded. "Okay. Just let me know if you need any help."

"Thank you."

The atmosphere on the bus was not unlike that of a team bus traveling to a football game: heavy with nervousness and anxiety. We were on our way to the first real test of the week: building tetrahedrons in a swimming pool. Ethereal moniker notwithstanding, in a few minutes we would all be vividly reminded of the competitive nature of Space Camp. As the bus rumbled on I became concerned that perhaps our kids were wrapped just a little too tight. Most of the campers had been here before and knew what to expect; at the very least, they were familiar with the *process* of competition, of expectations. They knew how to handle it. Our kids? I thought back to some of the more disappointing moments of the previous year—the first trip to the pool, the first timed practice mission—and I began to fret. *What if they panic? What if they forget that this is supposed to be fun?* I felt as though I had to do something to lighten the mood.

The bus driver was a grizzled Southern fellow of indeterminate age. With thin, gray hair and weathered skin, he looked as if he might have been in his sixties, although decades of doing real work might have added a few years to his appearance. He smiled as the bus bumped and rolled, and occasionally sang a line or two from one of the country-western songs crackling through the radio. Suddenly, the old Kenny Rogers hit "The Gambler" came on, and I just couldn't help myself. I stood up and walked to the front of the bus.

"Would you mind turning that up?" I asked.

He gave me a big smile. "Sure thing."

The driver cranked the knob and the song screeched through tinny speakers and rattled off the walls of the bus. Several of the campers squirmed in their seats; a few put their hands over their ears.

Since the bus also was used to give tours to visitors, there was a microphone perched alongside the driver's seat. "Mind if I use that?" I asked.

His smile broadened. "Be my guest, partner."

I keyed the mike once or twice, just to make sure it was working, and then, without so much as a mild warning, launched into the loudest, most pathetic rendition of "The Gambler" you'd ever want to hear. Or not want to hear.

"You've got to know when to hold 'em, know when to fold 'em."

While my students immediately started laughing out loud, and shouting, "Go, Coach!" the other campers, who were doubtless now convinced that the Burger King teachers were just as whacked as the Burger King team members, stared in disbelief.

I kept singing, louder and louder, faking the parts I didn't know, my voice cracking and straining. I walked up and down the aisle of the bus, clapping my hands, encouraging the kids to sing along. Ben was the first to join in, naturally, since he was completely uninhibited. Then Steve, and then Stephanie. Before long they were all singing, clapping, stomping their feet . . .

"*YOU'VE GOT TO KNOW WHEN TO HOLD 'EM, KNOW WHEN TO FOLD 'EM . . .*"

As they sang and laughed, the tension seemed to drain from their faces. Nervousness became relaxation, probably because the focus was no longer exclusively on them, but on me as well, the crazy coach with the microphone. What I wanted them to know, quite simply, was this: If anyone was going to make an idiot out of himself, or give the other campers reason to make fun of someone, it was going to be me. I think they appreciated that. It reminded them that Robynn and I were more than just their teachers; we were part of their team.

THE LOOSENESS OF the bus ride carried over to our performance in the first real competition of the week: constructing tetrahedrons underwater. In the locker room, as we all changed into swim trunks (teachers were allowed to be in the pool with their students, although strictly as spectators), the mood was decidedly light. The kids weren't exactly clowning around, but neither did they seem paralyzed with fear and anxiety. Ben Schmidt was so excited that he could barely sit still. He bounced around the locker room, shouting, over and over, "Coach, don't worry. I can hold my breath for a really long time!"

"That's good, Ben. If ever there was a time when I wanted to know that your lungs were good, it's right now."

I had planned to give some sort of a pep talk before we left the locker room, but it just didn't seem necessary. Admittedly, as I reflected on some of the dreadful performances we'd turned in during training—in particular, that first session at the Grand Rapids YMCA—my stomach knotted a bit. But then I remembered some of the other sessions, more recent practices during which we had worked seamlessly, flawlessly, and the trepidation melted away. If the kids thought they were ready, fine. Then they were ready. This was the start of a long, challenging week. Might as well just throw them in the water and see if they sink or swim . . . in a manner of speaking.

The tetrahedron competition was interesting on several levels, not the least of which was the fact that it required a greater combination of physical, emotional, and intellectual skills than any other event. That there would be no separate award presented to the winner of this competition didn't matter. It was the first real test of the week, and the performance of each team would be factored into that team's overall score to determine the winner of the top prize: Best Mission. In other words, the stakes were sufficiently high to produce an electric atmosphere around the pool.

We were one of the last teams to compete. The counselors instructed the kids to jump into the water in groups of five, then asked them to swim across the pool and back, just to be certain that everyone was competent. That task completed, they were lined up by the side of the pool and given their directions. The team would be divided into two groups of ten. Each group would use the supplied nodes and rods— which were piled on the deck—to construct a tetrahedron in the deep end of the pool. The faster of the two times would be the official result for the Burger King team. The groups were divided randomly, although we were fortunate to have a few of our strongest swimmers—Scott Goudy, Ben Schmidt, Steve Bennett—on one team. This greatly enhanced our chances of turning in a respectable performance. To be perfectly candid, that's about all I hoped for. Despite the fact that we seemed confident, I had no illusions about winning this contest—or anything else at Space Camp, for that matter. I hoped only for a good effort, one that at least reflected all the work we'd done, and the bond we had formed. Whether that put us in first place or tenth place was almost irrelevant.

The first group jumped into the water and waited for the counselors to give them the signal to begin. Scott looked at Steve and nodded. Steve looked at Ben and smiled. Stephanie Reinks, Rebecca Shriver, and Pat Zerfas were also part of this team. I couldn't help but notice how calm they all seemed, how perfectly at ease. As the counselor in charge of the competition finished his final instructions, the kids pulled down their goggles and took a few deep breaths. As with nearly everything at Space Camp, a countdown preceded the event.

"Five . . . four . . . three . . . two . . . one . . . *go!*"

The water boiled. Like a school of piranha, the kids from Burger King thrashed mightily, purposefully, and then disappeared beneath the surface. Once there, they collected themselves and began working smoothly. The piranha were replaced by dolphins, the most elegant and graceful creatures in the sea. Not a single node was dropped, not a single rod was misplaced. Components were passed from student to student, and messages, instructions, and encouragement were shared through sign language or telepathy, resulting in a gorgeous symphony of team-work. It was like nothing I had ever seen, or even imagined.

Thirty seconds passed without any of them coming up for air. Then forty-five seconds. Around the one-minute mark, with their lungs ready to burst, a few of them broke the surface for a quick gasp, but then they were gone again. Finally, with the clock showing 2:48, they burst out of the water together, all ten of them, holding the tetrahedron over their heads, smiling, laughing, sputtering, wheezing . . . and I swear it looked like the lost city of Atlantis rising out of the ocean.

They ripped off their goggles, rubbed their eyes, and caught sight of the clock.

"Oh, my God!" Stephanie screamed.

"Yeah!" added Steve.

Scott clenched a fist and smacked the surface of the water.

They knew . . . we all knew. This wasn't just a good performance. This was a great performance.

"Way to go, guys!" I shouted. But they didn't hear me. They were too busy hugging each other, exchanging high fives, celebrating. It was all the counselors could do to get them out of the pool so our second group could compete. And they did compete. That group, too, did a nice job, although the time was significantly slower than the first group. But there was no shame in that. As we found out just a short while later, when the last of the teams had completed the competition, we had recorded the fastest time of the day!

What an astounding development this was. There had been two tests in as many days, and the misfits from Forest Hills Northern High School . . . the students who really weren't even considered to be students at all . . . had received the highest grade in each. As we walked into the locker room to shower and change before catching the bus back to camp, I found myself fighting back images of our team sweeping all of the major awards that Friday. I imagined ticker tape parades back in Grand

Rapids, and a hero's welcome for all of us. Silly stuff, but it was hard not to dream. We were two-for-two in competition against a couple hundred gifted and talented students.

Anything seemed possible.

My fantasy was interrupted by the sound of a harsh voice, someone from one of the other teams leveling an insult at Rob Johnson and Lewis Dayhuff as they toweled off.

"You know," the voice said, "any idiot can swim. Let's see how you do when you have to go into a classroom."

I froze for a second, thinking, *The next sound I hear will be the sound of a body being thrown against a locker.* Once again, though, I had underestimated my own students. Lewis didn't move. Neither did Rob. Instead, they just ignored the kid and finished getting dressed. The only person who responded at all was Steve Bennett, who said, in a thoroughly dismissive, almost condescending manner, "Hey, buddy . . . look at the scoreboard on your way out."

Then I thought I heard a door slam, although it was hard to tell amid the laughter echoing off the locker room walls.

24

At breakfast Tuesday morning one of the counselors approached me with a clipboard. Her name was Vicky, and she was a small young woman with a big, friendly personality, and a Southern twang so sharp that when you engaged in conversation with her, you found yourself curling your vowels and talking like a native.

"Okay, here's what we're looking at," Vicky said. "You let me know if you have any complaints or suggestions."

Vicky then proceeded to read the list of position assignments for our first mission. After the entrance exam, Robynn and I had been asked to make suggestions, but we had decided that it would be best to let the counselors do their job, with little or no input from us. That's the way it worked for every other team, and we neither wanted nor expected preferential treatment. The lone exception to that rule was a request that Ben Schmidt not be assigned the role of pilot or commander—not because he wasn't capable of handling the job, but simply because Down's syndrome had a pronounced effect on his speech. Under the best of circumstances it was difficult to understand exactly what Ben was saying; in the heat of competition, while shouting through microphones, using precise, scientific language and hundreds of acronyms, Ben would be at an enormous disadvantage. It wasn't fair to ask him to accept that responsibility (although he surely would have), to place him in a position virtually guaranteed to cause him great embarrassment and to frustrate his teammates. We suggested that Ben be given a role in the space lab, where he'd have to complete challenging experiments, but where the deficiencies in his speech would not be a problem. The staff graciously agreed.

I had mixed feelings about the assignments for our first mission. On a positive note, Scott Goudy was named flight director, the most demanding job in Mission Control. As long as I'd known him, Scott had been a complicated kid, someone who could be very hard to read. The frustration of being labeled special ed pained him, and he would on occasion lash out at his classmates, but there was a sensitive side to him, too. He treated his girlfriend like a queen, bought her flowers on a regular basis and gave her the sappiest Hallmark greeting cards you could imagine. Prior to the Space Camp training program I had never thought of Scott as a leader, although he certainly had some of the necessary characteristics. He was competitive, aggressive, assertive, smart. Something happened to him, though, as the months went by. Perhaps more than any other student in the program, Scott was transformed. Not in a loud or ostentatious way, but in subtle ways. He became less volatile, less hostile toward the people closest to him. He became more helpful and patient, as if he suddenly understood that while he may not have been blessed with the brilliance or athleticism of some of the students at Forest Hills Northern, compared to most of his Burger King teammates, he'd gotten off relatively easy.

So I was relieved to hear that Scott would be in charge of the mission, and I was happy to hear that Steve Bennett would be working beside him in Mission Control. Most of the assignments, in fact, caused me no concern at all. Ben would be in the space lab along with Marion Mills and Andrea Burke. Brooke Fuller would be the weather tracking officer. Mission specialists were Mark Tyler and David Ward (one of our quietest but most capable students), which was encouraging, because both of them were good with their hands. Our pilot would be Stephanie Reinks. The only person I worried about was our commander, Shannon Hathaway.

Shannon was one of the nicest girls in our class, probably one of the nicest kids in the entire school, and while she was academically and intellectually challenged, she was a fiercely determined young woman who accomplished a lot with what God had given her. If Shannon had a flaw, it was that she sometimes suffered terribly from anxiety and nervousness, so she would not have been my choice for commander on the very first mission. The commander was in charge of everything that happened aboard the shuttle, and she worked in proximity to the pilot, who was responsible for actually flying the shuttle itself. Both were high-stress jobs, and they would be filled on the first mission by two of our more tightly wound personalities. But what could I say? Although we had stressed the importance of teamwork and stated repeatedly that no role was more important than any other, everyone knew that wasn't quite true. While a successful mission was dependent on twenty people performing twenty different jobs well, some positions were undeniably more difficult and more high-profile than others. These positions were assigned to the students who seemed most capable of handling them, as indicated by their performance on Sunday's entrance exam. Shannon, Stephanie, and Scott had recorded scores that were among the highest in the camp. They had earned the right to play these roles. They had earned the right to be challenged.

After breakfast we gathered the team together and revealed their assignments. Most of the kids were pretty excited. There was no complaining, no whining—they just wanted to get to work. As I anticipated, the one person who experienced a bit of anxiety was Shannon Hathaway.

"I'm the commander?" she asked, a look of disbelief on her face. "Why?"

"Because you deserve it," I said. "Don't worry. You'll do a great job."

Tuesday morning was devoted to practice. The first mission would be Wednesday, and the second would be Thursday, so this was our only chance to rehearse. With an attitude that was at once businesslike and enthusiastic, the kids took their positions: Ten reported to Mission Control, while the other ten took their places in either the space shuttle or the lab. I observed from the cockpit of the shuttle, while Robynn monitored the action in Mission Control. As with the actual mission, our roles were severely restricted. Since some of our kids were dyslexic, we were allowed to help them read lines if they stumbled on a word, but that was about it. We couldn't answer any questions or assist in the solving of anomalies; interference of that nature was absolutely forbidden.

Not that it was needed, anyway. The kids were very serious, focused, and it was obvious from the way they breezed through their scripts that they had put a lot of effort into preparation. Practice was designed to be somewhat loose, so that any student who wasn't quite sure of his role could seek clarification from the counselors, but our team had no such questions. They knew what a pilot did, they knew what a flight director did. They understood the role of every person involved in the mission. Having that depth of knowledge heading into the practice session gave us a big advantage, because we didn't have to waste any time acquiring information that had been available months earlier. Instead, we could concentrate on reading scripts, solving anomalies, and, maybe most important of all, just getting comfortable in this setting. You could conduct a hundred missions on computer screens at Forest Hills Northern and still be overwhelmed the first time you set foot in one of the space shuttles at Space Camp—it was that vivid a re-creation. Walking into Mission Control, with its massive projection screen, myriad computer terminals, and wall after wall of high-tech equipment, elicited a similar feeling of awe. So the desensitization that came with Tuesday's practice was invaluable.

The entire session lasted about ninety minutes. The counselors took the team on a tour of the shuttle and Mission Control, then walked us through a portion of one script, and then, after placing everyone in his or her assigned positions, ran the clock for thirty minutes—just a little dry run to give the kids some confidence and hands-on experience. And that was it. There were no major problems, no disputes or meltdowns. Granted, it was only a snapshot of a mission—tomorrow's would span two hours—but their performance was nonetheless impressive. Afterward, I called everyone together and asked for an honest self-appraisal.

"I think we did pretty well," Scott Goudy said, and the others nodded approvingly.

"Good," I said. "Now . . . I'm going to give you one chance here, and one chance only. Anyone have any complaints . . . concerns . . . questions? If you want to get something off your chest—if you don't like your assignment, or you're worried about any of your teammates handling their assignments—now is the time to speak. Tomorrow it's real. No whining allowed."

They looked at each other, said nothing. Finally, Steve Bennett broke the silence.

"Coach?"

"Yeah, Steve?"

"We're pretty lucky to be here, huh?"

"Yes, you are. We all are."

He smiled. "Don't worry, Coach. We're going to be okay."

ALTHOUGH LESS INTENSE, the remainder of the day was a blur of activity. I had assured the kids that they would have precious little time for rest and relaxation while at Space Camp—that there would be no need for portable CD players or comic books—and that prediction proved true. After our practice mission we spent a couple hours taking classes in the Space & Rocket Center's Space Museum and Rocket Park. This amounted to an overview of the history of space and rocketry, and while the material was not new to our students, it was presented in a way that was far more interesting than anything Robynn and I could have done in Grand Rapids. Standing three feet away from an actual Lunar module has a far more dramatic impact than reading about it in a textbook or seeing it on a videotape. The kids carried notebooks with them throughout the day, as they were expected to take notes and absorb as much information as possible. The information presented in these classes would form the basis for Thursday's Space Bowl, the final competition of the week.

The afternoon brought more classes, more instruction, this time with the focus on rocketry and propulsion. A history of the Redstone Arsenal was presented, highlighted by a speaker from the Marshall Space and Flight Center, a man who had once worked alongside Wernher von Braun. For me, an adult space junkie, it was an invigorating, enlightening day, listening to this man put his work in a historical contest, explaining what a dramatic effect von Braun's team had on space exploration—from Gemini to Apollo to the space shuttle missions of today. It was more history than math and science, although there was some fairly detailed discussion about engines and propulsion and the physics behind space flight. The intention was to give the campers an overall sense of how man conquered the once unimaginable—space flight—so that when they began building their model rockets, they would have a greater sense of perspective.

I thought the program was exceptional, but there was no question that it was rigorous, even for the most intellectually advanced students.

Several hours of lectures, classwork, and tours, right on the heels of a tough practice session in the shuttle, were enough to leave any teenager bleary-eyed; for a kid with special needs, it was utterly exhausting.

When classes ended, around two-thirty, the students were given a short break, about forty-five minutes to play basketball, volleyball, or just soak up the sun. Our kids needed this time. I could see it on their faces—they were starting to drag, to drift. After the break we were summoned to a big, open room and given a bag filled with rocket parts: fins, clips, cones, parachutes . . . everything needed to construct dozens of model rockets. Instructions in this exercise were limited. The counselors did little more than drop the bag on a table and say, "Show us what you can do."

Lewis Dayhuff reached into the bag first, fished around a moment, and then pulled out a handful of parts. He stared at them quizzically, then dropped them back into the bag. "Where are the instructions?" he asked, somewhat testily.

The counselor in charge of the exercise chuckled. "There aren't any. Use your imagination."

Imagination we had in vast supply, of that much I was now certain. We also had a wealth of knowledge on this subject, thanks to our community rocket launch. What we lacked, at this time, anyway, was energy . . . patience . . . inspiration. As often happens on good teams, however, strength came from an unlikely source. Our first experience with model rockets had been hugely successful primarily because of the creative effort and commitment of a handful of male students, most notably Lewis and Grant. Karen Treffiletti had produced the exquisite Saturn V that we presented to Dr. Muth, but much of the credit for that project belonged to her brothers. This time, though, it was the girls who took the lead. Perhaps because they sensed Lewis getting tired, irritable, or perhaps just because they were more confident than they'd been the first time around, Karen and Shannon Hathaway dived right in. They scooped up parts and enthusiastically began designing some pretty ambitious rockets. Predictably, this lit a fire under the boys in the class, who, in typical male fashion, had presumed the girls would flounder without their help and leadership, and were now reduced to protecting their damaged egos.

This development was precisely what I had hoped to see, and what

I had in fact witnessed on countless occasions in my years as a football coach: the emergence of talent, confidence, teamwork in places where you'd least expect it. In the parlance of the modern-day professional athlete, who is hopelessly addicted to clichés, it is known, quite simply, as "stepping up." As I watched Karen and Shannon, as well as Stephanie Reinks and several of the other girls, busily assembling their rockets, rebuffing overtures of assistance from their male classmates, it was hard not to be impressed. Call it anything you want—these girls were stepping up.

AFTER DINNER WE attended an instructional session on designing team space patches. Unlike the constructing of model rockets, which was more of a team building exercise and thus not factored into the final team scoring, the space patch competition was exactly that: a competition. A slide of each photo would be shown to a panel of judges, and a separate award would be presented on Friday morning to the team who had designed the most creative and compelling space patch. Like everything else at Space Camp, this event was intended to reflect the spirit of NASA. Indeed, even today, every crew that is launched into space is required to design its own team patch, one that symbolizes as succinctly as possible the goals of the mission and the personalities of the men and women on board.

The campers were instructed to adhere to only a few basic guidelines in designing their patches, the most stringent of which was this: Each patch had to include the name of the team, and all twenty members of the team had to be represented. So, the patch had to have twenty stars, or twenty planets, or twenty rockets . . . whatever. Basically, though, that was it. Our kids were given a ream of paper, colored pens and pencils, and a bunch of old patches to use as a frame of a reference. Then the counselors led them to an empty classroom and, once again, told them exactly what they needed to hear:

"Go in there and be creative!"

Unfortunately, they responded not with the vigor of the morning's shuttle practice, but with a sluggish resolve. It was almost nine o'clock at night by now, and most of them were beginning to wilt.

Robynn clapped her hands and tried to offer some encouragement. "Come on, guys. This is exactly the kind of stuff you do better than anyone else. Let's work hard and it'll be over soon. Then we can get some rest."

Ben shouted, "Yeah! Let's work hard!" But from the others there were only grunts and groans. Their reticence was cause for concern, because historically, with these kids, the distance between grumpiness and belligerence was pretty short. When they got angry and frustrated, they tended to lash out at each other. In this setting, that was an indulgence we couldn't afford.

Robynn and I tried to get them started, but in truth, we didn't really understand the whole process either. We hadn't spent any time at all preparing for the space patch competition. If we had, we might have been able to formulate a few ideas before leaving Grand Rapids, and thus taken some of the pressure off the kids. As it was, they were simply tossed into a room and told to work as a team. There was no organizational structure, no hierarchy . . . *no plan*. This was a recipe for trouble.

Optimally, the patch would be developed along the lines of an advertising campaign, with team members contributing suggestions, sketching out ideas, and then agreeing on a final concept. Of course, that required leadership and direction, neither of which we had at the moment. With attention spans dwindling and energy flagging, the team quickly devolved into a collection of individuals—twenty kids talking at once, shouting out ideas, no one listening, no one taking charge. Some of the guys, most notably Steve Bennett, were fooling around, making ridiculous suggestions, drawing goofy characters and shapes, and generally refusing to take the exercise seriously.

At one point, Karen Treffiletti tried to exercise some leadership, but her methods only fanned the fire.

"Come on, Steve!" she shouted. "Grow up!"

Well, that was all Steve needed to hear. Suddenly the old animosity bubbled to the surface, and Steve and Karen began fighting for power again, with the rest of the students egging them on, choosing sides. It was a sad and surprising development, to see how quickly this team could unravel—how easily they could reject the lessons of the previous year.

Robynn and I wanted to stay out of it, because just as it wasn't our place to design the patch for them, neither was it our job to solve their disagreements. As much as anything else, Space Camp was supposed to be about teamwork, about working toward a common goal and vision. But right now it was obvious that we had no vision.

"All right, everyone quiet down!" Lewis Dayhuff yelled. He was seated at a table, about five feet long and three feet wide, paper and pencils fanned out in front of him. Lewis was our best artist—our only artist—so naturally the team had chosen him to sketch our patch, and he had obliged. Now, though, Lewis was getting frustrated. Either the ideas were coming too fast, or they weren't coming at all. Some of the kids drifted away from the group, figuring, selfishly, that Lewis would do a better job anyway, so why not just let him handle it? Others bombarded him with scraps of paper covered with doodles and half-baked ideas. They shouted each other down, made fun of each other, and generally behaved in a manner entirely inconsistent with the ideals we had established prior to this trip.

"Try this, Lewis!"

"No, that sucks . . . try this!"

"Shut up! Use this one, Lewis!"

I could see in Lewis's eyes that he was nearing the breaking point, but I was more concerned with the kids who were screwing around. If something really bad was going to happen, I thought, they would be the instigators, and it would happen right here, in front of the counselors and in front of a woman whose name I did not know, but who had been following us around almost from the moment we arrived. She was middle-aged and well-dressed—clearly a professional woman—and while she did her best to blend into the background, it was fairly obvious by now that she had more than a passing interest in our progress; wherever we went, she was there, and I hadn't noticed any other team receiving such blanket coverage. What her job was, and whether she wanted to see us fail or succeed, I did not yet know. But I did not have a good feeling about her presence, especially now, with the room about to break apart.

"Come on, Lewis . . . this one's best, don't you think?"

"Use this star, Lewis . . . pretty cool, huh?"

I looked again at Lewis, noticed his foot tapping furiously beneath the table as the group hovered over him. Suddenly he stopped sketching and began rubbing his forehead.

Uh-oh . . . big trouble.

"That's it!" Lewis shouted. He pushed himself back, stood up, and as everyone stared in amazement, he flipped the table over, sending paper and pencils flying in all directions.

"Screw this!" Lewis said, his voice cracking. "I'm outta here!"

The room fell silent as Lewis marched toward the door. The counselors seemed to be in a state of shock, as if they feared for their lives. Their reaction was understandable—I'm sure they'd never seen anything like this, not at Space Camp, anyway. I imagined them, and the mystery woman, reporting back to Ed Buckbee and Deborah Barnhart that night and recommending rather enthusiastically that the incorrigible kids from Burger King be placed on the next flight back to Grand Rapids. Along with their teachers. Out of sheer desperation, I ran for the door and tried to block Lewis's path.

"Where do you think you're going?"

He stared at the floor, said nothing.

"Answer me, Lewis."

He looked up, his eyes glassy and bloodshot. It was a look I'd seen before, usually after Lewis had been in some sort of fight. It was a look of anguish, turmoil. "Get out of my way," he said. I looked at him again, so small and fragile, and yet so filled with anger, and I felt immeasurable sadness for having allowed this to happen. I stepped aside and let him pass.

As the door slammed, Vicky came up to me with another counselor and said, "Do you want us to bring him back?"

I shook my head. Pursuing Lewis right after an outburst was not a good idea—it would only fuel his rage. He needed time to cool off, to process what had happened.

"No," I said. "Let him be for a few minutes, and then I'll go get him."

I watched through the door as he paced the hall, perhaps fifteen to twenty yards away. He shook his head, scuffed the floor with his feet, and appeared to be talking to himself. Then he backed up against a wall, slid to the floor, and hung his head between his legs. I could tell he was crying.

Meanwhile, the rest of the kids argued among themselves, blaming each other for what had happened to Lewis. As I listened, I felt the anger rising in my throat. I was mad at the kids for their lack of sensitivity, I was mad at myself for not sensing the inevitability of Lewis's outburst sooner, and I was mad at the interloper, the woman who stood quietly in a corner, scribbling in a notepad.

I turned to face the rest of the class. My head was throbbing. "Are you happy?" I said. "This is exactly the kind of thing we have been talking about for the past year: treating each other with dignity and respect."

They hung their heads; no one said a word.

"Quite a display," Robynn said, picking up where I had left off. "Where's the 'team' in this?" She gestured toward the door. "Look what you did to him. I hope you're proud."

Stephanie was the first to speak up. "Sorry, Coach."

"Sorry doesn't get it done," I said. "Look around this room. You know what's going to happen? This incident is going to get back to people, and they're going to say, 'See, I told you something like this would happen. These kids do not belong here!' They'll send us home and never invite another special ed class. That will be your legacy." In all my years of teaching, I'd rarely been as angry as I was at that moment. More than that, though, I was disappointed. "I don't understand. You guys know what Lewis is like. He's your teammate. He's your *friend!* You know how sensitive he is. You know you have to be patient with him. Why didn't you just back off?"

There was no fight left in them, no suitable explanation for their behavior, and so they didn't offer one. After a while I ran out of breath and gave up.

"I want you all to sit down and be quiet and behave for Ms. McKinney," I said. "I'm going to get Lewis and try to bring him back here."

I turned and started to walk out of the room, but as I reached the door, I felt someone tugging at my arm. It was Steve Bennett, followed closely by Scott Goudy. I was fully prepared to shout them down one more time, to spank them like insolent children, when Steve said something so surprising, so forthright that it took the breath right out of me.

"Coach . . . we don't need you anymore."

At first I thought it was another of Steve's jokes, albeit one that was in particularly poor taste, but I could see by the look on his face that he was completely serious. Behind him, Scott nodded.

"What are you talking about?" I said.

"We'll talk to Lewis and bring him back in here," Scott answered. "We can handle this on our own."

Neither of them broke eye contact with me. They were taking a stand. I looked at Robynn, who seemed every bit as surprised as I was, and then stepped away from the door. "Go ahead. If he'll come back with you, that's great."

As they passed through the door, Scott said, "Don't worry. He will."

How do you respond to something like that? With pride? Awe? Anger? How about pain? When I heard those words—*"We don't need you anymore"*—my knees weakened; I had never realized just how badly I could be hurt by my own students.

"We don't need you anymore . . ."

How could that be? They had always needed me. They had always needed Robynn. And they always would. When the initial shock wore off, of course, I understood exactly what they meant. The intent was not to hurt me, but rather to make a point: *We got ourselves into this mess, and we can get out of it.* Intellectually, I knew this was a good thing— that they were taking complete responsibility for their actions, to the extent that they were actually reaching out to a teammate and trying to console him. It represented a significant level of maturity. It was, in fact, precisely the type of gesture that should have made me proud. So why did I feel like my heart was breaking? I knew the answer: Because I had always been the hero. I'd always been the one to bail them out, to come to their rescue when no one else cared. Truth be told, I liked it that way.

With mixed emotions I watched through the door as Scott and Steve approached Lewis. They kept their distance at first, but after a while they, too, slumped to the floor. Steve threw an arm around Lewis, like a big brother, and Lewis began to sob. At that point I turned away.

TEN MINUTES PASSED before the three of them returned to the room. Steve nodded reassuringly as they entered, so that everyone would know Lewis was all right. He walked slowly, calmly back to the drawing table, which Rob and Ben had turned upright, and sat back down.

"Okay," Lewis said. "I'm ready."

A few of the kids applauded. Several said they were sorry.

"Forget it," Lewis said. "But let's try to have a sense of order around here, all right? Give me your ideas . . . *one at a time.*"

And that was it. For the next hour and a half the process of designing a team space patch went as smoothly as I had originally hoped it would. The kids splintered off into groups, came up with various concepts, and then patiently presented them to Lewis, who brought them beautifully to life. They shared ideas, exchanged feedback and criticism without hesitation. Miraculously, they became a model of efficiency.

The central conceit of our patch was, naturally, Burger King.

"Wouldn't it be kind of funny if we had a Burger King restaurant in space?" one of the kids had suggested, and after they finished laughing, their imaginations kicked in. Pretty soon Lewis had sketched out a celestial BK with a fly-thru lane. At the service window, a remote manipulator arm dropped whoppers, by parachute, into the cargo bay of a space shuttle. Additionally, shuttles were parked all around the restaurant, like a 1950s drive-in, and service was provided by twenty cyborgs (representing our team) on jet-powered Rollerblades.

"What do you think?" Lewis asked as he held up the sketch for Robynn and me to inspect. It was funny, smart, imaginative, and extremely well executed. But I didn't say that out loud, and neither did Robynn.

"It doesn't matter what we think," she said, taking the words out of my mouth. "This is your project. What do *you* think?"

Lewis held the sketch at arm's length, looked it over, and then nodded approvingly. "I like it."

THAT NIGHT, DESPITE being utterly exhausted, I slept poorly. Like any parent, I had mixed emotions about the emerging independence of my kids. One of the primary goals of any special education teacher is to instill a sense of independence in his students, so I should have been pleased. It was the speed of the transformation that caught me off-guard. I was waiting for the cake to finish baking, and someone had stuck it in the microwave.

As I tossed and turned in bed, I tried to convince myself that what had happened earlier was the best thing possible, for the next day the kids would have their first mission, and there they would be entirely on their own. Still, I couldn't get it straight in my mind . . . or my heart.

In that place where I should have felt satisfaction, there was mainly sadness.

"What's wrong?" my wife asked after my thrashing woke her up for the third or fourth time.

I let out a sigh. "They don't need us anymore."

There was a long pause. Finally she rolled over, put an arm around me, and said, "Isn't that what you wanted?"

"Yeah . . . I guess so."

25

Wednesday. Hump day. Three days down, three to go. By Wednesday of Space Camp you have a pretty good idea of how your team is performing. You know who's homesick and who isn't, who's taking the competition seriously, and who considers the entire week to be little more than a vacation. Tuesday night's debacle notwithstanding, our students had acquitted themselves well thus far. A few of them obviously had experienced pangs of loneliness and homesickness, and yet hadn't said too much about it. Even the most pampered and sheltered of them turned out to be pretty strong. Exactly how strong they were, and how they would handle some of the most intense pressure of their lives, would be determined today, when they flew their first mission.

When I arrived at the space habitat early that morning the kids were in surprisingly good spirits, almost as if they had completely forgotten about what had transpired the night before. So I didn't bring it up. Our mission was scheduled to begin around three o'clock that afternoon, which made it the last of the day. The timing was good and bad. Good . . . because we had plenty of time to prepare and study. Bad . . . because we had eight or nine hours to think and obsess and perhaps become crippled by nervousness.

Fortunately, the people who run Space Camp are well aware of the hazards of free time, so they give the campers virtually none of it. After breakfast we attended a presentation on what it's like to live in space. Then the real fun began, the part of Space Camp that was most like an amusement park. First came a ride in the multi-axis trainer, an exact duplicate of one of the instruments NASA used to train astronauts. I'd been in the multi-axis trainer the previous summer, and I knew the kids would love it. Horrific in appearance, with a chair spinning wildly inside a gyroscope, the trainer looked like a device guaranteed to induce queasiness, if not outright nausea. In reality, it was quite the opposite. A passenger in the multi-axis trainer was positioned in such a way that the equilibrium in his inner ear was kept in constant balance, so while there was considerable torque on the body, even the most delicate stomach would not be upset.

Not that our students believed any of this when they first laid eyes on the machine.

"No way," Rob Johnson said, holding a hand against his midsection. "I'll hurl."

The counselor in charge of the equipment laughed. "That won't happen," he promised. "You'll be fine."

"He's right," I added. "It's a piece of cake."

"Oh yeah?" Steve Bennett said. "Then let's see you go first."

"Guys . . . look—"

"Good idea, Coach," Stephanie Reinks said. "Show us how it's done."

Before I could get another word out, they all began clapping, chanting, exhorting: "Coach! Coach! Coach!"

To add a bit of drama to the situation, I pretended to panic as they strapped me into the chair. My hands shook, my knees knocked. As the multi-axis trainer came to life, I yelled, "No! Please! I've changed my mind. I . . . *can't* . . . do . . . this!"

The kids weren't particularly sympathetic. As the machine lurched and rolled, spare change spewed from the pockets of my shorts and onto the floor.

"Faster! Faster!" they yelled, and the counselor happily obliged. He kept shifting directions, jerking me back and forth, until finally, after I had dropped about three dollars in nickels, dimes, and quarters, the machine came to a stop. As the straps were removed and I stood to exit the trainer, I deliberately stumbled as if drunk and pretended I was going to be sick.

"Coach! No!"

The whole class jumped back as I opened my mouth wide and . . .

"Okay, give me my money back," I said.

"Oh, man! That's not funny, Coach!"

"Sure it is," I said. "Now, come on. Who wants to go next? If an old guy like me can handle it, you guys shouldn't have any problem."

Ben Schmidt's hand shot up. "Me!"

"You're a good man, Ben."

Pretty soon Ben was strapped in and rolling around, laughing uncontrollably, that smile of his lighting up the room. After Ben got off and gave a four-star review in only one word—"Awesome!"—the rest of the kids couldn't wait for their turn to ride. Everyone tried the multiaxis trainer—everyone, that is, except Robynn, who, despite being goaded and harassed by the kids, by me, and by the counselors, steadfastly refused.

"That's okay," she said. "I get the idea."

While it may have seemed like a carnival ride, the multi-axis trainer, like everything at Space Camp, had a deeper purpose. It was intended not merely to be "cool," but to give the campers an idea of what it would be like to be a passenger in a space capsule as it reenters the Earth's atmosphere, tumbling and spinning wildly. The idea is to just hold on and go along for the ride . . . and not panic.

Similarly, while the kids also enjoyed working out in the "one-sixth gravity trainer," because it, too, was almost unspeakably cool, the goal was to educate as well as entertain. The one-sixth trainer—essentially a chair attached to a giant springlike device—was so named because it afforded its user the opportunity to experience the sensation of walking on the moon, where the gravitational pull is one-sixth that of the gravitational pull on Earth. Some of our bigger kids were a little nervous about using the one-sixth trainer, because they were concerned that the more you weighed, the higher you'd bounce, and they were legitimately worried about hitting the ceiling and getting hurt.

"Uh . . . guys. It doesn't work that way," I said. "Anyway, you're tethered to a chair—you can't go through the roof."

"Oh."

BY THE END of our sessions on the multi-axis trainer and one-sixth trainer, it was time for lunch. After lunch we finished building our model rockets. That left about an hour to review scripts and make final preparations for our mission.

At around 2:30 P.M. Vicky suggested we return to the space habitat to get changed into our flight suits. No one said much of anything as we dressed. Again, the atmosphere in the bunk reminded me of the atmosphere in a locker room before a football game: the way they took such care with their uniforms, the way they primped and preened in front of the mirrors. Everything had to be perfect. These kids, so many of whom routinely came to school in unwashed clothes, wanted to look their best in the shuttle. They combed their hair, washed their faces, brushed their teeth. If their sleeves were even an inch or two long, they cuffed them precisely. Same with their pant legs. As they marched quietly, in single file, out of the habitat, Robynn nudged me with an elbow. She looked like a proud mother watching her children go off to school.

"Gosh," she said. "They look like astronauts, don't they?"

Indeed they did.

We walked as a team from the space habitat to the simulator center. No one said much of anything as we climbed the ramp to the front door, walked inside, and sat down on a long bench, not far from the gleaming, white space shuttle *Discovery*. Vicky came over, told us the day was right on schedule and that we'd be up in a few minutes.

"Good luck," she said. "I'm sure you're going to do great." She turned to me. "Coach, if you want to say anything, now is the time. After this, they're on their own."

I had rehearsed a little speech in my head, and God knows I had given enough pregame pep talks that I shouldn't have been nervous about delivering this one. For some reason, though, my mouth was dry and my hands were trembling. Never had I felt such anxiety, such pressure, before the start of a competition. Not even as a coach leading a team into the state football playoffs; not even when I'd been a college player. The stakes here were much higher. Granted, Space Camp wasn't a matter of life and death, but it was a heck of a lot more important than any football game. My quandary, as I stood in front of them, was whether to be honest, to spell out the implications one more time, or to minimize the pressure by simply telling them to have fun.

I took a deep breath . . .

"I want you to look at each other," I began. "Look into the eyes of the person sitting next to you. Remember how you felt about that person a year ago, two years ago, and measure that against the way you feel today. That's what teamwork can do. It can change the way you perceive your friends, your classmates, even yourself. You guys are a team, and that's something no one can ever take away from you. But you're not just any team. You're the first team of special education students ever to set foot inside that space shuttle. The first team from the state of Michigan, the first team from the United States, the first team in the entire world . . ." A few of them smiled at that description, event though they'd heard it before. A couple fidgeted uncomfortably. "That's a huge responsibility, isn't it?" I continued. "Because whatever happens in there today will have a ripple effect. Get the job done, and other special ed kids will be lining up right behind you."

Steve Bennett cleared his throat. "And if we don't?"

I shrugged. "I'm not worried about that. We've spent seven months training for this day . . . for this moment. You guys can do this with your eyes closed. No other team in this whole camp has put in more time than you have; no other team is as well prepared; no one has as much to prove." I paused and looked at Robynn, whose jaw was clenched, her arms crossed stoically. I knew her well enough to know that she was even more nervous than I was, and probably more nervous than the kids. "Ms. McKinney, do you want to say anything?"

Robynn bit her lower lip and said, "Just do your best. That's all we can ask."

I nodded. "Anyone else want to add anything?" They looked around, shook their heads. You could almost feel the adrenaline in the air. "Okay . . . everybody in." I held out my right hand, palm down. The kids stood up and formed a tight circle around me and Robynn. "Put your hands on mine," I said. It was not an unusual gesture—our football team did it before every game, as did most teams in most sports. The great majority of these kids, however, had never been part of a team, never put their hands together in a display of brotherhood or unity. But they did it now. One by one they reached into the center of the circle, until we had a stack of twenty-two sweaty hands, from which the synergy fairly flowed.

"I know you guys come from different schools, and from different towns," I said. "But right now, we're all representing Forest Hills Northern. We're all Huskies. So, on the count of three, let's show a little Husky pride." They all smiled.

"One, two, three . . . *Husky pride!*"

My God, it was loud! Our voices reverberated off the walls of the building, prompting people to stop dead in their tracks and stare at us. At the same time, we threw our hands skyward, sending a shower of perspiration into the air.

"Game time, huh, Coach?" Ben Schmidt said.

What a great big teddy bear of a kid he was. "Game time, Ben."

WE WERE SEPARATED into three distinct groups. One group went into Mission Control, another went into the space lab, and the rest—including the flight crew and mission specialists (the latter of whom would eventually don full space walk regalia for extravehicular activities)— boarded the space shuttle. Robynn and Darcy also went to Mission Control, where they would be permitted to help with reading problems that might arise. I followed Stephanie, Shannon, and the rest of the flight crew into the shuttle to watch them get set up. I stood quietly in the back as they strapped on headsets, got a first look at their flight scripts, and prepared for the countdown. Originally I had intended to put on my teacher's hat one more time and warn them about being on their best behavior, about not farting into the microphone or making silly noises or yelling at each other. But that hardly seemed necessary now. They were all business. I took one last walk through the shuttle, said "Good luck," and left, just as the counselor who ran the shuttle missions announced, "All right, we're going to start the countdown at T-minus nine minutes. Let's go!"

In both the shuttle and Mission Control, everything seemed to be going smoothly. The kids were reading their scripts flawlessly and running through various checklists in preparation for liftoff. We didn't expect any problems at this point in the mission, because it was highly unusual for a team to be given any anomalies prior to leaving the launch pad. Still, it was a possibility, and the fact that the kids seemed calm and focused was reassuring. How often, after all, had I seen talented, well-prepared football players fumble on the first possession of a game, for no other reason than because their nerves had gotten the best of them? Remembering what had happened the previous fall, when we'd lost our football opener to Paw Paw, I closed my eyes and anxiously rolled up my script. I wanted so badly to say something, to help, to offer words of encouragement, but that time had come and gone. All I could do . . . all Robynn could do . . . was hope for the best.

"T-Minus two minutes."

The words, delivered in a dull, lifeless monotone, came from Rob Johnson, who, as public affairs officer in Mission Control, was responsible for the countdown. I'm sure Rob was trying to project an air of authority, a cool confidence born of experience. He hoped his tone said, "Been there, done that . . . no need to worry." Instead, I thought, it said, "Anybody mind if I take a nap?"

"Come on, Rob," I whispered to no one in particular. "Show a little emotion."

Robynn and Darcy said, in unison, "Shhhhh!"

The countdown continued without incident. The kids didn't miss a cue. They delivered every line perfectly, executed every command in the prelaunch protocol.

"T-minus ten seconds," Rob moaned. "Nine . . . eight . . . seven . . ."

"Can you believe this?" I said. "He's been hanging out with Grant too much."

"Six . . . five . . . four . . ."

What kind of freaking count is this?!

"Three . . . two . . . one . . ."

Please, Rob. Finish with a bang.

"We have liftoff."

The words were so soft, so devoid of emotion, that they were all but drowned out by the rumbling of the shuttle's engines and the roar of the booster rockets. With its nose tilted up, the shuttle shook madly, thereby giving its passengers the sensation of liftoff (without the unpleasant G-forces, of course). Meanwhile, in Mission Control, an image of an actual shuttle leaving the launch pad was projected onto a giant screen. Here we were, in the midst of this thrilling experience, with all the elements of a once-in-a-lifetime adventure, and all I could think was, *This kid just gave us an Eeyore countdown.*

"Geez, I'm sure the counselors are *real* impressed by that," I said sarcastically.

Robynn shot me a harsh glance. "What do you want from him, Mike? He's handling things calmly. That's good, isn't it?"

Sheepishly, I replied, "Yeah, I guess so." The truth was, Rob did just fine. If anyone was behaving inappropriately right now, it was me. I decided to keep my thoughts, and my anxiety, to myself, even if it meant biting my own tongue off.

The first critical moment of any shuttle simulation is the solid rocket booster (SRB) separation, which typically occurs at around the two-minute mark. As with a real shuttle mission, in order to have SRB separation, the pilot and commander have to be working in perfect synch with Mission Control. The right switch has to be thrown at precisely the right time. The difference, obviously, is that in a real mission, a failed SRB separation can have life-threatening consequences, while here, in the shelter of Space Camp, it would result in nothing more dramatic than a botched simulation and a dismal score on the mission. But our timing was precise. Scott gave the right command and Stephanie threw the right switch, resulting in a glorious image of SRB separation on the Mission Control screen.

Great job! Now we're cooking!

The next important task, approximately eight minutes into the flight, was the separation of the external fuel tank. I had stressed during training that we had to be prepared for an early anomaly, such as an aborted mission, which would require us to immediately make the adjustments necessary to return to the launch site, after which we'd resume the mission. But it didn't happen. Eight minutes passed, the external fuel tank was released, and the mission went on.

"They're handling everything pretty well," Robynn said.

"I know. Maybe this is our day."

It did seem that way. The kids appeared to be on their game, as if nothing could disrupt or disturb them. Even the first few anomalies—a faulty switch, an electrical problem—failed to induce panic, or even agitation. The kids addressed the problems professionally, referring to their handbooks and conferring with each other to deduce the quickest and simplest solutions. There was no hand wringing, no crying, no bickering. One after another, the team solved each anomaly and moved on, seemingly oblivious to the pressure of the ticking clock. In fact, though, a subtle shift had occurred, one I hadn't anticipated at all. They weren't coping with the time element; they were ignoring it.

Around the eighteen-minute mark Robynn tapped her watch. I

checked the script. In five minutes the crew would be expected to perform one of the major tasks of a shuttle mission: the release of a satellite into orbit. It wasn't a particularly difficult task, but it did require the systematic execution of a series of steps within a small window of time (approximately one minute). As our kids continued to focus on solving anomalies, it became apparent that they had forgotten about the impending satellite release. The anomalies, as it turned out, were serving their function, which was not merely to test the students' knowledge, but to distract them from their primary objective.

At twenty-one minutes, immediately after solving yet another anomaly, a reminder came from the flight director.

"Okay, people, we're coming up on the satellite launch. Take your places, please."

Scott Goudy's voice was deep, calm, reassuring, exactly as it should have been. In the cockpit, everyone seemed poised. There was no indication of what was about to happen.

We had prepared for this part of the mission dozens of times. It was the responsibility of the pilot and commander to walk to the rear of the cockpit, hit the right switch, and launch the satellite. But as the flight director said, "One minute to satellite launch," no one moved.

Come on, Stephanie. Get up!

At Shannon Hathaway's urging, Stephanie finally left her seat, and even from Mission Control, watching on grainy, closed-circuit monitors, the fear on her face was evident. Stephanie had frozen. And everyone knew it.

"Flight director to pilot . . . are you all right?"

Stephanie said nothing, just stood there trembling.

"Stephanie," Scott said, his voice rising only slightly. "In the back. You can do it."

"I . . . I . . . I can't remember!" Stephanie stammered.

A pause. "Yes, you can," Scott said. He had the right idea. As one of Stephanie's former tormenters, he knew better than most how fragile she was, and that shouting at her, or at Shannon, would only make the situation worse. Unfortunately, he was alone in his awareness. Within seconds panic spread throughout the flight crew and into Mission Control. Stephanie and Shannon pleaded with Scott for guidance, but his advice was drowned out by the chaos of the cockpit.

"Hurry up, Stephanie!"

"We're running out of time!"

"Throw the switch . . . it's right there . . . on the panel!"

A successful satellite launch is depicted on the screen in Mission Control. Within a few seconds after the last switch is thrown, a satellite drops out of the payload area of the shuttle and disappears into the blackness of space. In our case, after Stephanie and Shannon finally found their way to the control panel and threw the proper switch . . . nothing happened. The window had closed. We were too late.

I dropped my head into my hands and waited for the inevitable explosion to occur: an all-out war among teammates that would rival anything I'd witnessed in my classroom. Finger pointing, name calling, maybe even a physical confrontation. Under this kind of pressure, anything was possible. Instead, there was only stunned silence, as if they couldn't believe what had happened, and how suddenly the mission had gone awry. Stephanie and Shannon began to cry, softly at first, and then violently, in heavy, full-throated sobs.

"I'm sorry," Stephanie said. "I'm so sorry."

"Me, too," Shannon blubbered. "I blew it!"

They fell into each other's arms and cried as if standing beside the casket of a loved one at a funeral. Across the room from me, on the other side of Mission Control, the mystery woman scribbled in a notebook. Her face was expressionless. As Shannon and Stephanie continued to weep, and the clock continued to tick, some of the other members of the flight crew became irritable.

"What do we do?" asked David Ward, a mission specialist who had always been a bit more driven than his classmates, and thus occasionally intolerant of their shortcomings. "We're screwed now!"

Although I didn't approve of his response, I didn't disagree with him. We had made a very big mistake. The flight crew should have released the satellite and then finished addressing the anomalies, because these were not life-threatening problems. We had discussed this so many times in our training—the importance of prioritizing—that I was surprised and disappointed by their failure to recognize what was happening. Such are the mistakes kids make, especially in the heat of competition. The trick now was to get back on track, to remember that less than one quarter of the mission had been completed. At this moment, with Stephanie and Shannon crying, and the rest of the team immobilized by shock and indecision, it seemed possible that they might just quit. Ditch the shuttle, walk out, and never come back.

I waited for the final blow, for someone to call Stephanie a "stupid gump." She'd reply with a hearty curse and then kick a hole in the wall on her way out. Instead, I saw Scott Goudy slowly lean forward in the flight director's chair. He cleared his throat, loud enough for everyone to hear, and began to speak.

"I want everyone's attention." It wasn't an order, exactly, but it might as well have been. "We have an hour and a half left in this mission," he continued. "This is not over. Remember what Coach said: 'If you make a mistake, put it behind you.' We can make this up as a team."

He paused to let the words sink in, then continued.

"Pilot? Commander? Is that clear?"

Stephanie wiped a hand across her face. She and Shannon both nodded. "Good," Scott said. "Now . . . everyone get back to your positions. We've got a lot of work to do."

As I watched them scurry to their posts and resume the mission, I reflected on what had happened the night before, and I could almost hear Steve Bennett's voice: *"We don't need you anymore."* Maybe he was right, for now, thanks to Scott, they were responding as adults, trying to pick up the pieces of their fractured journey.

The counselors cut our team no slack either, throwing a handful of tricky anomalies at them in the next twenty minutes, thereby increasing the likelihood that they'd stumble again at the next critical juncture: connecting the shuttle to a space station. Docking the shuttle is a more demanding maneuver than releasing a satellite, and I wondered whether Shannon and Stephanie would be up to the task, given their delicate emotional states. But they breezed through it. With one hour left in the mission, the shuttle docked cleanly, and our mission specialists—David Ward and Mark Tyler—put on their space suits and did their jobs, which included repairing a dead battery in a satellite. (The space suits were so hot that the kids had to wear ice packs to reduce the risk of heat exhaustion.)

While the crew completed their EVAs, I decided to take a walk over to the space lab, mainly to check on Ben Schmidt. I anticipated no problems with Ben, and indeed there were none. When I entered the lab, I could see him hunched over a computer monitor—his glasses were so thick that he practically had to climb through the screen in order to read the text. When he heard me, Ben looked up, smiled, waved, and then went right back to work. His primary responsibility was to relay to Mission Control all the information given to him by the rest of the crew, and he seemed to be completing his duties well.

In fact, throughout the second half of the mission the entire team performed almost perfectly. Even some of the more serious anomalies, such as a crew member falling ill, were dealt with in a calm, professional manner. As a result, the mission was resurrected.

"These kids have really picked themselves up off the floor," I said to Robynn when I returned to Mission Control. "We may do all right after all."

The scoring system used to grade missions was highly subjective, with each crew rated on a scale of one to ten in ten different categories. The highest possible score was one hundred. Because the judging was splintered in this way, it wasn't out of the realm of possibility for us to salvage a decent score. In much the same way that an Olympic figure skater could commit an apparently horrific error by tumbling to the ice and yet still win a medal, our performance in the final three quarters of the mission could offset our botched satellite launch. If the rest of the mission went well, I thought, we could score in the eighties. Since our final score in the best mission competition would be determined by combining our two missions, this would, in all likelihood, put us out of medal contention, but at least the result would be respectable. We had rebounded from a near-fatal mistake, and that was worth something. Actually, in my book, it was worth quite a lot.

"Here they come," Robynn said, pointing to the screen. The shuttle was entering the Earth's atmosphere. All that remained was the landing.

Please let it go well . . .

It did. The shuttle touched down gently and cruised to a stop. In Mission Control, Scott and Steve exchanged a high five. There was applause from every corner of the room.

"Okay," one of the counselors said. "Turn off your microphones, take off your headsets, put everything down. Congratulations. The mission is over."

We exited Mission Control at the same time that Ben and the others were coming out of the space lab. Together we watched from a few feet away as the shuttle settled back into a crouch and disgorged its passengers. Most of the crew members were smiling and congratulating each other, but Shannon and Stephanie hung back and kept to themselves. Suddenly, they both began to cry again.

"I'm so sorry," Stephanie said. "I can't believe I messed up like that."

In an instant the other kids gathered around them, hugged them, told them not to worry. The intolerance and hostility that once typified their behavior in situations such as this was gone; in its place was compassion.

"You did just fine," Scott said.

"That's right," said Brooke Fuller. "We all did."

THE WAIT WAS to be mercifully brief. We were sent to an empty classroom and told that within fifteen or twenty minutes the scores would be tabulated and we'd have our result. Robynn and I were more nervous than the kids, probably because they were completely worn out from the mission—indeed, from the entire week. I went out and got each of them a soda, but before they even had a chance to start drinking, Vicky walked into the room, a sheet of paper in one hand, a big smile on her face.

"Let me tell y'all something right now," she said, her Southern twang thicker than ever. "Y'all got an eye." I tilted my head for a moment, not sure I had heard correctly. The kids were similarly perplexed.

"We got a what?" I asked.

"An eye!" she repeated. "Isn't that great?"

Still no reaction.

What is she talking about? An eye? An eye? Ohhhh . . . an EYE!

"Vicky, are you trying to say we got an A?"

Exasperated, she threw her hands into the air. "That's what I said. An eye! Y'all scored a ninety-six point five out of a hundred!"

As the news finally sunk in, the kids erupted. They jumped into each other's arms, slapped hands, whooped and cheered like champions. Stunned, I turned to Robynn, whose mouth was agape.

"Well, I'll be damned," I said. "They did it."

Robynn nodded. Then, knowing that ours had been the last mission of the day, she asked Vicky an important question: "How did the other teams do?"

Vicky shook her head. "I don't have all the scores, but I'm pretty sure you're in the top three or four."

Suddenly, the celebration stopped.

"Really?" asked Lewis Dayhuff. "Top three?"

"Three or four," Vicky repeated. "You're in the hunt, that's for sure." She paused. "Hey . . . y'all gotta be hungry after that mission. Why don't you go get something to eat? They'll be serving dinner in a few minutes."

The kids looked at each other. No one moved.

"What's wrong?" I asked.

Scott Goudy answered for the group. "Coach, would it be all right if we go back to Mission Control and practice reading our scripts for a little while, to get ready for tomorrow's mission?"

"You're kidding."

"Uh-uh."

I deferred to Vicky. "Is that allowed?"

She shrugged. "It's your time. Do what you want."

With Scott Goudy leading the way, they filed out of the room and headed back to Mission Control, their stomachs empty, their minds full . . . "A" students after all these years.

26

By Thursday morning exhaustion had set in. Robynn and I met the kids in the space habitat bright and early, before breakfast, and went over the day's agenda. We'd all been up late the previous night, working on our space station presentation, and now, understandably, everyone was dragging. The cumulative effect of medication, sleep deprivation, and intense competition was finally taking its toll. Physically and emotionally, our team was running out of gas.

Unfortunately, on this road, there were no service stations; there wasn't even a rest area or a breakdown lane. In terms of competition, Thursday was the final, and busiest, day of Space Camp. On the schedule: another simulated mission, presentation of our space station, a campwide rocket launch, and the Space Bowl. By the end of the day we'd have a pretty good idea how we had done, and on Friday, when awards were handed out, we'd know for sure. Whether we still had a shot at winning the most coveted prize—Best Mission—would be determined in short order, since ours was the first mission of the day. I wasn't sure whether this was a good thing or a bad thing, but I understood it to be a necessary thing. Fairness was the goal, and to that end, the order of competition was reversed: The team that had flown the first mission on Wednesday would go last on Thursday, and the team that had flown last on Wednesday would now move to the front of the line. That team was Burger King. On the one hand, I was pleased that we'd dispense with our mission early; on the other hand, we had done rather well flying late in the day Wednesday. Then again, we might be too tired to think straight by late this afternoon; of course, watching the kids stumble around the space habitat, wiping sand from their eyes, tripping as they climbed into their space suits, it was hard to imagine them being any less energetic than they were at this moment.

So . . . who knew what to expect? As Robynn said, "I don't know about you, but I don't have a clear read on them right now."

Neither did I. I had planned to give them another pep talk, another "rah-rah" speech, but that hardly seemed appropriate right now. A lighter touch was warranted. I asked everyone to take a seat, and then I opened the floor for comments.

"What do you guys want to talk about?"

They scratched their heads and yawned.

"Nothin', Coach," Scott said.

"You're sure? Because I don't have a lot to say. You guys told me a couple days ago that you don't need me anymore—"

Steve Bennett cut me off. "Come on, Coach. That's not what we meant."

I held up a hand. "I know what you meant, and believe me, it's all right. I respect it. That's what I wanted to hear . . . it's what I *needed* to hear: that you can stand on your own feet. But understand something: You've made a choice. You've decided, as a team, that you're capable of completing this week without any help from Ms. McKinney and me." I paused and searched for the right words. "We've coached you, we've worked with you, and we're very proud of you. But this is your time now. We're here to support you, to cheer you on . . . the rest is up to you. Tomorrow is graduation. What happens at that ceremony is entirely in your hands."

Initially there was no response. I think perhaps they had expected something else, probably another fiery speech, similar to the one that had preceded Wednesday's mission. Instead, I addressed them straight from the gut, just as I would have addressed my own kids. No bull, no psychobabble. We'd been together long enough, and they had performed well enough, that I thought it was safe, and even appropriate, to simply state our expectations. Bo Schembechler had a theory, and I subscribed to it: In any given season, you can only fire up your team two or three times. The rest of the time, the motivation has to come from within. I felt as if we had played a game sixteen hours earlier, and

I had used up my Big Speech. A repeat performance now would have been a waste; worse, actually—it would have seemed false . . . a lot of fake screaming and emotion. I didn't have that in me, and the kids didn't need it.

"Don't worry, Coach," Scott said on the way to the cafeteria, where we'd have time for a quick breakfast before the mission. "We're not going to let you down."

"That's not important," I said. "What matters is that you don't let yourselves down."

He smiled. "No chance."

EACH STUDENT WAS moved to a new position for the second mission. Steve Bennett (pilot) and Karen Treffiletti (commander) were in charge of the shuttle. Brooke Fuller (flight director) took over for Scott Goudy in Mission Control; Scott, meanwhile, became a mission specialist. Once again the prelaunch routine went smoothly, and this time, with Pat Zerfas serving as public affairs officer, the countdown was a rousing, emotional experience:

"Three . . . two . . . one . . . *We have liftoff!*"

Well . . . that's more like it!

The first twenty-five minutes of the flight went by without incident. SRB separation was achieved, followed by external tank separation and satellite launch. Along the way, the crew easily solved a few simple anomalies. Approximately thirty minutes into the flight, however, trouble presented itself. Dozens of lights on the back panel of the shuttle began to flicker and flash. An alarm sounded. Steve raced to the back, looked over the wall of lights, and stood there for a moment, assessing the situation.

"Oh, God . . ." I whispered to Robynn.

She nodded. "I know . . . Christmas Tree."

Yup. We'd been handed the most infamous and potentially devastating anomaly of the mission. In a few seconds, Steve would either recognize the anomaly for what it was—a trick—or he would panic and begin solving each problem individually, in which case the mission was all but over.

Steve stroked his chin. Then, slowly, a smile came to his face. "Hey!" he shouted. "It's the Christmas Tree! Cool!"

I let out a sigh of relief as the crew went to work. Within two minutes they had solved the problem, which was nothing more than a minor short circuit, and proceeded with the mission.

"This is too good to be true," I said to Robynn. "I think we've got a perfect score so far."

It *was* too good to be true. Around the forty-five-minute mark, one of the counselors walked into Mission Control and told us that Marion Mills, who had been working in the space lab, had become ill. This wasn't an anomaly—she was legitimately sick. Marion had begun to feel faint, nauseous, and had to be removed from the lab. Whether her condition stemmed from nervousness, exhaustion, or some residual effect from her leukemia treatment, I had no idea, and it really didn't matter. The point was, we were now missing a crew member, and a crucial one at that, since Marion had been in the middle of an experiment when she'd taken ill.

I left Mission Control and walked to the space lab. Marion was sitting outside on a bench, her face drawn, her complexion a milky white. I sat down beside her and put a hand on her shoulder.

"How are you, Marion?"

"Not so good. I'm sorry, Coach, but I don't think I can go back in there."

Inside I was thinking, *Well, that's it, then. There goes our chance of winning Best Mission.* I couldn't say that, of course. There was no question that Marion had done her best, and that she was thoroughly incapacitated. "That's all right, hon," I said, giving her a hug. "We'll be fine."

The urge to enter the space lab was almost overwhelming, and even though the rules restricted my presence there, I was pretty sure an exception would have been made under the circumstances. But it wasn't my place to try to make everything right. Whatever happened . . . happened.

A few minutes later one of the counselors came out of the space lab to check on Marion.

"How's she doing?"

Sipping a cup of water, Marion just moaned. "I think she's had better days," I answered.

"Well, I wouldn't worry too much. Another young lady has taken over her experiment, and it looks like she's got it under control."

"Which young lady?" I asked.

"Andrea Burke."

What?! I was stunned. If there was one person on the entire team I least expected to step in and do something heroic, it was this sad, pathetic little girl.

"You're kidding, right?"

"No. As soon as she finished her own experiment, she walked right over and asked for permission to complete Marion's. I told her to go right ahead."

Flabbergasted, and suddenly buoyed by optimism, I returned to Mission Control to watch the rest of the flight. As far as I could tell, we did not make a single mistake in the final hour. Our EVAs went well, we solved every anomaly; the reentry and landing were executed flawlessly. Assuming we hadn't messed up any of the experiments in the space lab, our score had to be in the nineties . . . again.

Interestingly, when the shuttle touched down this time, there was no wild display of emotion in Mission Control. Instead, it was as if they were twenty-year veterans of NASA: *Another day, another mission. Hohum.* And when they came out afterward, their first response was not to congratulate each other, or even to assess the mission and fret over whether they still had a chance to finish first, but rather to check on Marion, to see if she was all right. Their primary concern was for the health of their teammate and friend. This blew me away. Nine months earlier they wouldn't have cared. Rather, they'd have whined and complained about their misfortune; more than likely, the mission would have collapsed and they'd have blamed Marion for its unraveling.

Now, not only were they refusing to hold Marion accountable, they were offering her sympathy and compassion; at the same time, when the kids in Mission Control and the space shuttle found out that Andrea had assumed the responsibility of finishing Marion's experiment, they expressed only confidence.

"Hey, that's great, Andrea," Steve Bennett said. "How did it go?"

"Okay . . . I think," Andrea responded, somewhat sheepishly. "I'm not sure."

It almost didn't matter. As far as I was concerned, this mission had already been an extraordinary success. Still, there was a part of me, the part that coached football and loved not just to compete but to *win*, that desperately wanted another high score, and a shot at taking the highest honor at Space Camp.

"Hey, Coach," Vicky said as she entered the room where we waited for the news. This time the look on her face was somewhat somber, and I thought briefly that perhaps I'd gotten some bad information about Andrea's work in the space lab. Maybe the estimates of her performance had been greatly exaggerated, and now Vicky was here to break the news. But then her face lit up again, just as it had the day before.

"Y'all are startin' to make a habit of this, huh?"

"What do you mean?"

She waved our scorecard in the air. "I mean . . . this says ninety-eight point five. Y'all got another eye!"

Good Lord! I couldn't believe it. A nearly perfect mission, which meant we really did have a chance to win the team title. The day was young and there was no telling how the other teams would fare, but this much was certain: We had put ourselves in a position to win. More than that, we could not have asked.

As the other kids celebrated, I rushed right over to Andrea and gave her a big hug. "I didn't know you had it in you."

Andrea laughed, which was another thing she rarely did, and I was struck by what a nice smile she had. "Me neither."

AFTER THE MISSION we turned in the final version of our space patch and then went outside to launch our model rockets. Although there was no judging of their work, our kids were excited about this exercise, not only because it represented an opportunity to flaunt their craftsmanship (which was as advanced as that of any of the teams in camp) but also because they wanted to strut and show off just a little bit following their exemplary shuttle mission. Many of the other campers were also at the launch site, and the Burger King team wasn't shy about letting everyone know that they had just aced their second mission. They were cool about it, of course. They didn't run around screaming or thumping their chests, but they did walk with a noticeable bounce in their step, and when another camper asked how the mission had gone, the response was delivered without hesitation.

"Not too bad—ninety-eight point five."

Interesting, too, were the reactions of the other campers, which typically went something like this: "Wow! That's great, man. Good for you!"

Gone was the condescension of the first two days, and in its place was respect. Rumors had been floating around for most of the week that the special ed kids from Michigan were doing a pretty good job; better than that, even—they were among the top groups in camp. Several counselors told me that other teams had at first been suspicious of our performance, that they wondered aloud whether the special ed kids were getting special treatment. Assured they were not, the other campers invariably shook their heads and said, in effect, "I can't believe we're getting beat by these guys." With each passing day, however, and with each successive display of grace under fire, the evidence mounted, and the doubt diminished. Now, on the last day of competition, we seemed a virtual lock to finish among the top five teams in the category of best mission, and we had a chance to finish first. Within a few hours, as other teams competed, that might change, but there was no way our kids were going to squander their time in the spotlight.

To be honest, it made me a little uncomfortable to hear them bragging (albeit low-key bragging), since this was something I rarely tolerated from my football players. Eventually, I always reminded them, the shoe will be on the other foot. So show a little humility, a little class. The difference was that most of the football players at Forest Hills Northern had at least a passing familiarity with the concept of victory. Our special ed kids were losers; they'd always been losers, and most people thought they were destined for a lifetime of losing. Now, suddenly, they were winners. Or, at least, they were *winning*.

"Let them have fun," Robynn said. "Let them talk about themselves for a change. They've earned it."

Out of the twenty rockets we built, seventeen soared off the launch pad and floated safely back to Earth. Three simply fizzled, for one reason or another. Although no scores were kept, I later learned that our success rate (85 percent) was among the highest in camp. No surprise, really, since a lot of campers just didn't take the exercise very seriously. They were looking ahead to their final shuttle missions, or to their space station presentations, or, perhaps, to the Space Bowl.

The Space Bowl did not play to our strengths, since the contestants were required not only to answer difficult questions about space and science and history but to do so quickly and in the heat of competition. The content, really, was not much more dense than what we had encountered on the entrance exam, but this time the answers had to be provided orally. The format was uncomplicated. One representative from each of two teams would sit at a table and listen to a question. The first person to hit his or her buzzer earned the right to answer the question. If the answer was correct, the team earned a specific number of points. Then two more students would take their places. The team with the most points advanced to the next round.

We fared reasonably well . . . until we met the team from Costa Rica in the semifinals. Their kids were quick on the buzzer and highly knowledgeable. Our kids just seemed to have lost interest. They were lethargic, even distracted—it seemed as though their comparatively short attention spans were finally becoming relevant, and as a result the Costa Rican team ripped us. In all candor, this was way overdue. Our kids were naturally restless, if not clinically hyperactive, and to have made it this far without losing focus was a noteworthy achievement.

By late Thursday afternoon, especially while the kids were foraging in the gift shop, looking for souvenirs, Robynn and I were beginning to hear more and more comments about "getting home," "sleeping in my own bed," "seeing my parents." Most of the kids had just about run out of money by now, so Robynn and I pulled out our credit cards and told them to get whatever they wanted—within reason, of course. We dropped several hundred dollars, but it was worth it. Most of the kids picked up a T-shirt or sweatshirt for themselves, and then a few things for their friends and relatives. The one exception was Lewis Dayhuff, who approached me in the checkout line holding only a Space Camp key chain and a T-shirt obviously too small for him to wear.

"That it, Lewis?"

"Uh-huh."

"For your little brother, right?"

"Yeah, he'll like this stuff."

"Why don't you get something for yourself?"

Lewis furrowed his brow, as though it was a ridiculous suggestion. "Nah. I'm cool."

WHEN WE ARRIVED at the auditorium after dinner for our space station presentation, the mystery woman was seated in the back row, taking notes as usual. I stared at her for a moment, tried to make eye contact, but she never looked up. I wondered what she was writing, and to whom it would be addressed. At that point, though, I really didn't care.

The space station presentation was designed to test not only the creativity and teamwork of each group but also their composure and stage presence. With the other teams and the entire staff looking on, each team took its place at the front of the auditorium. One by one, each member of the team would read a few descriptive lines, written on three-by-five index cards, while a videotape of the space station played on a screen behind him. The judges would then evaluate the overall presentation. Each space station was made out of small plastic parts and occupied approximately twenty-five square feet. Each team was allotted fifteen minutes to make its presentation.

Our space station had been conceptualized, constructed, and videotaped late Wednesday night, at a time when the kids were utterly exhausted, and yet they had done an exceptional job. Marion Mills, doubtless inspired by personal experience, had come up with the idea of building a hospital in space—more specifically, a hospital that was capable of coping with the increased levels of radiation often found in space. The other kids liked the idea and began firing questions at Marion, pressing her about radiation treatment, and what she had been through at St. Jude's Children's Hospital. This was deeply personal stuff, and Marion wasn't accustomed to sharing it with others, but in this setting, under these conditions, she opened up, and before long they had outlined their entire script. How ironic, then, that Marion became sick the next day, and even now, as she took the stage, still appeared to be a bit wobbly. But she was tough. She managed to choke down a few bites of dinner, drink some water, and take a handful of Rolaids to settle her stomach. The space station presentation was important to Marion, especially after what had happened during the shuttle mission, and she wasn't about to miss it.

We were the third team to make our presentation. When we were introduced, there were no catcalls, no nasty remarks, no laughing, in part because such behavior would not have been tolerated by the staff, but also because Burger King was no longer a team to be mocked. It was a viable and worthy competitor, if one with a slightly offbeat view of the universe, as our presentation would clearly demonstrate.

"Good eeeee-ven-ing," Steve Bennett began, in a voice borrowed from Bela Lugosi. "Welcome to our space station presentation." I squirmed in my seat. *Oh, boy. Here it comes. Steve's schizophrenic personality is finally coming out. He's going to turn this thing into his own personal showcase.* But everyone laughed . . . not in an uncomfortable way, and not in a condescending way. They laughed because they thought Steve was funny, endearing, interesting. I looked at the judges—even they were laughing. I looked at the mystery woman—she wasn't laughing. She just scribbled. *Ah, the heck with her!* My only concern was whether Steve would show enough restraint to pull back and get on with the meat of the presentation.

"Thank you," he continued, after the laughter had died down. And then his voice lowered, his cadence slowed. "Our space station is a medical hospital dealing with the study of radiation and how it affects the human body."

Steve read a couple more lines, without injecting any levity, and then stepped to the side. As the other members of the team recited their parts, Steve provided subtle sound effects to accompany the images on screen: the whirring of a small vehicle, the humming of laboratory equipment.

Oh, God. Here we go . . .

But, once again, the audience loved it. Steve, who had driven so many teachers to the brink of madness with his antics, this time knew just where to draw the line. His gift for mimicry proved to be an asset in this situation, as it created a soundtrack for the presentation, a supplement rather than a distraction. The narration covered all of the pertinent information—how astronauts would live in the space station, what type of work they would do, how food and oxygen would be produced—and the sound effects made it all somehow more engaging. Yes, there was laughter, but it was quiet, appreciative laughter, and it didn't detract from the presentation at all. When it was over, as the audience applauded enthusiastically, Steve took a deep, theatrical bow.

Overall, it was a thorough and highly entertaining presentation, and easily one of the best of the day. Whether it was a bit too quirky and irreverent remained to be seen. The results of the space station competition, like the contest for Best Mission, would be revealed Friday at graduation.

"So, what did you think, Coach?" Steve asked afterward. "Not bad, huh?"

"I thought it was . . . *interesting*," I said, choosing my words carefully. "I just hope it doesn't backfire."

Steve rolled his eyes. "Ah, you worry too much, Coach."

I couldn't argue with him on that one.

27

Although we weren't scheduled to fly out of Huntsville until Saturday morning, Friday promised to be the wildest day of the week, largely because even though we had an additional night in town, we would not be allowed to spend it at Space Camp. The session ended on Friday, right after graduation, which meant all campers had to be off the premises by that afternoon. So we were obligated to pack up twenty kids and move them from the space habitat to the Marriott for a single night. No small task, as any parent (or teacher) would surely attest.

Most of my attention was focused on the logistics of this move. Thursday night, after the space station presentation, I had instructed everyone to return to the habitat and pack their bags so they'd be ready to roll first thing in the morning. I'd also been working closely with the staff at the Marriott to ensure that our students would all be placed on one floor, preferably in proximity to Robynn or me.

For better or worse, I had neither the time nor the energy to fret about Friday's awards ceremony, which would begin at eleven o'clock. There was just too much else to do. Nor was I quite as nimble a social director as I might have been. A handful of parents, including Mike Schmidt and his wife, had gone to extraordinary lengths to fly down from Grand Rapids so they could witness graduation. I tried to be polite and accommodating, but I was so tired and distracted that I failed to fully express my appreciation for their help and concern. Without their unwavering support, this trip and this program would not have been possible in the first place, and it meant the world to me, and to their kids, that they showed up for graduation.

I cannot say the same for the presence of our regional special education coordinator, who had shocked us all by arriving at Space Camp on Thursday evening. Denise had not called in advance to say she'd be coming. In fact, our correspondence had dwindled to virtually nothing in the weeks leading up to our departure. She had tolerated the program and feigned approval when she stood to benefit from it, but there was no disguising her dislike for Robynn and, especially, me. When I bumped into Denise at the Marriott, I felt not even a twinge of gratitude that she'd traveled all the way from Grand Rapids. Maybe that was a mistake on my part; maybe I should have cut her some slack, but I didn't think so at the time, and I really don't think so now. As Denise sashayed through the lobby, and proceeded to act as if we were the best of friends, I felt nothing but resentment.

"I've been getting wonderful reports," she said. "Congratulations."

I tried to be polite, but I just didn't have it in me. This was a woman who had never had a kind word for our program, or for the kids. *Especially* the kids. In her eyes, the students were, at best, a nuisance.

"Thank you," I said. "But it's really not much of a surprise . . . is it?"

She didn't respond. I let the words dangle in the air for a moment, and then I excused myself. The next morning, at breakfast, when the kids saw Denise, they were equally offended.

"What is she doing here?" several of them asked. "I thought she was against this whole trip."

"She was." I winked at Robynn. "I guess she's changed her mind."

"Yeah . . . right."

A far more welcome, but no less surprising, guest greeted me after breakfast. I was in my hotel room, packing, when I got a phone call from the front desk saying I had a visitor in the lobby. Having endured Denise Boitano's grandstanding, I feared the worst: Maybe Tom Keller, our principal, was here, too. When I stepped out of the elevator and saw the smiling visage of Jack Lousma, I could not have been more relieved.

"Jack! What brings you here?" It was a legitimate question, for while he was a former astronaut and thus always welcome at the Space & Rocket Center, I wondered what coincidence had led our paths to cross on this very day.

He took my hand in his, shook it vigorously. "I'm giving the graduation speech. Hope you don't mind."

Mind? I was thrilled . . . and honored. It turned out that Jack had not been invited to be the guest speaker; rather, he had specifically asked for the job, because he felt an attachment to our students and wanted to congratulate them, in person, on their accomplishment.

"Wait until I tell the kids," I said. "They'll be so excited."

Jack pursed his lips. "Do me a favor. Don't tell them. I want it to be a surprise. I'll just meet them in the auditorium before graduation."

With some time to kill after they'd finished packing, the kids walked around the park, did a little more shopping, and hung out with some of the other campers. A few of them even exchanged phone numbers, which I thought was kind of poignant, even though it was doubtful they'd actually keep in touch, for once they left Huntsville there was little to bind them any longer. Most of the campers would be returning to their comfortable homes and elite schools and advanced placement classes; our kids were going back to my classroom in Grand Rapids . . . back to special ed. For many of them, this week, this trip, was as close as they would come to being viewed as "normal."

FRIDAY WAS THE hottest day of the week. By ten-thirty in the morning, as the campers began lining up for the graduation ceremony, it was already eighty degrees. And humid? Oh, man, even the slightest movement provoked a river of perspiration. Flight suits were not mandatory for the ceremony, but a lot of campers opted to wear them; most who did came to regret their decision, for the uniforms became sweatsuits in the most literal sense of the word.

Thankfully, a decision had been made to move graduation inside, to the climate-controlled comfort of the auditorium. With generic processional music playing in the background, some three hundred campers, counselors, administrators, and guests—parents, mostly—marched quietly, proudly into the theater. By this time my focus had indeed shifted to the outcome of the competition, to the extent that I couldn't even sit down. I was so filled with nervous tension that I paced back and forth in the rear of the auditorium. Our kids, on the other hand, seemed completely at ease. Not once that morning had any of them said, "Hey, Coach—think we have a shot at winning Best Mission?" Or even, "How many awards do you think we won?" Not that they didn't care—I'm sure they did. Far from being a sign of apathy, their lack of anxiety was a clear indication of how they felt about their performance. They had done the best they could, and they knew it. Win or lose, there would be no shame. Not for them, their school, their parents, and certainly not for their teachers.

Their placid veneer, however, was shattered as they walked down the aisle of the auditorium to take their seats, and suddenly realized an old friend was in their midst.

"Hey, Jack!" Steve Bennett yelled, loudly enough for everyone in the auditorium to hear. "Guys, it's Jack Lousma!"

Pretty soon the whole team was waving, yelling, doing everything they could to get Jack's attention. Class act that he was, Jack didn't mind in the least. From the stage he waved and smiled, then saluted. Our kids responded in kind.

This exchange naturally aroused the curiosity of some of the other campers, who had not recognized Jack but had been smart enough to figure out that he was someone important. Standing at the podium, tall and trim, Jack Lousma looked like a pilot. He looked like a soldier. He looked like an *astronaut*.

"Who is that guy?" one of the campers asked Steve Bennett.

"That's Jack Lousma," Steve replied. "He flew the space shuttle."

"No kidding?"

"Nope."

"And you know him?"

"Uh-huh."

"How?"

Steve crossed his arms majestically, triumphantly, playing the moment for all it was worth.

"He worked with us when we were training. Helped out with our rocket launch, too. We're tight." With that Steve raised a hand, yelled, "Yo, Jack!" and took off on dead sprint down the aisle. The rest of the team followed suit. Within a few seconds they were all huddled around Colonel Jack Lousma, decorated war veteran and distinguished astronaut, laughing out loud, hugging, shaking hands, talking the way old friends do.

AS THE LAST of the campers filed in, I felt a tap on my shoulder. When I turned around, I was surprised to see the mystery woman standing by my side, notepad and pen in hand. She fidgeted nervously, shifting her weight from one foot to the other, and then finally, with a thin smile, introduced herself.

"Mr. Kersjes," she began. "You don't know me—"

Tactlessly, I cut her off. "No, I don't know you, but I've sure seen you around a lot this week. What are you, some kind of spy?"

She lowered her head, as if embarrassed. "Actually, that's not far off. My name is Mary Spencer, and I work for the Huntsville public school system. Mr. Buckbee hired me as a consultant. He asked me to follow your team, take a lot of notes, and then file a report on how your students performed."

"I see."

"No, I don't think you do." Her demeanor—the way she rocked uncomfortably on the balls of her feet, the way she averted her eyes, the way she struggled for just the right words—indicated a significant degree of discomfort; something was really bothering this woman. "I was instructed to look specifically for flaws and not just strengths."

Although none of this information came as much of a surprise, hearing it was surprisingly painful. Here we were, nearly two thousand miles from Grand Rapids, and some twenty months removed from the initial wave of ignorance and resistance that had met our initial inquiry, and still we were being treated with skepticism. Would it never end?

I let out a sigh of frustration.

"Why are you telling me this?"

Suddenly Ms. Spencer's lower lip began to tremble; her eyes glazed over. "Because I thought you should know. And I also want you to know that when I turn in this report, a lot of people are going to be surprised."

Now I was more confused than ever. She'd been shadowing us all week. Hadn't she accumulated enough dirt to bury us ten times over? I thought again of Lewis's outburst, the table flipping over and the craziness of that entire night. I thought of Stephanie and Shannon losing their composure in the shuttle, and the way our second mission nearly fell apart. I thought of all the times that week that our students had been more boisterous, more lively, more energetic than the other camp- ers . . . all the times they had acted, well, like themselves, and I couldn't imagine that her little pad wasn't overflowing with bad news.

"What?! Why?"

She began flipping through her journal, turning the pages furiously, searching for something. "I don't even know where to begin. All I can tell you, and all I can tell Mr. Buckbee, is that I think you have the most wonderful students at this camp. This notebook is filled with ob- servations about how hard they worked, how much they cared for each other and supported each other, how they handled themselves with maturity and professionalism . . ."

She shrugged her shoulders. "What else can I say? I came here ex- pecting to find a class of juvenile delinquents, and what I found, instead, was a great bunch of kids. I can only hope that when the students from my school go through this program, they conduct themselves half as well."

Ms. Spencer tucked her notebook into her pocket and extended her hand again. Had I not been caught completely off-guard by her appraisal and confession, and distracted by the upcoming awards ceremony, I might have hoisted her into my arms and showered her with affection and gratitude. Surely it would have been easy for her to overlook the accomplishments of our team, the gestures of kindness and considera- tion, and the legitimate displays of knowledge and expertise; it would have been easy for her to file a negative report. But she didn't, and for that I am eternally grateful. At the time, however, I could muster no better response than to simply say, "Thank you." And just like that she was gone, back to her seat, and back to her notebook, which I now recognized as an ally, and not an enemy.

Robynn had witnessed but not heard the whole exchange, so when Ms. Spencer departed, she stepped closer and asked, "What was that all about?"

"She's a hit man," I said with a laugh. "But she couldn't pull the trigger."

"Come again?"

The music had stopped now and Deborah Barnhart was approaching the podium. The ceremony was about to begin. "Never mind. I'll explain later."

DR. BARNHART'S OPENING remarks were brief and doubtless similar to those she had made at countless other Space Camp graduations. She thanked the counselors for their dedication and hard work, the teachers for their support and guidance, and, above all, the campers, for making it all possible. Then she introduced the guest speaker. As Jack Lousma stood up and walked slowly to the podium, the audience applauded warmly but politely. Most of the audience, anyway. In the middle stood twenty kids, some dressed in blue flight suits, some wearing Burger King T-shirts, and all pumping their fists and screaming at the top of their lungs.

"All right, Jack!"

"You da man!"

"Knock 'em dead, Jack, baby!"

Robynn dropped her head into her hands and tried to stifle a laugh. Here was Jack Lousma, a world-famous astronaut and fighter pilot, and the honored guest at this ceremony, and our kids were shouting at him as if he were one of the gang working the grill at Burger King. But Jack didn't mind at all—it was precisely this type of raw emotion that had attracted him to our program in the first place. There was nothing false about these kids, not a hint of pretense. Whatever they said or did, it came directly from the heart. So Jack merely smiled and waved and then cleared his throat and took control of the room.

A gifted speaker with an uncanny knack for seemingly addressing each member of the audience individually, Jack delivered a commencement speech that was relevant to the entire group, yet clearly written with our team in mind.

"You all came here with specific goals," he said. "And while those goals may have differed, you shared a common desire: to perform to the best of your abilities."

His body language—the way he moved his hands, cocked his head, the attempts to make eye contact with the rowdy group in the center of the room—may have been imperceptible to others in the audience, but to me, and to Robynn, the message was clear: *I'm proud of you.*

It was brilliant the way he did it, the way he layered his address, the way he wove a personal message of congratulations to our students within the fabric of a broader discussion. When Jack said, "You've worked hard as a team, and you've succeeded because you are a team," I suppose he could have been talking to any of the groups in that auditorium, but it resonated more powerfully with us, for Jack had been along for part of the journey, and he knew what we had been through, what obstacles we had faced. To us, these were not generic words.

"I wish you all the best of luck in the future," he said in conclusion. "Remember—don't be afraid to go after your dreams. It may take a lot of hard work on your part, but if you're willing to make the sacrifices, there is nothing you can't accomplish."

Taken out of context, those words may sound trite, but they could not have been more meaningful to our team. These kids had worked hard, extraordinarily so, and they had made tremendous sacrifices . . . every one of them. And now, here they were, about to graduate from Space Camp, perhaps with honors—we'd find out in a few moments. Regardless, it was an accomplishment of staggering proportions. As Jack strode back to his seat, to the accompaniment of vigorous applause, I reflected on that first day, some eighteen months earlier, when I'd floated the idea of Space Camp to these very same kids, and they had reacted with sarcasm and self-loathing. That they would all end up here, in this auditorium, accepting praise from an astronaut . . . well, it was unfathomable.

The actual graduation ceremony began with each team being individually recognized. The team's name was announced (usually a corporate sponsor), along with the town and state it represented. Then each member of that team was introduced and summoned to the stage, where he or she was presented with a set of wings, signifying graduation from Space Camp. The entire team then posed for a photo.

This portion of the ceremony passed slowly, and by the time it ended my stomach had once again been invaded by butterflies, for now all that remained was the presentation of awards. Knowing that it was ridiculous to feel such anxiety over awards that really didn't matter, I tried to beat back the silly creatures. We were already "winners" after all. Who cared whether we won Best Mission . . . or any other competition?

Well, to be perfectly candid, I cared . . . quite a lot, probably more than our students. They wanted to win, too, obviously, but they seemed to have a better sense of perspective than I did. Win or lose, they'd be happy. I wasn't so sure I could say the same thing. Whether it was validation for my own work that I sought or recognition for the students . . . or whether it was merely a case of my hypercompetitive nature taking control . . . at that moment I was nearly overwhelmed by a desire to succeed . . . to *win*. For some reason a fleeting glimpse of the Academy Awards ceremony flickered in my mind's eye, and I thought of all the actors over the years who had sat there, trying to smile for an audience of several hundred million, clenching their teeth as they choked back the disappointment of hearing, "And the Oscar goes to . . ." followed by the announcement of someone else's name; and then nodding warmly as that person clutched his statuette, emblematic of the sweet salve of recognition following a lifetime of work and struggle and pain, and said, with a straight face, "It's an honor just to be nominated . . . to be in the company of such an extraordinarily gifted group of artists."

Yeah . . . right.

How easy it is to be gracious in victory, and how hard to be noble in defeat. That much I had learned from my years as a football player and coach. It was nice to be nominated, which in our case meant simply gaining acceptance to Space Camp, and it was enormously satisfying to have discovered, along the way, just how much we were capable of accomplishing, and to prove that our presence here was not a fluke, not a gift, not a concession, but something we had earned and deserved.

An honor to be nominated? Sure. No question about it. But to say it was enough . . . to say I craved nothing more for myself or my team would be a lie.

The first award was for Best Team Patch. Dr. Barnhart read a brief description of the event and the criteria used to judge the entries. "Teamwork," she said. That was the key. Artistry was nice, certainly, and appearance was not unimportant. But it was the concept that mattered most, the ability to convey twenty students united in a common goal. She paused briefly as one of the counselors stepped to the edge of the stage and prepared to hand out medals to the top three finishers. The entire auditorium fell silent. Dr. Barnhart looked at her notes.

"Third place in the category of Best Team Patch goes to . . ." She paused, looked up, smiled. "McDonnell Douglas."

There was polite applause as the students from the McDonnell Douglas team walked to the stage and received their awards. They strode confidently, assuredly, as if they knew all along they'd be making this walk, and that by the end of the day, after taking home a pile of hardware, they'd be able to find their way to the stage blindfolded. I don't mean that as an insult—it's merely an observation. There was an air of entitlement to this team, just as there was to most of the teams at Space Camp . . . a sense that it wasn't so much a matter of *whether* they would, but rather *how much* they would win.

Watching the kids from McDonnell Douglas accept their third-place awards, I didn't know whether to be relieved or depressed . . . happy or sad . . . excited or anxious . . .

We didn't get third. Okay, well, maybe we got second. Then again, maybe we got nothing. Naaah . . . not possible. Our patch was awesome . . . wasn't it?

I smacked myself in the forehead. *Get a grip, Kersjes, or you're going to blow an embolism before this thing is over.*

"Congratulations," Dr. Barnhart said as the stage cleared. She was back at the mike, trying to keep things rolling. "Now, second place in the category of Best Team Patch goes to . . ."

I held my breath.

Second would be good. No, check that . . . second would be great. Please, God, just let us win something . . .

". . . Burger King."

For an instant, I swear, time stood still. There was no sound, no reaction, no movement at all, and I wondered if perhaps I'd experienced some sort of auditory mirage. I felt as though I'd been immersed in water, so difficult was it to move, hear, speak . . . even think. But then I saw them—Lewis, Steve, Scott, Stephanie . . . all of them—jumping, dancing, slapping hands, hugging like brothers and sisters, and as the fog cleared I saw Jack Lousma beaming from the stage, giving them, us, a hearty thumbs-up, and suddenly the air left my lungs in a great, exhaustive rush, and my knees buckled. I reached for Robynn, not merely to share this moment with her, but, quite literally, to keep from falling down.

"We did it," she said.

Speechless, I simply nodded. A montage of images flooded my mind: Lewis flipping over that table just a few nights earlier, and then slumping to the floor, crying, overwhelmed by the pressure and anxiety and the craziness of being here in the first place; Steve Bennett and Scott Goudy comforting Lewis in the hallway—*"We don't need you anymore"*—and then leading him back to that table, back to the work he did so well, back to the teammates who needed him; the patch itself, such a quirky, irreverent, and innovative design, one that not only paid homage to Dan Trierweiler, whose generosity had made this trip possible, but, in depicting a space-age Burger King, poked gentle fun at the hardscrabble roots of our team. More than any other entry, it was a patch that announced, *"This is who we are."*

I knew that night, when I saw the prototype, that it was a good and honorable bit of work, but now I saw it as something else, something so fiercely proud and utterly lacking in ambivalence that it was in its own way . . . well, brilliant.

By the time I regained my composure, Dr. Barnhart had already announced the first-place winner and moved on to the next category: Best Space Station Presentation. Third place went to the team sponsored by Boeing, and as they strolled to the stage and accepted their awards, I turned to Robynn and said, half-jokingly, "Wouldn't it be cool if we got another second?"

The words had barely escaped my mouth when Dr. Barnhart said, "Second place in the category of Best Space Station Presentation goes to . . . the Burger King team!" She seemed somewhat startled herself, although not the least bit disappointed. Deborah, after all, had taken a chance on our behalf; in recommending that we be admitted to Space Camp, she had issued an open challenge to her boss, Ed Buckbee. If we had failed, she stood to lose a great deal, perhaps more than any of us.

Not that I can honestly say I was dwelling on the repercussions of her gamble as our kids scrambled up to the stage a second time. Watching them now, falling all over each other, riding each other piggyback down the aisle, reveling in their hard-earned success in a way that few other students in the audience could even comprehend, I felt a tightness in my chest. I pulled out a handkerchief and dabbed at my eyes as Ben Schmidt came running back up the aisle. He threw his arms around me and laughed out loud.

"Hey, Coach. It's okay. You don't have to cry. We're doing good!"

Snorting, laughing, weeping . . . all at the same time . . . I held Ben close, held him tightly, as if afraid to let go, the way I'd embraced my own children hundreds, maybe thousands of times over the years.

"Thanks, Ben. I appreciate that."

After I released Ben he continued on up the aisle, to where his parents were seated. They swept him into their arms and rocked back and forth, the three of them forming a tiny, sobbing scrum. What vindication this must have been for them, what profound and immeasurable joy, to see their son, their child, in such a triumphant pose; and how distant and mad must have seemed the words of the doctors they'd heard years before, the ones who urged them to place the heavy-lidded boy in an institution, so evident and severe was his disability, so obvious his need for lifelong custodial care. Where were they now, these insensitive and imperceptive members of the medical fraternity, these geniuses, and what would they think if they were here . . . seeing the boy at sixteen . . . doing quite well . . . *thank you very much!*

In another part of the auditorium a group of students actually rose from their seats and cheered, and I recognized them as members of the team from France. These were good kids, more accepting and supportive of our students, I'm a bit saddened to say, than any of the students from the United States. Perhaps it was their lack of provincialism, their wonderful ignorance of American class structure and commercialism, that led them to open their arms and hearts to a group of special-needs students; then again, maybe it was something much more basic, primal, such as the obvious affection bestowed upon a couple of the more attractive French girls by some of our boys, most notably Lewis Dayhuff.

It was a measure of Lewis's growth that he expressed his interest not with some crass comment, as he so often had done in the past, when he indulged his raging hormones and emotional insecurity in the hallways of Forest Hills Northern, but with a genuine and unique sensitivity. Lewis was an artist, and what better way for an artist to impress someone than with a gift created with his own hands? So Lewis drew for them. He sketched scenes and landscapes and cartoons . . . he even sketched their portraits. The girls were naturally flattered, and so now they returned the affection, letting everyone on our team, but Lewis in particular, know exactly how they felt.

BY NOW THERE was a buzz in the room, people whispering to each other, making comments. Perhaps this was merely a result of there being only one team award remaining, the biggest award, and so the excitement was naturally mounting. It seemed like more than that, though. I sensed an awakening to the capabilities of our team, an awareness that maybe the special ed kids from Michigan knew what they were doing after all.

But there was so little time to process any of this, so efficiently was Dr. Barnhart pushing through the awards ceremony.

"And now the one you've all been waiting for," she said. "Best Mission."

The buzz dissipated; all talking, twitching, and fidgeting ceased. Never before had I seen so many teenagers so quiet. They hung on every word as Dr. Barnhart explained the objective of the missions and outlined the procedure for scoring. She did a wonderful job of breaking down the shuttle mission into its various parts and providing an overview of a pretty complicated subject. This was great for the visitors in the audience—the parents and school administrators—but an agonizing digression for those of us who had been here all week and now were aching to hear the results.

"Every team endured two rigorous missions," Dr. Barnhart said, "each precisely two hours in length . . ."

For God's sake . . . get on with it!

A flood of conflicting emotions cluttered my mind, making it hard to think straight, to breathe. I knew we had finished in the top five, and that should have been enough. Surely it was sufficient to justify our trip, and to prove to the doubters and cynics and critics back home in Grand Rapids that this was not merely some fool's errand, nor a selfish and self-destructive ego trip on the part of two crazy teachers. It was much, much more than that.

Our point had been made: Given the right amount of support and encouragement, given the room to succeed as well as fail, these kids were capable of almost anything. Whatever happened next, whether we finished first or fifth, was almost irrelevant. Nothing could detract from what we'd already achieved, from the indelible mark we had made on

Space Camp, and the blow we had struck for all students with special needs.

And yet . . .

There was this feeling, this burning in the pit of my stomach that I knew so well, that any coach or athlete would recognize as the insatiable need to win. I swallowed hard, hoping it would go away, but there it was, and there it would remain. After runner-up efforts in the two previous categories, my hopes were soaring, and there was no practical way to keep them tethered. Maybe, I thought, we really were the best team. Maybe, in a few minutes, the allegedly troubled and troublesome kids from Forest Hills Northern would be standing on that stage, accepting the highest award at Space Camp . . . and what a miraculous, impossible, unthinkable thing that would be!

"Okay . . ." Dr. Barnhart's voice pulled me back. "Third place in the category of Best Mission goes to . . ."

I closed my eyes. *Not us. Not yet . . . Not yet . . . Not—*

"The Burger King team!"

The kids leaped out of their seats and charged the stage once more, stumbling over each other and hugging each other every inch of the way, rolling toward the front of the room en masse, like a great, surging wave of adolescent energy. That the wings they accepted as trophies were painted bronze rather than gold did nothing to diminish their excitement. From the edge of the stage they held their prizes tightly, stared at them in disbelief, then waved proudly to the crowd, and it hit me then, watching them, that they had not shared my definition of "victory." For the first time in their lives these kids had been singled out for their accomplishments, rather than their deficiencies; they had been *recognized*, and that was a wonder beyond almost anything they had dared to envision. Sure, they had wanted to win, and they had given their best effort in pursuit of that goal. To them, first would have been nice . . . but third was just as good.

My reaction? I felt my shoulders sag beneath the sudden and unexpected weight of disappointment. I scuffed the floor with the toe of my shoe and muttered the word "Damn . . ." under my breath, an ungracious display that did not go unnoticed.

"Hey, Kersjes. Lighten up!" I felt an elbow in my side. It was Robynn. "Just this once, try not to act like a football coach . . . okay?"

I smiled. "Okay."

Man, did she have a point. Greed had gotten the best of me. Three categories and three top-three finishes, and somehow I'd interpreted this as anything less than a complete and utter triumph? What had come over me?

The answer, of course, was . . . *ambition*. Imagination, the ability to dream and to work hard enough to make the dream real had gotten us this far, and so, for a few minutes, at least, I had indulged in a Rocky-esque fantasy: the little guy who beats the longest of odds. Then I remembered: Wait a minute! Rocky didn't win! Not in the first film, anyway. (And isn't that the only one that matters?) And yet, even in defeat, he remained a winner . . . one of the biggest winners, in fact, in the annals of storytelling . . . of history . . . right up there with such legendary underdogs as David and the 1969 Mets.

The journey was more important than the destination, the struggle more meaningful than the outcome. I knew that. Hell, I'd *preached* that. Considering where these kids had come from, and what their lives had been like . . . especially when compared to the other students in camp . . . well, theirs was an accomplishment of almost immeasurable proportions.

PERSPECTIVE NOW REGAINED. I went into escape mode, my full attention quickly diverted to details small and large that would consume the next twenty-four hours: escorting the kids out of the auditorium and over to the Marriott; getting them settled in their rooms; arranging dinner, double-checking airline reservations and transportation to the airport in the morning. Running through a checklist in my head as the awards ceremony continued, I barely noticed the students from Boeing accepting their first-place award for Best Mission; similarly, as Dr. Barnhart introduced the final award of the week, the only individual award, I was already on my way out the door—mentally, if not physically.

"The Right Stuff Award," she explained, "is presented to the individual who best displays the characteristics of a true astronaut . . . who has been invaluable to the accomplishments of his or her team. In choosing this person, the judges looked for someone who was a true leader . . . someone who never complained, who supported his or her teammates, and who was respectful of counselors, classmates, and fellow competitors throughout the week."

I glanced at my watch. The ceremony was nearly an hour old, and I was eager to get going. The pressure and anxiety associated with the team awards were gone now. I looked around the room, a room filled with brilliant kids—future scholars, scientists, captains of industry, maybe even an astronaut or two—and found it inconceivable that any of our students was even in the running. We had been a team in the truest sense of the word: In our case, the whole really was greater than the sum of its parts. That each student had some sort of learning disability, some perceived deficiency, didn't matter, because here, at Space Camp, we were not individuals. We were one.

The Right Stuff Award? Who cares?

Dr. Barnhart announced the name of the third-place winner, and then the runner-up. I surveyed the room again, tried to think of someone who had truly stood out, someone who seemed destined to fill Jack Lousma's shoes one day, or maybe Deborah Barnhart's. Nothing came to me. The faces and names all blended together, and I realized just how intensely I had been focused on my own team. A few rows down sat a kid with curly hair and a ruddy complexion, part of the Boeing team, a kid who always seemed to know exactly what he was doing, the most confident kid on a team brimming with confidence.

Maybe him.

Or, perhaps, the blond-haired girl from the French team. She seemed smart, too, and friendly, and admired by the other campers. Or maybe that thickly muscled kid from Coca-Cola, the one who looked like a football player. Or the girl from Costa Rica, the one with whom some of our girls had struck up a friendship. Or maybe . . .

Oh, forget it. Just tell us who it is.

"And the winner of the Right Stuff Award is . . ."

Gotta be the kid from Boeing . . .

". . . Scott Goudy from the Burger King team!"

Oh, my God . . .

Whatever surprise or elation I had felt before paled in comparison to what I felt now. Suddenly an award that had seemed meaningless became the most important thing in the world. From the center of the crowd, in a roomful of students whose average combined SAT hovered slightly above the fourteen hundred mark, emerged a learning disabled student from Grand Rapids, Michigan; a kid who just one year earlier had found his greatest pleasure in picking at the wounds of his classmates. And now he represented the ideal of Space Camp, the ideal of NASA, the image, spirit, and maturity of an astronaut.

What a strange and incomprehensible turn of events; and yet, when I thought about it, when I tried to step back from my role as teacher and coach, and consider the award objectively, I realized just how fitting a choice it was. The Scott Goudy I had known from my special ed class had all but disappeared, his place taken by a stronger, more thoughtful young man, and it was that person who was honored on this day.

As Scott walked calmly to the stage, his classmates cheered wildly. All of them, that is, except Steve Bennett, who stood on his chair, threw his arms into the air, and shouted, "Hey! What did he do? Why not me?"

It was just a good-natured bit of ribbing, of course. When Scott returned to his seat—after Jack Lousma had placed around his neck a medallion attached to a beautiful ribbon—Steve was there to greet him with a big hug. Robynn and I embraced him, too. Scott, though, was remarkably cool about the whole experience, so emotionless that I actually wondered whether something was wrong—that perhaps he was overwhelmed, or had come to believe this was the way a "real" astronaut would respond to such an honor, with an icy detachment. Either way, it didn't seem natural.

A few minutes later, after Dr. Barnhart gave her closing remarks ("have a safe trip home . . . hope to see you back next year!"), our team was surrounded by some of the Space & Rocket Center staff, as well as a handful of reporters. Naturally, Scott was the person with whom they were most interested in speaking, but he seemed distracted.

"Hi, Scott. Congratulations!" said one woman, a local television reporter accompanied by a cameraman. "Can we talk?"

Scott squinted, tried to look beyond her, off into the distance. "Not right now. Sorry."

"It'll only take a few minutes."

"I can't."

As he started to walk away, I chased him down and put a hand on his shoulder. "Scott, what's the problem?"

"No problem, Coach. I just have to do something."

"Like what?" I couldn't imagine anything that required such urgency. All around us were the sights and sounds of celebration: kids laughing, embracing friends and relatives, chatting with their opponents in that easy, relaxed way that comes in the wake of competition. At the center of all this was Scott Goudy, winner of the Right Stuff Award . . . the single most impressive and outstanding student among a class of more than two hundred.

A student with special needs . . . and obviously special gifts. The mind boggled at the significance of it all.

What should have been the biggest moment of Scott's life, however, seemed to be something else entirely, for rather than embracing the adulation . . . rather than basking in the warm glow of the spotlight, he appeared to be backing away from it.

"I need a pair of scissors," he said quietly.

"Scissors? What in God's name for?"

"Please . . . I just need them."

"Scott, I don't have any scissors. I'm sorry. Now do me a favor and go back there and talk to the reporters."

He turned away and began walking purposefully into the crowd, pushing past people, occasionally stopping to say something, and then moving on, until finally he disappeared completely. A few minutes later he returned, a small Swiss army knife in his hand.

"Where did you get that?" I asked.

"From one of the counselors."

"And exactly what are you planning to do with it?"

"This . . ."

With his thumb and forefinger, Scott extracted a tiny pair of scissors from the Swiss army knife. Then he removed the Right Stuff Award from his neck, squatted down, and placed it on the floor. After smoothing out the wrinkles, he inserted the top of the ribbon between the blades of the shears, and slowly, carefully, began to cut.

"Scott! Have you lost your mind?" I couldn't believe what I was seeing. And I was one of the few people who could see it, since we were a good fifteen to twenty feet away from the center of activity.

He looked up, smiled. "I don't think so."

"Then what are you doing?"

"Sharing my award." Although almost comically small, the scissors were sharp and well maintained, for they did their work perfectly, slicing neatly through the ribbon and separating a thin slice of fabric. "We're a team, right?"

"That's right."

"Then everyone should have a piece of this."

I took a step back, so startled that I nearly lost my footing. It wasn't so much his generosity that impressed me—I knew Scott had that in him, somewhere—but rather the manner in which it manifested itself. This was an act of supreme sacrifice and selflessness, one that required far more than just a casual respect for one's teammates and friends. It was a gift that came from somewhere much deeper, much closer to the soul.

"Okay," he said after making the final cut, and then he scooped up the once-perfect ribbon, now twenty shards of nylon, and pressed them into his palm. "Let's go."

The crowd had started to thin out by the time we returned, but the reporter was still waiting for Scott.

"Can you handle an interview?" I asked as we walked together.

Scott frowned. "It makes me nervous, Coach. Anyway, I really don't have all that much to say."

"That's all right. Something is better than nothing. Just be yourself."

I stepped aside as the reporter introduced herself once more and congratulated Scott again on his award. Scott nodded, said thanks, and then they chatted for a few moments as the cameraman readied his equipment. After a short time the reporter straightened her hair, cleared her throat, and gave the cameraman a signal to begin taping. She seemed not to notice what Scott had done with the ribbon.

"How do you feel about winning the Right Stuff Award?" she asked.

"Pretty good."

The reporter stood there, microphone extended, obviously expecting a slightly more long-winded response. When it became apparent that one was not forthcoming, she pressed on.

"Scott, I understand you have a learning disability. Is that correct?"

"Yes."

"And that your team is the first group of special education students to attend Space Camp?"

"That's right."

"You must be very proud of your performance."

Scott didn't respond right away, and for a few uneasy moments it appeared as though he might not respond at all. In reality, he was merely taking his time, reaching for just the right words. He cocked his head, looked into the eye of the camera.

"We really didn't think we were going to win . . . because sometimes people don't like special people." He paused again, glanced down at the pieces of ribbon in his hand. The corners of his mouth turned up just a bit. "But we did win . . . and we love it. And that's all I have to say."

THAT AFTERNOON, AT the Marriott, we held a small party for the team. Nothing too extravagant, just a hot-fudge-and-brownies social, followed by some swimming in the hotel pool. A couple of the parents helped out, which was nice, since it gave Robynn and me a chance to relax. I told the kids how proud of them we were, and how much we appreciated their hard work; Robynn said something similar. Then we gave them a chance to speak. It wasn't in their nature, of course, to bare their souls, to engage in cloying sentimentality, so most of them just shook their heads and continued to eat and talk, almost as if this were just another day.

In the back of the room, however, I noticed Scott fumbling with something beneath the table. Our eyes locked as he nodded subtly and pushed his chair back. As he stood to speak, and everyone turned to face him, the clinking of glasses and spoons abated.

"Yes, Scott?" I knew what he had done, and what he had in mind, but I wasn't sure how he planned to proceed. Scott was not the type to grandstand. He was not inclined to make speeches. If he had become a leader, he was nonetheless a quiet leader.

"Here," he said simply, holding up a clenched fist, from which pieces of the Right Stuff Award protruded. "This is for everybody."

The room froze as Scott walked casually from table to table and handed a strand of ribbon to each of his teammates. He said nothing as he went about this task. There was no hand wringing, no hugging, no outpouring of emotion. Just a simple presentation. One by one the other kids scooped up their trophies, looked them over, smiled approvingly, and said, "Thanks, Scott." And then they went back to their hot fudge and brownies.

The response was so cool, so devoid of excitement or elation, or even appreciation, that I actually felt a pang of sympathy for Scott. Imagine a college quarterback winning the Heisman Trophy, then hacking the statue into bits and distributing chunks to his offensive linemen. To me, this was an equivalent gesture.

"What's wrong with them?" I whispered to Robynn. "Don't they understand what he just did?"

She looked around the room, saw twenty tired kids happily digging forks into mounds of chocolate, and nodded. "Yeah, I think so."

And then it hit me: *They knew!*

Their reaction was not born of envy or apathy or any other petty emotion. It was far purer than that. They knew Scott was going to share his award. In fact, they *expected* it! Not because he had said anything, not because they had pressured him, not because it was some sort of heroic gesture . . . but simply because it was the right thing to do. And each one of them would have done precisely the same thing. Theirs was a bond forged of trust, friendship, respect . . . maybe even love. At some point in the past eighteen months they had become more than individuals, more than friends, more than teammates. They had become family, and in every family, some things, maybe the most important things, go unspoken.

EPILOGUE

The trip home was quiet, uneventful. No one needed Dramamine, and there were no disputes over who would get to sit next to Robynn or me or my wife. Quite frankly, no one wanted to sit next to us. It was amazing, really, the way these twenty kids had, in less than a week, morphed from accidental tourists into intrepid explorers. From Huntsville to Atlanta, from Atlanta to Chicago, and Chicago to Grand Rapids, they behaved impeccably, just as they had on the way down, really, although without the nervousness that had characterized that end of the journey.

On the last leg, as the plane cruised over Lake Michigan, Robynn and I naturally, out of habit, went into teacher mode.

"Any suggestions as to how we should handle things after we land?" I asked.

"How about if I run up front and make sure everything goes smoothly on that end? You can stay back here." We were seated in one of the last rows. "That way we're covered—fore and aft."

I looked around the cabin. Steve was listening to his Walkman. Scott was sleeping. Stephanie and Shannon were playing cards. The others were either chatting quietly or reading or looking out the windows.

"You know what?" I said. "There might be quite a few people waiting for them at the airport." I knew this was true, for I'd been told we could expect at least a small reception upon arrival. Friends, relatives, some students, and the local media. "Why don't we just hang back, let them have their moment?"

Robynn smiled. "Good idea, Kersjes."

The plane touched down neatly, smoothly, and we taxied back up the runway to the terminal. Robynn and I remained in our seats as the kids stood up, gathered their backpacks and coats from the overhead storage bins. I said nothing, just watched as they went about their business, indistinguishable from the rest of the passengers. There was nothing in the way they spoke, moved, or behaved that betrayed their status as special education students. They seemed like normal kids. Good kids.

We watched from the back of the pack as they trudged up the jetway, stiff and sore from a day of air travel, exhausted from a week of labor. As the first few members of our group stepped through the door and disappeared from view, I could hear something, a slight hum that grew into a rumble . . . the faint sounds of laughter, shouting . . . the sound of loved ones being welcomed home. Then something else, something I recognized from years of football, a wonderful sound, the sound you hear when you're a coach, trailing your players, walking from the locker room to the field, through the hallways, and out into the Friday night air, where the crowd waits for you with open arms.

A sound every kid should hear at least once in his life. A sound our kids had never heard before, at least not directed solely at them. Not like this.

Clapping . . . cheering . . . whistling . . .

The sound of . . . *acceptance*.

POSTSCRIPT

The success of the Forest Hills Northern team helped pave the way for other special-needs students to attend Space Camp, which now offers numerous programs for the learning disabled, as well as for the hearing impaired and visually impaired.

In addition to working as a consultant specializing in instruction for the Forest Hills Public School District, Mike Kersjes today is the president of Space Is Special, Inc., a not-for-profit organization dedicated to providing special education students with the opportunity to enhance their skills in science and mathematics by using space as a motivational theme. Through grants from NASA and the National Science Foundation, the Space Is Special program has expanded into seven states and each year provides scholarships for several hundred students to attend Space Camp. The success of the program was featured in a documentary television program that aired on the Learning Channel in 1997.

Mike is also an assistant football coach at Forest Hills Central High School.

As for some of the other members of the team featured prominently in this book . . .

Steve Bennett is a certified paramedic living in Ada, Michigan. He also runs a successful video production company specializing in the coverage of automobile racing.

Lewis Dayhuff owns a woodworking business and also has a job installing office furniture for Steelcase, Inc., in Grand Rapids, Michigan. He owns his own house, which he shares with his wife and seven-year-old son.

Brooke Fuller lives in Grand Rapids, where she works in the catalog division of J. C. Penney.

Scott Goudy is employed by the Corona Door Corporation in Grand Rapids.

Robynn McKinney still works for the Forest Hills Public School District. She is now an administrator in charge of alternative education.

Marion Mills works in the food service department of a Grand Rapids hospital, where she designs and bakes pastry for patients. She has a steady boyfriend and is in good health. She has never had a recurrence of leukemia.

Stephanie Reinks lives with her mother in Rockford, Michigan. For more than a decade she has worked as a nurse's aide at a local hospital.

Ben Schmidt holds down two jobs: one in the printing department of the Forest Hills Public School District, and another as a stock clerk at D&W Food Stores in Cascade, Michigan. He lives with his parents.